Palgrave Studies in Relational Sociology

Series editor
François Dépelteau
Laurentian University
Sudbury, Canada

In various disciplines such as archeology, psychology, psychoanalysis, international relations, and philosophy, we have seen the emergence of relational approaches or theories. This series seeks to further develop relational sociology through the publication of diverse theoretical and empirical research—including that which is critical of the relational approach. In this respect, the goal of the series is to explore the advantages and limits of relational sociology. The series welcomes contributions related to various thinkers, theories, and methods clearly associated with relational sociology (such as Bourdieu, critical realism, Deleuze, Dewey, Elias, Latour, Luhmann, Mead, network analysis, symbolic interactionism, Tarde, and Tilly). Multidisciplinary studies which are relevant to relational sociology are also welcome, as well as research on various empirical topics (such as education, family, music, health, social inequalities, international relations, feminism, ethnicity, environmental issues, politics, culture, violence, social movements, and terrorism). Relational sociology—and more specifically, this series—will contribute to change and support contemporary sociology by discussing fundamental principles and issues within a relational framework.

More information about this series at
http://www.palgrave.com/gp/series/15100

Jamie Cleland • Mark Doidge
Peter Millward • Paul Widdop

Collective Action and Football Fandom

A Relational Sociological Approach

palgrave
macmillan

Jamie Cleland
University of South Australia
Adelaide, SA, Australia

Peter Millward
School of Humanities & Social Science
Liverpool John Moores University
Liverpool, UK

Mark Doidge
School of Sport and Service
Management
University of Brighton
Eastbourne, UK

Paul Widdop
Leeds Beckett University
Leeds, UK

Palgrave Studies in Relational Sociology
ISBN 978-3-319-73140-7   ISBN 978-3-319-73141-4   (eBook)
https://doi.org/10.1007/978-3-319-73141-4

Library of Congress Control Number: 2017963367

This Palgrave Macmillan imprint is published by Springer Nature
The registered company is Springer International Publishing AG
The registered company address is: Gewerbestrasse 11, 6330 Cham, Switzerland

FOREWORD

The authors of this book are to be congratulated, not only because they have written a great book about a fascinating subject, nor even for their innovative cross-pollination of ideas from the sociology of leisure and sport, on one side, and social movement studies and the sociology of collective action on the other. They have done both of these things and should be congratulated for these achievements but no less important, in my view, is their decision to take relational sociology out of the realm of pure theory, where it still largely resides today, into application and empirical analysis. Theoretical innovations come thick and fast in sociology. There have been so many 'turns' in the last 20 years that we must all be a little dizzy. This makes sociology exciting, and there are, of course, many reasons to value such innovations and evaluate them. I cannot help feeling a little disappointed, however, that so many of these revolutions leave the practice of sociology, as an empirical discipline, more or less unchanged. Our vocabulary changes as do the Gods to whom we express devotion in the 'theory section' of more or less everything we write, but other than that we carry on as before.

Relational sociology has the potential to achieve much more than this and I believe that the authors of the present study are setting the ball rolling, if I can be allowed that pun, in the right direction. They make a strong, persuasive, and fascinating case for using relational sociology to make sense of football, particularly collective action in football, discussing how and why these theoretical ideas are of use. More than this, however, they do so using case studies and empirical data and employing methods, such as social network analysis, which exemplify relational sociology in action. They don't just talk about relational sociology. They do it. The example will, I believe, inspire many others to follow. This is a genuine and significant step forward for relational sociology and hopefully one which will usher in a new phase in the development of the theory.

Our understanding of football benefits considerably from this work, but so too does our understanding of relational sociology. The various chapters of the book illustrate key concepts from relational sociology, but also, inevitably, in applying them they sharpen them, refine them, and allow us to see them in a new and different light. In this way, moreover, the authors not only apply theory, they do theory, in the field (or on the pitch), so to speak.

I hope that relational theorists and social theorists more widely will see the book in this light and embrace the lessons it has for us all. This is a major study in relational sociology and deserves the attention and discussion that this description suggests.

Manchester   Nick Crossley
17 August 2017

Acknowledgements

Howard Becker published the first edition of *Art Worlds* in 1982. The book argued that although a piece of art might be credited to an artist (or occasionally a group of artists), it was the product of a collective enterprise of all who existed in, worked in, or just interacted with an 'art world'. As such, the 'art world' and the development of fine art comprised everyone involved in producing, commissioning, presenting, preserving, promoting, chronicling, criticizing, and all pieces. Far from being an individual piece of work, each painting, sculpture, or composition was the product of the influences and ideas emerging from the networks of networks of networks made up of interactions. This book is credited to the four of us but is the product of the networks of networks of networks made up of interactions within and away from work that we keep. Acknowledgements have never been more clearly owed.

So with this in mind, Jamie would like to acknowledge the love and support of his family, particularly his mum and dad who supported him financially during his post-graduate studies that set him up on a career in academia. He would also like to acknowledge the research collaborations with Ellis Cashmore, Kevin Dixon, Rory Magrath, and Ted Kian that directly fed into this book.

As this book highlights the relational aspects of football fandom, it is the product of so many relationships, both scholarly and fandom related. Consequently, Mark would like to thank so many of the fantastic fans he has met on his European and non-league journeys. There are too many to mention individually, but special mentions definitely need to go to Endi and Dani at Football Supporters Europe. Their tireless work has brought together so many people for the good of fans. At Dulwich Hamlet, Alex is an incredible force, and without her, so much of this could not have been done. And last but not least, thanks to the Whitehawk Ultras who have shown what football fandom should be!

Pete would like to express deep gratitude to family and friends. In particular, he would like to thank his partner, Anna, who at the time of the first submission of the manuscript was almost eight months pregnant with their first child. Less than a week after that submission, Layla Rose Millward arrived five weeks early and life had changed for the better. Anna probably could have done without this book project invading Pete's waking (and often sleeping) thoughts during the entire period they were expecting! Into the 'academy', Pete would like to warmly acknowledge colleagues at Liverpool John Moores University and past and present PhD researchers he has supervised, the discussions with whom have fed into many thoughts that grew in this book. Also thanks are due to Robin Canniford, Matthew David, Richard Giulianotti, Michael Halpin, John Hayton, Tim Hill, Laura Kelly, Neil King, Andrew Kirton, Susan O'Shea, Dan Parnell, Renan Petersen-Wagner, Emma Poulton, George Poulton, and Karl Spracklen for their joint research enterprises with Pete on other research project and outputs. Their work, and collegiality, has directly and indirectly fed into shaping his thoughts on the material across this monograph.

Paul would like to dedicate this book to Jayne, Heidi, Paddy, Elsie, and Betsy. He would also like to thank his mum for her love and support and his Grandads Bill and Peter, who loved Burnley and Middlesbrough Football Clubs. Finally, he would like to thank Daniel Parnell, a great friend and scholar.

In addition, we would like to collectively recognize the help and support offered by a number of friends and colleagues. Particular thanks in this regard are owed to Palgrave Studies in Relational Sociology series editor François Dépelteau for his support and patience in our delivery of this monograph and Nick Crossley for being a sounding board for ideas across this and connected projects. Gratitude is also due to both for their strong work in the field that influenced our thoughts in establishing a cultural relational framework to explore football fan movements. We would also like to thank the support received from the Football Collective, Political Studies Association Sports Group, British Sociological Association Sport Study Group, and Mitchell Centre for Social Network Analysis, and not only on this book but throughout our academic life. Needless to say, extreme thanks are also owed to all of those journalists and football supporters who spoke to us and allowed us into their 'social worlds' to collect data in this research. We quite literally could not have produced this book without you.

Jamie Cleland
Mark Doidge
Peter Millward
Paul Widdop

CONTENTS

LIST OF FIGURES

LIST OF TABLES

CHAPTER 1

Relational Sociology, Collective Action, and Football Fandom

INTRODUCTION

Despite the grey skies it was the height of summer 2017 and, across many countries in Europe, it was association football's (hereafter football) 'close season'. There would be no competitive football matches in the UK for a full month and around a month had passed since the last ones took place—but this was 'fan activist' season. The week before, Pride in Football had run their 'Call It Out' conference—a meeting of supporters from across Europe engaged in challenging sexuality-themed prejudices at all levels of the sport. The following week, Football Supporters Europe (FSE; see Chap. 7) would run their fans' congress in the traditional rival cities of Gent and Lokeren in Belgium. Here, supporters from across the continent would get together to debate issues ranging from the ways in which they can help refugees to alternative approaches to the use of pyrotechnics at football matches. But today it was the annual 'Supporters Summit'—a meeting of football fan activists organized jointly by the national organizations of the Football Supporters' Federation (FSF; see Chap. 6) and Supporters Direct (see Chap. 5)—held at the Football Association's (FA) St George's Park facilities. The opening panel turned to 'Clubs in Crisis' hearing the voices of supporters from Coventry City (see Chap. 4), Leyton Orient, and Blackpool. These fans talked about how the practices of their club's 'owners' (of business and financial rights) had negatively affected their team 'on' and 'off' the field of play, along with the actions they had

© The Author(s) 2018   1
J. Cleland et al., *Collective Action and Football Fandom*,
Palgrave Studies in Relational Sociology,
https://doi.org/10.1007/978-3-319-73141-4_1

undertaken to bring about a change to circumstances. Later panel discussions would include leading on themes including 'safe standing' (lobbying to reverse a government and FA decision that supporters had to sit rather than stand at matches, see Turner (2017) for more details) and affordable match ticket admission prices (see Chap. 6). Fans from around 90 clubs sat in the audience and engaged in debate. Many more joined in and continued this debate on social media platforms such as Twitter. FSF chair, Malcolm Clarke, spread shared feelings of hope among fans by declaring that the 'supporters' movement had never been in such good shape' (field notes, 1 July 2017). The following day members of his organization unanimously voted to collectively lobby football clubs and news outlets to stop engaging with and selling the UK's largest selling newspaper, *The Sun*, principally in the light of the lies it had been found to have told about the conduct of Liverpool supporters in 1989 at the Hillsborough disaster from which 96 football fans unlawfully died, mainly as a result of poor policing and a stadium that was unsafe (Scraton 2016).

The 2016/17 season that had been one in which supporters' protests were highly visible in men's football in England and Wales. 'Wenger Out!' was the ubiquitous slogan of a section of Arsenal fans around the world. Signs adorned with this mantra were held aloft at matches, flown behind planes, and even appeared in St Peter's Square during the Pope's Easter address. Fans across the world regularly vent their frustrations at football managers like Arsène Wenger when results decline; yet football fans are increasingly campaigning around other issues affecting their clubs. In particular, as per discussions at the Supporters Summit, many of these campaigns are directed at owners who rarely consider the opinions of fans when making decisions. The end of the season in England especially highlighted a number of these criticisms. Blackpool fans boycotted the League Two playoff final against Exeter City in protest at the claim that the club's owners, the Oyston family, were extracting money from the club. Exeter City, in contrast, is the only football club in the Football League that is wholly owned by its fans. In the same league, Leyton Orient fans frequently protested against owner Francesco Becchetti in a season that resulted in the East London club being relegated out of the Football League for the first time in 112 years. Nearby, Charlton Athletic fans have had a long-standing dispute with the club's Belgian owner, Roland Duchâtelet. Elsewhere, fans of Blackburn Rovers, Carlisle United, Nottingham Forest, and others have protested against owners who they view as draining economic resources from football clubs, rather than supporting football success. During the same season, success was felt at clubs where fans have taken active involvement in protesting owners, campaigning around stadiums and rescuing clubs from financial problems. Brighton and Hove Albion, Newcastle United, Millwall, Portsmouth, and Plymouth Argyle all have had active involvement from fans in recent years. This book highlights this important phenomenon and seeks to explore these bouts of fans' collective action using an approach we call 'cultural relational sociology'. This approach draws upon the wide-ranging relational sociological approach but particularly borrows from Nick Crossley's *Towards Relational Sociology* (2011), which he neatly concludes with the following statement:

> Connections matter. Indeed for sociologists they are or should be 'what it is all about'. This is often recognized in relation to the microcosm but is no less important in relation to the macrocosm. Social life doesn't cease being about what actors achieve in interaction, whatever scale we choose to analyse it and whatever abstractions we bring to bear. From children in the playground to the 'world economic order', societies are networks of interacting and co-constituting actors, orientating to conventions, exchanging resources and more generally 'being social'. (Crossley 2011: 206)

Football fandom is an excellent way of assessing the networks of interactions. Football fans are heterogeneous and come from a wide range of backgrounds and interests. They share a love of the game and their clubs, and as we shall see, this is increasingly becoming an area of political mobilization. The social worlds of football comprise a diverse network of players, coaches, owners, fans, administrators, journalists, and more that have a variety of interests in the sport. In this way we can start to see how fans interact and intersect across groups. We follow Crossley and Edwards (2016) in adopting a relaxed position on the methods we utilize providing they capture the connections between social actors. As Crossley states '[c]onnections matter' because they are stamped across all domains and scales of social life and for sociologists 'should be "what it is all about"'.

This chapter is split into three distinct parts, utilizing the literature base to introduce and begin to unpack the three fundamental dimensions of our project: first relational sociology, second collective action and social movements, and, third, football fandom before adding a fourth dimension in discussing the methods we utilize in our empirical work. We start these discussions by outlining our understanding of relational sociology, by describing its common ontological roots and variations of its use before describing how it might operate using two conceptual levels which are, first, the central concepts in the approach and, second, the dimensions of relations, networks, and interactions.

Placing a Stake in Ground: Unpacking Relational Sociology

Society does not consist of structure and agency but of the social relations between human beings. Life is not the struggle of the individual against structure, nor the reproduction of the structure by the agent but an eternal round of interactions through which social relations between humans are made, transformed and destroyed. Even the vast and apparently faceless institutions of modern society are ultimately reducible to the social relations between humans. In every case, these institutions involve groups of humans in social relations coordinated in special ways and with access to certain resources. In this way, these social groups have the extraordinary powers which are so recognizable to individuals in modern society. The reality which individuals confront is human; it is others, even when these others are gathered into very large and powerful groups. (King 2012 [2004]: 17)

Anthony King neatly sums up the broad starting point of a relational sociological approach, namely, that sociological concerns with the individualisms of a specific agency approach or the holism of a reduction of society to its structures are intellectual red herrings. Society consists of humans who, in their networks, make up the systems and conventions that guide the behaviour and actions of others. It makes no sense to study individuals in either isolation or structures without the people who have built and maintained (or resisted) those structures. Instead we must look at the interactions of those individuals that shape past, present, and future systems and actions of individuals: for Crossley (2011: 23) 'relations are real and that the social world comprises actors-in-relation' (2011: 23), and for King (2012 [2004]: 17) 'society consists of human social relations which are the basis of even the most powerful associations'. Predating Crossley and King, Emirbayer (1997: 281) laid out 'a fundamental dilemma' which was the ontological question of whether we should be conceiving 'the social world as consisting primarily in substances or in processes, in static 'things' or in dynamic, unfolding relations'. It was clear he favoured the former as a world made up of interactions of interactions of interactions and networks made up of networks of networks. Despite the influence of the article—20 years from its publication Google Scholar data recorded it having been cited over 2200 times—it is debatable how much the ontological gauntlet has been picked up with Diani (2015: 4) arguing that the 'amount of systematic empirical research conducted from a relational rather than an aggregative perspective is still relatively limited'. In this book, we pick up the challenge of adding to this knowledge base by empirically profiling relational collective action in the context of football fans' projects.

The variety of social actors in the social worlds shaping football means there are many networks that pattern social relationships. Despite a unity in the belief 'that transactions, interactions, social ties and conversations constitute the central stuff of social life' (Tilly 2002: 72) and a rejection of 'the notion that one can posit discrete, pregiven units of analysis such as the individual or society as ultimate starting points of sociological analysis' (Emirbayer 1997: 287), there exist a number of different variations of relational sociology (Crossley 2011, 2013, 2015a; Dépelteau and Powell 2013a, b; Donati 2010; Donati and Archer 2015; Emirbayer 1997; Mische 2003, 2011; Tilly 2002; White 1995, 2002). Dépelteau and Powell (2013a: 3–4) identify some of these areas of debate:

Are social relations emergent entities, having a reality or an explanatory force unto themselves that is irreducible to individuals or to individual action? And if so, are they the building blocks of all other social formations—that is, is all of society relational—or are they only one type of social formation among others, so that society can be more relational or less relational from one time and place to another? Or, alternatively, are relations nothing more than patterns in the actions of individuals, patterns in the ways that individuals are constrained by each other's actions and are therefore dependent on one another? Or are they some third kind of thing, an elementary force out of which both individuals and collective phenomena are constituted? Do relations depend on humans' subjective perceptions of them to have any effects, or are they in some way independent of individual subjectivity? Are they imbued with meanings and defined by the meanings they carry, or are they essentially morphological and meaningless? Are relations concrete ties among actual people, or are they relative positions in some kind of social space? How does one observe relations? Can we measure and analyze them quantitatively, or qualitatively, or both, and if so, how? Are they something about which we can have objective knowledge, or does the relationist abolition of dualism extend even to the abolition of subject–object dualism, thus calling into question the very notion of objective knowledge and of science itself? Is relational thinking a vehicle for social critique, or is it a reactionary assault on Enlightenment humanism, or is it neither of these, being instead politically protean or polymorphous? Different relational sociologists give, or would give, differing answers to these and other fundamental questions.

This list of questions is comprehensive and a review of the literature shows the answers are not always clear, with little consistency running through the relational sociology 'project/paradigm' (Dépelteau and Powell 2013a: 10). Prandini (2015) describes the tensions and similarities in the contemporary work of Donati, Dépelteau, and Crossley as exemplifying these issues, while we add the 'New York School of Relational Sociology' (see Burt 1992, 2004, 2005; Tilly 2002; Mische 2008, 2011; Mische and White 1998; White 1992, 1993, 2002, 2008) to these debates.

One branch of relational sociology derives from critical realism (Donati 2010, 2015; Donati and Archer 2015). Donati (1983) brands this a 'relational theory of society'. This approach borrows from Bhaskar (1997 [1975]) who argued against the empirical realism offered by the tradition of positivism and the transcendental idealism offered in social constructivism. Instead, he offered a realist ontology that 'things' 'exist' even away from human experience of those things and argued for a structured and differentiated account of reality in which difference, stratification, and change are central: thus calling for *a new* ontology. Donati (2010, 2015; Donati and Archer 2015) picked up these threads, sharing a belief in avoiding both methodological individualism and holism. His social ontology is that relations might be invisible but this does not endanger their existence and researchers should not necessarily explore it through symbolic mediation, projections of individuals, or expressions of structures. Rather than viewing society as a space in which relations are contained and played out, he saw it as the tissue and makeup of those relations, meaning that his relational theory sees society *as* a relation rather than *having* relations within it (Donati 2015). Accordingly, he views a relation as having three properties:

(1) it says that between two (or more) entities there is a certain distance which, at the same time, distinguishes and connects them;
   (2) that such relation exists—i.e. it has a reality—in itself (from Latin 'exsistere', which means 'to be out having its own consistency' with respect to its generators) with its own qualities and causal powers;

(3) that such a reality has its own modus essendi (the modality of the being which is inside the relation), i.e. a structure, be it more stable or more volatile. (Donati 2015: 89)

Donati (2015) contrasts his ideas from Emirbayer's (1997) who he argues to be opposed to his relational theory of society and crudely reduces its relations between measurable transactions between actors. Thus, he argues that his work is different in the way social relations are defined and the types of reality that are attributed to those relations. Donati's (2015) contrast with Emirbayer (1997) could equally be provided in connection to Dépelteau (2011, 2013, 2015), who is comfortable placing transactions at the core of relational sociology. Dépelteau (in Dépelteau and Landini 2014) draws influence from Elias to develop the concept of the 'field of transaction' which relates to fluid social processes made by interdependent action, by interdependent actors that exist across spatial and temporal fields in the form of 'conversations', 'communications', 'couples', 'protests', 'social movements', 'fandoms', 'states', or 'empires' (which relates to Elias' concept of 'figuration', 1978). Such interdependent actors can be either human or non-human in Dépelteau's (2015) ideas; however, Crossley (2015a: 66) 'bracket[s] out' the latter favouring human and corporate actors (which he includes because they are composed of humans and their actions). Thus, there is disagreement over what an 'actor' might be, as well as how we see (if we can see) that relationship, in the relational paradigm.

There is also debate about the causal shape of social mechanisms. Dépelteau (2008, 2011) rejects 'codeterminism', as the study of interaction between social structures and agency. This guides him to reject the idea that a networked social structure leads to specific outcomes, offering this to be 'a soft version of the old deterministic structures' when, rather, 'relational sociology should move beyond the positivist principle of causality' (2011: 395). However, Harrison White formed deeply complex mathematical models of social structure that were primarily based on patterns of relations instead of the attributes and attitudes of individuals, that is, he viewed society as networks rather than as aggregates of individuals. In *Identity and Control*, White (1992) reminds us that the social world, and an individual's position in it, emerged from patterns of relationships, using models based on equivalences of actors across networks of multiple types of social relations to demonstrate this. Two important followers of White's were Mark Granovetter and Ronald Burt; their research made a huge impact upon network science showing how social networks play a central mediating role between micro and macro level of societies, impacting upon how relational approaches to sociology. Granovetter's (1973) weak ties is an important idea, given correlations between movements and tightly bound groups (Granovetter 1995; González-Bailón and Wang 2016). In this argument he presents that novel information is more likely to come from acquaintances rather than friends, so it is those ties that bridge across network structure that are important and a source of social capital, while strong ties are needed to gain coordination and cooperation, to pool resources and allow trust between participants to grow (Crossley 2008a). For Burt (1992) individuals with ties into multiple networks that are largely separated from one another may enjoy strategic advantage (Granovetter 2017). That is, they can act as broker when resources and information have to pass through them to reach other parts of the network. They have potential to exploit this 'structural hole' and enjoy substantial social capital (Granovetter 2017).

As a result of the rising recognition in the importance of social networks, not least as a consequence of Harrison White and followers, their study moved from being considered a method to a paradigmatic approach. Wellman (1988) notes that network analysis is a way of examining social structure by studying directly how patterns of ties allocate resources in a social system. However, most relational sociologists reject the idea that social life can be studied and explained entirely by attention to social networks (Granovetter 2017). Rather Crossley (2011) notes that network analysis is an invaluable methodology and set of tools for relational sociology.

Football is a cultural practice, and consequently, an acknowledgement of culture is important to our understanding of social relations in football fan movements. Prandini (2015) refers to Crossley's (2011, 2013, 2015a, b) ideas as a cultural approach to relational sociology. This form of relational sociology has flexible boundaries of inclusion. For Crossley (2011, 2013, 2015a, b), as long as relationships, networks, and interactions are core to the analysis of the differing levels of society, the work can be relational. As such, his relational sociology reminds us that ideas ranging from Marx, Durkheim, Simmel, Blumer, Mead, Goffman, and Merleau-Ponty and rational choice theory paid key attention to relationships in their analyses. Crossley's (1999, 2003, 2004) prior work had been influenced by critical engagements with Bourdieu's (1986, 2004 [1990]) ideas. This is evident in his relational approach although he argues Bourdieu 'lacks any

plausible mechanism to explain either the formation of habitus or the con-
centration of particular habitus within specific regions of "social space"',
correcting the argument to suggest that 'dispositions and interactions/
relations are mutually influencing. The former is in no way prior to or
determinate of the latter' (Crossley 2011: 27).

Crossley's aim of relational sociology is to find the mechanisms of interaction, network, and relationship that shape society and its outcomes. This
is 'cultural' because it provides a useful way of explaining social worlds
without reducing them to individuals or collectivities. Social structures
may enable or constrain actors but are the product of conventions and
resources that emerge from sociality people and groups of people in the
social world. 'Culture' is the things people do in common and derives its
meaning through emergent interaction between individuals and groups.
As such, Crossley argues (2011: 13) 'society is not a thing but a state of
play within a vast web of ongoing interactions' and a coordination of
efforts. He takes three empirical case examples which concretely illustrate
his relational approach: gym practices and behaviours (Crossley 2008b),
social movements (Crossley and Ibrahim 2012; Stevenson and Crossley
2014), and, most clearly, music scenes, especially those from 'punk' and
'post-punk' periods (Crossley 2008a, 2009, 2014, 2015b; Crossley and
Bottero 2015; Crossley and Emms 2016; Crossley et al. 2014; Hield and
Crossley 2014). In particular, two influences loom large over Crossley's
empirical articulations of his cultural relational sociology: Howard Becker's
(2008 [1982]) work in *Art Worlds* and the 'New York School of Relational
Sociology' which drew together strands of cultural sociology, political
sociology, comparative historical sociology, and collective action, with
social network analysis (SNA), creating a cross-fertilization of networks,
culture, and historical analysis (Mische 2011).

Becker (1974, 2008 [1982]) approached art as a coordinated form of
'collective action' comprising networks of both cooperating and competing individuals (who sometimes, and under some conditions, both cooperated and competed with each other). For Becker, art comes from 'art
worlds', and this is composed of not just the artist but all social actors who
are involved in the commission, promotion, production, presentation,
criticism, and chronicling of fine art who work together, even if this collaboration is not always intentional and not necessarily in the same physical space. Therefore, Becker (1974, 2008 [1982]) discusses how the
divisions of labour of the work of many individuals goes into the production of the tools and routines the artist owns which plays roles in the

creation of art work, alongside how coproduced shared meanings play in ascribing cultural value art. In essence he explored how ideas and realities in music and art saw compositions produced through the pooling of economic and cultural resources to produce collaborations that are 'more than the sum of their parts' (although Crossley 2015b notes that it is not exactly clear how the outputs that are produced through these artistic networks can be 'measured' to be 'more'). In doing this, art worlds rely upon conventions. A convention is broadly thought of as a social rule set of agreed and culturally encoded standards, social norms that may take the form of customs (Melucci 1996a). As we shall see, football can be considered a social world. Competing teams have to cooperate in order to hold competitions and comply with conventions and rules over signing players, hosting matches, and participating in matches. We follow Crossley's lead in a cultural relational approach to now dig out five central concepts in cultural relational sociology: (i) relations/relationships, (ii) interaction, (iii) networks, (iv) social actors, and (v) power/counter-power.

CULTURAL RELATIONAL SOCIOLOGY: CENTRAL CONCEPTS AND DYNAMICS IN SOCIAL WORLDS

The sociology of relationships is broadly dominated by the analysis of personal relationships between people (Jamieson 1999) but can involve engagements between people (and groups of people in organizations or nation-states) on any level of society. *Social relations* are 'live trajectories of iterated interaction' (Crossley 2011: 28) or, put simply, an engagement between two or more actors. This might change into a *social relationship* if that engagement is enduring with the expectation of an indefinite number of future interactions. Relational sociology is focused upon social relations and relationships although they may assume different forms, with different properties. For instance, Crossley (2011: 230) lists these properties as including friendship, hatred, economic exchange, slavery, sex, trust, and political alliance. These may shift in alignment with changing cultural processes of social interaction. Equally, as Crossley (2011: 38) points out, relationship formation involves an actor allowing another to move closer to them, permitting intrusions and sharing information that would otherwise not happen. However, Crossley also points out that relationships have limits on those processes, not allowing complete absorption. To be clear, the actors holding each other at a distance (in length and in what ways) define the different types of relationship.

Interactions are key to relationships. In mapping out 'symbolic interactionism', Blumer (1969) sets out three basic premises: first, that social actors respond towards 'things' (which could include other actors) on the basis of the meanings they ascribe to them; second, the meaning of such things is derived from, or arises out of, the social interaction that actors have with others; and, third, that such meanings are handled in, and modified through, an interpretative process used by the actor in dealing with the things that are encountered. The result of these interactions broadly forms 'meaning' and the webs of interactions something that could be labelled as 'society'. Crossley (2011) elaborated that interactions mutually modify the interactors conduct as, together, they form a whole that should not be reduced to the sum of its parts. Actors 'mutually tune in' to one another, each having 'a feel' for what the other will do and at what point in time (Crossley 2011: 32). This means that understandings and explanations of the interactions of either actor are impossible without reference to both; this is the case in both consensus formation and disagreement. As such, Crossley argues that actors will frame and conduct their debate within the parameters of what they feel is 'acceptable' (with such judgements arising out of current and past interactions).

These interactions and social relationships take place within the context of *networks* which Mische (2003: 258) argues are composed of 'culturally constituted processes of communicative interactions'. In their crudest sense networks are the patterns of connection across a society. Across sociology, networks are closely associated to two theoretical perspectives: 'actor network theory' (Callon 1991; Latour 1987, 2005; Law 1991, 2004) and the 'network society' (Castells 2000 [1996], 2004 [1997], 1998, 2000, 2013 [2009]). In actor network theory objects, ideas, and processes are seen as just as important in creating social situations as humans, an argument that Dépelteau has greater sympathy for than Crossley. Latour (2005) implies that the social structures with causal powers in which 'contexts' are external, constraining forces should be distinguished from the idea that 'actants' are interdependent social forces to give 'agency'. Thus, Latour offers that social forces do not exist in and of themselves, meaning that they cannot be used to explain social phenomena, favouring that a strictly empirical analysis should be undertaken to 'describe' but not 'explain' social activity. To be sure this means that, first, social phenomena are the relations between sets of human and non-human 'actants' and, second, attention is not paid to explanations of why a network exists but towards descriptions of their infrastructure, formation, and how they can fall apart. In Castells' work the 'network society' is a network of 'local' societies that are defined on the basis of the symbolic and communicative codes that regulate them rather than a territorial basis. Capital, in the form of people, money, and information, flows between potentially spatiality distant points. Donati (2013: 20) argues that the network society can be thought of as 'relational' because it 'gives rise to contexts for living where what is crucial is the quality of the relational *patterns* prevailing in the social spheres that constitute these contexts'. We depart from Crossley's ideas in that he omits Castells from his work but he does centralize networks in his cultural relational sociology by arguing that they 'make a difference. We can no more understand a relationship in isolation than understand an individual in isolation. How relations are configured in wider networks affects them' (Crossley 2011: 40). Networks are filled with the mechanisms and conventions that shape all forms of interaction and their products which may also become embedded within that network. They 'make a difference', he contends, in the sense of both who is known (part of the network) and who is not, so in the patterns of connection and non-connection. In other words, networks pattern relationships in the way they pattern '"social worlds" which centre upon specific shared or overlapping interests which bring actors together in collective action' (Crossley 2011: 22).

Crossley (2011: 42) points out that 'there are no interactions, relations or networks without actors, but actors take shape within those interactions etc. in a constant process of formation or becoming'. We follow Crossley in viewing *social actors* as humans, trade unions, business organizations, and national governments but drawing the line where actor network theorists would not by not including objects and places. Actors are not self-contained or self-sufficient but are agents in relation. We are comfortable with Jasper's (2014) parallel of actors to 'players' who act out their (potentially multiple) roles in specific arenas but may be governed by different rules and norms in relation to each other. Deriving influence from the 'New York School of Relational Sociology', in Crossley's work, specific actors may play specific roles in the relationship, interaction, and network such as gatekeepers or brokers—once again, we embrace this idea. We also accept the ideas of the 'actor' from Touraine (1988) who argued that 'society' is a field of social action in which structures are constituted by those actions or networks of action. Actors in their networks both shape and are shaped by such structures and social change comes about through aggregations of social actors bringing about social action through expressions of power and counter-power, which we pick up in our discussions about collective action.

Our understandings of *power* and *counter-power* are shaped by Castells (2013 [2009]: 10), who defined the former to be the 'relational capacity that enables a social actor to influence asymmetrically the decisions of other social actor(s) in ways that favor the empowered actor's will, interest and values'. Thus, power is attributable to relationships that give rise to economic, social, cultural, and political ways of controlling other actors in a network and 'resides in the complex sets of alliances and joint activity constituted around particular projects and interests in networks' (Castells 2013 [2009]: 45). For Castells (2011: 772) 'wherever there is power, there is counter-power' which is 'the deliberate attempt to change power relationships [...] by reprogramming networks around alternative interests and values, and/or disrupting the dominant switches while switching networks of resistance and social change' (Castells 2013 [2009]: 431). In other words, counter-power could be the power of protest groups or networks of individuals in protest and collective action. Undoubtedly power might be related to resources, while counter-power might be realized through such resources. Castells outlines information, the flows of which might be enabled by information and communications technologies, as a key resource. Crossley spreads his net wider, with power existing in the balance of interdependence between actors who are organized in their networks and social relationships through their interactions in the various contextual (and potentially connected) *social worlds* that might include football fandom and collective action with their social structures that can both cause and constrain action.

The coming together of the five core concepts of social relations, interactions, networks, social actors, and power has multiple dimensions in the composition of the social worlds in society. Cutting across these concepts, there are six dimensions that need to be considered in the analysis: temporal, spatial, symbolic, emotional, narrative, and structured. Football is saturated with stories and memories of events that take place throughout a season, and these provide emotional meaning for fans. First, social worlds have *temporal dimensions*. As Crossley (2011: 29) notes, 'what happens early on in the interaction may both facilitate and constrain what happens later'. In other words, networks, relationships, and interactions are the product of a history of previous networks, relationships, and interactions but may change over time. Similarly, the resources and situations that render 'power' are not temporally static: what is desired or not desired at one moment may not hold such value in a future or past moment in time. Football fandom is constantly changing as new social actors emerge or disappear or if regulatory frameworks change. Second, social worlds also entail *spatial dimensions*, which is to say that the power dynamics that hold in one place do not in others (Löw and Weidenhaus 2017). Following Castells, we are not confusing space with territory—networks can cross-cut nation-states, as we shall see in Chap. 7 with the importance of FSE. Yet mobilization often occurs around specific geographical spaces. As Crossley (2015a, b) points out, the punk and post-punk musicians were originally organized around the 'foci' of nightclubs, recording spaces, and 'hang-outs' through where friendships and ties were formed. In football, fans have stadiums, pubs, and supporters' clubs as foci. This provides the opportunity to share ideas, devise strategies, and provide emotional support.

Third, given that actors read each other's actions and, on the basis of that, classify/typify each other, interactions in the social world hold *phenomenological* and *symbolic dimensions* (Schutz 1972; Crossley 2011). Actors also reflexively read and respond to their own actions, in the meanwhile establishing situational definitions of who and what they are engaging with and internalize their given 'roles' in that environment. In other words, actors read the symbols of a social world (that is relationally created) and these filter into their internal thoughts about themselves and others in that environment. Football is saturated with symbolic meaning, from club colours, badges, legendary players, and 'sacred' stadiums. These provide meaning and sustenance to fans and fan movements. This connects with the fourth dimension of the social world—namely, that they are *affective* in that the thoughts, memories, perceptions, and impressions of others generate a range of emotions which may spread across the network and may even provide the 'moral shocks' needed to motivate action (Castells 2015 [2012]; Crossley 2011; Jasper 1998). In making this point, Burkitt's (1997, 2014) argument that emotions are not expressions of inner processes but are modes of communication within relationships and interdependencies highlights the affective dimension of the social world in so far as: 'Relations of conflict may stir in people feelings of aggressiveness towards certain others with whom they are interdependent—those who may not have fulfilled their responsibilities in the relationship, or who may have betrayed or undermined it—but aggressiveness comes from the interrelations not, originally, from inside the person' (Burkitt 1997: 40). Football is imbued with emotion as fans share the rollercoaster of wins and defeats, the exhilaration of scoring goals, and the despair of conceding. It is this emotional connection that frequently motivates fans to mobilize in order to save their club or fight for their voice to be heard. Related to the affective and symbolic, the fifth dimension relates to narratives. Crossley (2011: 36) points out that 'we can and do tell stories about our relationships' such as 'relating how we met and what events we have been through together'. These narratives may elicit a range of emotions (Polletta 2006) highlighting the *storied dimensions* of social worlds. Crossley (2011: 96) points out that this is important given that stories allow actors to relate their own experiences to others in a range of ways, and White (1992: 65) argued that stories provide the phenomenological reality that links identities in a social network, highlighting the importance of this dimension of the social worlds for a cultural relational sociology. However, sixth, social worlds are also *structured*. This means there are networks of social actors who, in their relationships, structure human behaviours in the ways that White, Granovetter, and Burt argued but may have their actions shaped by memories, emotions, and perceptions in the way White, Granovetter, and Burt underdiscuss.

COLLECTIVE ACTION, SOCIAL MOVEMENTS, AND PROTESTS

A second key theme in this book is collective action. We explore this as a site of study rather than as an area to theoretically develop. This site is important as football supporters constitute one of the biggest social movements in the world (Lestrelin 2012). For instance, as Millward and Poulton (2014: 3) argue, the hundreds and thousands of Manchester United fans engaged in protests against the Glazer family makes them 'among the best supported social movements in the world'. The protest Millward and Poulton refer to takes into account supporters who are aggrieved at the socio-political and economic issues they associate to the financial ownership of 'their' club by external investors. This type of mobilization is picked up in Chap. 4 when we look at Coventry City supporters' protests, but Lestrelin (2012) considers the communal act of supporting a football team to be a collective action unto itself. When these diverse expressions of fandom are added together, it is clear that they constitute a significant form of collective action.

However, in a similar vein to 'relational sociology' there is some contestation around how the collective action is used and what it refers to in the social scientific literature (see Blanton and Fargher 2016; Coleman 1973; Chong 1991; Evrigenis 2007; Hardin 1982; Kelly and Breinlinger 1996; Lauman and Pappi 1976; Marwell and Oliver 1993; Medina 2009; Olson 1968; Schutz and Sandy 2011 for a few wide-ranging examples). In this regard, our understanding 'magpies' from various perspectives but broadly follows Alberto Melucci (1980, 1984, 1988, 1989, 1995, 1996a, b), and we therefore turn to his ideas before briefly also discussing other attractive theoretical propositions, such as those offered by Diani (2015) on networked social movements. More pertinent to understandings of collective action by football fans is that these political mobilizations are around a form of consumption: football. This is distinct from earlier forms of social movement that were centred on gaining political rights on the basis of class, race, sexuality, or gender.

Akin to Coleman (1993), Marwell and Oliver (1993), Olson (1968), and Melucci (1989, 1996a) broadly paralleled collective action to social movements and the group processes involved in protesting and campaigning. In doing such, his work—along with that of Castells (1976, 1983, 2004 [1997], 2013 [2009], 2015 [2012]), Offe (1985), Habermas (1981), and Melucci's 'mentor' (Diani 2015: 4), Touraine (1977, 1981, 1989, 1990, 1992)—followed trends and trajectories including rational action (see Coleman 1973; Gamson 1990 [1975]; Olson 1968), resource mobilization (see McCarthy and Zald 1977), and political process (see McAdam 1982, 1986, 1988; Tilly 2009) theories in the study of mobilization to form the canon of 'new social movements' theories (NSM, Buechler 1995). We do not have an exclusive commitment to the broad ideas in NSM, but it is important that Touraine (1992: 129) noted that they are 'usually traced back to the 1960s' where, in Europe, there was the rise of student protests, women's rights advocacy groups, and anti-war and anti-cold war protests, while in the USA there were 'civil rights and woman's liberation movements, anti-Vietnam war campaigns and new gay movements'. As such, Scott (1990: 26) argues that new social movements tend to be linked to a single broad theme or interest—such as peace, the environment or inequalities related to gender, ethnicity, or sexuality—rather than the interests of the working classes. NSMs are not conceived to develop any notion of total politics, or to subsume politics under a single focus and by the same token, they avoid 'political reductionism' (Melucci 1996a) that may 'bypass the state' (Offe 1985). In other words, change is sought by lobbying social spheres of society rather than the obvious political spheres of governments and only affects certain areas or groups. This accords with the relational football fan movements we profile: none are explicitly 'party political' or opposed to the specific state policy, with most linked to single broad issues—such as a rejection of the commercial values associated to elite football (Chap. 3), resistance towards owners' practices at football clubs (Chap. 4), gaining supporters a democratic voice in the running of a club (Chap. 5), ticket pricing (Chap. 6), or general belief in broadly defined anti-discriminatory values on a European scale (Chap. 7).

In his specific account of an NSM approach to collective action, Melucci (1996a) centralizes the concept of 'collective identity' as a pre-cursor to mobilization. He argues that this is important because potential participants must feel part of a group before they invest their time and other resources. In making this point, he is critical of resource mobilization theory, arguing that those such as McCarthy and Zald (1977) have based their work on a rational choice model of action and, by marginalizing theme of identity, have emptied the social dimension of the mobilization (Melucci 1996a). His ideas show collective action to be treated as the active creation, product, and accomplishment of actors, produced within the limits and possibilities posed by a 'complex society' (Melucci 1989, 1996a). This means that the collective action is not just the sum of individual actions involved in the mobilization but takes on its own life through the relational processes involved within it. However, Melucci (1995, 1996a, b) argues these relationships are based upon consensus, conflict (which is 'a struggle between two (or more) actors seeking appropriate resources regarded by each as valuable', Melucci 1996a: 22), and solidarity (which Melucci (1996a: 23) defines as 'the ability of actors to recognize, and be recognized, as belonging to the same social unit'). In making this point, Melucci (1989: 25) argues movements bring together diverse actors with a range of differing goals and aims in a 'multipolar action system'. This means that processes of collective action are necessarily based upon processes of interaction, negotiation, conflict, and compromise among a variety of different actors who fail or succeed in producing 'unity' and a collective identity of the movement (Melucci 1989: 217). Within this web of complex relations, the 'submerged reality of movement networks' exists, which is constituted through the relationships between participants in social movements that are hidden from public view, through which people communicate and exchange information with each other, while also negotiating a collective identity and developing a sense of belonging (Melucci 1989: 338). In effect, the 'impact or importance cannot be reduced to visible mobilization events or their impact on the polity' (Fominaya 2010: 396). Connections in collective actions make the 'action' 'collective', but these connections may not be immediately visible.

A frustration with Melucci (1996a) is that his theoretical framework is ultimately a sketch of thoughts around mobilizations. In other words, he does not strongly guide us towards an analytical framework, although the reverse of this point is that there is fluidity in his approach and the strong potential to use his work in ways that are useful to specific contexts. As such we are not rigidly glued to a single approach and can draw upon other influences alongside his theories. However we find three key foci of his work particularly appealing for our study of football supporters. First, we are attracted to his idea that social movements are the result of negotiation and interactive processes rather than taken as a pre-given object of study. Second, and connected, Melucci outlines the steps towards a relational theory of collective action and recommends basing the analyses on the forces that work for and against collective action. Third, Melucci's need to understand 'the submerged reality of movements' (1988: 338) through the observable and immediately non-observable connections that produce conflict, tensions, and interactions within and outside of the movement as well as those on the outside is appealing given the diversity of social actors in our work. This is because we follow Crossley (2011: 30) in viewing opinions and attitudes as relational stances 'form[ed] and lodge[d] between actors not within them'.

This is not to say that we do not take the opportunities afforded by Melucci's looseness of theory to take on board other influences in the understanding of fan collective action. In his work on social movements and networks, Diani (2015: 4) argues that 'the empirical scope of his [Melucci's] research was limited by his increasingly exclusive interests in the loose, informal networks' and called for more empirical work to be undertaken on networked collective action, which is a challenge we pick up in this book. Although Melucci was critical of some dimensions of the rational action approach to collective action, we are interested in Olson's (1968) claim that actors with more resources will carry a higher burden in action than poorer ones, giving rise to the 'free-rider strategy' in which those with fewer resources (defined in a range of different ways) will attempt to benefit without a full contribution to the action in those groups where that do not provide benefits only to active participants. Potentially all fans gain from fan activism, for example, getting cheaper tickets from the Twenty's Plenty campaign, but not all fans participate (see Chap. 6). Olson challenges the idea that if everyone in a group (of any size) has interests in common, then they will act collectively to achieve them by arguing that when the group grows, concentrated interests of 'free riders' may trump the majority interests. This is because large groups face comparatively higher costs when attempting to organize for collective action, while small groups face relatively low costs, and individuals in large groups will gain less per capita of successful collective action (Olson 1968).

UNPACKING FOOTBALL FANDOM: CONNECTIONS THAT MATTER

Our discussions around football fandom are located within the sociology of sport. It is not our intention to survey this large sub-disciplinary area given that these discussions can be usefully found elsewhere (see Malcolm 2011, 2012, 2014; Young 2016). Suffice to say Bourdieu (1998) argued that scholars in this area have been sidelined in 'mainstream' sociology, although the last three decades have seen investigations of football cultures afford studies into aggression, violence, and deviance (Armstrong 1998; Armstrong and Harris 1991; Dunning et al. 1988; Williams et al. 1992 [1984]), 'globalization' (Giulianotti and Robertson 2004, 2007, 2009), racism (Back et al. 1999; Burdsey 2006; Cleland and Cashmore 2014, 2016; Cleland 2014a), gender (Caudwell 2011; Dunn 2014), and homophobia (Cashmore and Cleland 2011, 2012; Cleland 2014b, 2015b; Cleland et al. 2016). By exploring the sociological interest of collective action through the prism of sport consumption/football supporter cultures, we follow the above-cited research down the path Elias (2008 [1986]: 10) laid out in suggesting that 'studies of sport which are not studies of society are studies out of context'. In the UK, research in this mould has disproportionately focused on studies that use football fandom as the arena to understand social process (Malcolm 2012; Horne and Malcolm 2016). For Ha-Ilan (2017: 13), football fandom 'is a form of collective behavior conducted within social networks' with Blackshaw (2008: 336) stating how 'football's community is a profound agreement of cultural identity, companionship, and breathing space, one of the most intimate things permissible in a modern public space'.

Frosdick and Marsh (2015 [2005]) offer that the first social scientific insights into football fandom arose from the desire to understand the contested phenomenon of 'hooliganism' from the 1960s. In the decades that followed, trends of describing and/or explaining these actions ranged from Marxist criminological approaches (Taylor 1971a, b), ethogenics (Marsh et al. 1978), process sociology and figurationalism (Dunning 1999; Dunning et al. 1988, 1991; Williams et al. 1992 [1984]), and ethnographic accounts (Armstrong 1998; Armstrong and Harris 1991; Giulianotti and Armstrong 2002; Giulianotti 1991, 1995, 1999; King 1997a, 2001; Pearson 2012). Although relational sociology is not explicitly discussed in this literature, relationality was a central theme in an area of debate that reached little consensus. For instance, Taylor's analysis of social and economic change at the end of the 1960s describes how this alienated young working class men from clubs who sought to attract a more affluent supporter base to generate more income at clubs to be able to improve players' wages. This, he argued, resulted in violent resistance as working class male supporters felt that the traditional relationship they had with clubs was broken. Similar accounts were presented in Dunning's accounts of crowd behaviour from the 1960s where the economic hardship resulted in a rough working class sub-culture whose perceived alienation from society led them to use violence at football to publicly demonstrate a collective resistance to authority. Marsh et al.'s (1978) account of violence among Oxford United fans found the existence of an internal hierarchical structure that operated within specific 'rules of disorder' where individual roles were assigned for the collective good of the hooligan group. Indeed, this collective element of resistance is also a continued feature of modern research on football violence such as the work of Giulianotti and Armstrong (2002) and Pearson (2012) who illustrate the interactions that take place between different hooligan groups to avoid detection by the police. Moreover, Stott et al. (2007, 2012) refer to how policing styles affected the fan groups' internal dynamics, patterns of collective action, and level of 'compliance' with the police. In some cases, a sense of victimhood led to the emergence of a 'social identity' among fans that could result in conflict, but changes in policing showed increasing interaction and dialogue between fans and the police. Interactions, relationships, and networks of association clearly mattered in all of these—in some respects—to the same extent they do in other empirical articulations of relational sociology, such as music scenes and gym cultures, as highlighted earlier in this chapter.

King (2012 [2004]: 19) saw relational sociology to be a 'social ontology which insists that society consists only of social relations: humans interacting with each other on the basis of shared meanings. Sociology should focus precisely on how these social relations come into being and are transformed by the humans engaged in them'. Some of his empirical research emerged from a two-part ethnographic study on the consumption of football particularly focusing on masculine bonds between male supporters of clubs in their supporter practices (King 2002 [1998], 2003). In particular, King's (1997b) analysis of the 'lads' at Manchester United found that their interaction and solidarity with each other produced the enjoyment and pleasure; it was not something that existed unto itself. Rather the 'craic' and 'buzz' came through collective demonstrations of loyal support that consisted of regular attendance, singing, and fighting, irrespective of whether the team was winning or losing. From his relational sociological work, these 'humans interact […] with each other on the basis of shared meanings'. This work allowed him to talk about the phenomena of 'football hooliganism' through some of the encounters he heard about although his focus was not explicitly on supporter violence (King 1997a, 2001). Malcolm (2011: 2) describes his work as important as 'mark[ing] the end of the dominance of hooliganism studies and thus a broadening out of the sociology of sport research agenda'.

The temporal period in which King's work was set was one in which there were profound structural changes to elite professional football with the emergence of the Premier League (in England) and the Champions League (across Europe). As such he keys into the accelerated commodification of professional football since the 1990s and how it was experienced by networks of supporters. Giulianotti (2002) pointed out that these experiences were not uniform but are often based on socialities in local economic, cultural, and legal contexts. Cleland (2010) outlined how this has led to the emergence of a significant number of 'active' fans who participate in football-related information, resistance, and interaction with other fans, clubs, and the media in order to instigate a sense of inclusion in the game. In their analysis of football fans as social actors, Perasović and Mustapić (2017: 3) illustrate how it is 'creating a common denominator, a covenant, a symbolic field—or expressed in sociological terms—a social movement'. On this point, Numerato (2015) refers to two inter-related layers of collective emotion when football fans establish a social movement: (1) the sociability, affective loyalties, rituals, and passions in the practice of football fandom and (2) how these emotions are subsequently protected when faced with anger and threat. Football fan movements can take many different structural forms depending on whether the focus is to challenge a particular issue or something more deep-rooted that requires a long-term strategy (Ha-Ilan 2017). This subsequently impacts upon the type of action that might take place given the contextual background. Thus, this book investigates some of the social and cultural processes behind particular collective mobilizations and the extent of their 'success'. It addresses particular outcomes and forms of conflict such as all-out confrontation, confrontation regarding particular decisions or issues and the different roles and element of cooperation fans have with relevant clubs and other external stakeholders (such as the local and national media).

The structure of football as well as fandom changed dramatically since the 1980s. One element of this was deindustrialization and growing importance of the service sector economy at the expense of manufacturing but also through significant changes to English and European football in the post-Hillsborough period. Initially this was based on the upgrading or building of new stadia, but it also led to the Football Association to effectively embrace neo-liberalism through the introduction of a Premier League in 1992 and subsequently a more commercially driven strategy, most notably through higher ticket prices and the league's relationship with satellite broadcaster, BSkyB. The result was a fundamental change in the historic fan-club relationship and emergence of significant fan activism and resistance in various contexts not just in the UK but also across the world. As suggested by Williams (2007: 129), 'it is routinely claimed now that elite soccer clubs in England today lack some of the earlier deep-rootedness and cultural and personal commitment traditionally provided by their previously loyal and local core soccer supporters'.

According to Crabbe (2008), the social, political, and economic changes to the culture of football fandom led to a cultural transformation that impacted on individual choices of consumption and subsequently enhanced a sense of individual reflexivity (Bauman 2000; Giddens 1991). In his analysis of football fandom as everyday practice, Stone (2007: 170) states how it expresses 'notions of self-identity, belonging and interpersonal relations; all of which are initiated, reinforced and challenged through the enactment, internalization, embodiment and contestation of structural influences within the daily practices of life'.

The increase in active fans can be traced back to the 1980s after the Heysel Stadium disaster in which 39 fans died and the negative portrayal of fans by the government and the media (Scraton 2016). One of the first signs of collective action at club level began with the publication of a print fanzine (a short magazine-type publication written by fans and sold at home matches that contained humour as well as a resistance to the government and football authorities). Indeed, three months after the Heysel Stadium disaster, the nationally focused Football Supporters' Association (FSA) was created with the aim of providing fans with a greater influence in the game (in 2002 the FSA was replaced by the FSF). The success of the print fanzine movement and national organizations led to the creation of more club-based Independent Supporters' Association (ISA) movements across the UK during the 1990s where supporters voiced their concerns at a local level (Nash 2000). Further changes aimed at increasing supporter representation at clubs emerged in 2000 through the creation of Supporters Direct with the emphasis on forging 'a new relationship between supporters, their clubs and the local community' (Hamil et al. 2001: 7). This consisted of legal and practical support for fans who sought to purchase enough shares to become more involved in the day-to-day running of clubs by gaining some form of representation on the board of directors. There had been often-cited example that occurred before then with supporters at Northampton Town rescuing the club from administration in 1992 and rewarded with a supporter on the board of directors. One of the most recent was at Portsmouth, with the club the first in the history of the Premier League to go into administration. In April 2013, with the club in another period of administration, the Supporters' Trust took over the club after raising £3 million. Other examples include Exeter City (Treharne 2016) and AFC Wimbledon (Couper 2012), but the best example of part-supporter ownership is at Swansea City, with the Supporters' Trust retaining its 21 per cent ownership of the club that was mostly accrued when the club was playing in the lower leagues (see Chap. 5). However, it is important to reiterate the composition of these trusts; they are not 'male-only' spaces as Dunn (2017) points out.

Despite the growth of active supporters across the world, we should also be mindful of the significant number of passive supporters, defined here as those who do not seek a participatory role in collective action or protest (Cleland 2010). Of course, this can be club and country specific, but in the case of clubs in the UK the financial resources needed to acquire enough shares to be able to influence the decisions made by clubs are often out of the financial reach of most supporters. It should come as no surprise, Swansea City apart, therefore that the success of supporter movements in terms of supporter representation at board level has often come in the lower leagues of British football.

Many cases of fan 'alienation' also exist. Although Taylor (1971a, b) offered this as an explanation for 'hooliganism', this theory has been broadly discredited with elite professional football's commercial operations growing at a far faster rate than fan violence (which is difficult to measure with any validity). Despite this, alienation is a motivating factor for some fan groups. The most high profile was the debt-laden takeover of Manchester United in 2005 that led to locally based protests and resulted in a new democratically run football club, F.C. United of Manchester, whose mission sought to 'maintain or re-establish the community' and to be 'an example of how to bring football back to ordinary people' (Brown 2007: 627). Perhaps as a result of this was the creation of the 'Spirit of Shankly' (SoS) group at Liverpool in 2008 to challenge a similar debt-laden purchase reportedly over £400 million by its then American owners, Tom Hicks and George Gillett (Millward 2012). Although Williams (2012) states that the eventual takeover by the Boston-based New England Sports Ventures (later becoming Fenway Sports Group) was a result of the global economic crisis, rather than fan resistance, the new owners did seek to immediately repair the damaged relationship between the club and supporters. Other examples of tangible forms of success can be found at Hull City in 2014, where supporters stopped the owner Assem Allam from changing the club name to Hull Tigers (Hayton et al. 2015).

In his analysis of expressions of fandom as a form of collective action that may not explicitly be concerned with the cultural politics of supporting a football team, Lestrelin (2012) suggests that friendly interactions and levels of sociability encountered over the course of fandom makes up the incentive to join this form of 'activism'. Friendships, ties, networks, and relationships are thus at the core of 'life' (Fischer 1982) of which the inherently interactive processes involved in football support is an important part for many fans. Numerato (2015: 125) refers to the socio-cultural reflexive actions of football fans and how 'collective actions to transform, redirect, and reorient contemporary football culture, to struggle against the negative impact of football's allegiances with business within the context of neo-liberal principles and the mass media, and to address corruption or mismanagement in football governance bodies'. Understanding this reflexivity to be a 'social practice of a discursive nature', Numerato explains the intrinsic role of emotions fans feel towards their club and its local community and how forms of protest can inhibit as well as facilitate social change. Reflecting on the potential of success as well as conflict, Ha-Ilan (2017) states that common interests and values within collective action encourages trust and collaboration. In some cases, the sense of community felt by fans became an important element in their collective identity and led to the fan-led creation of teams across the world, including Hapoel Katamon Jerusalem, Austria Salzburg, F.C. United of Manchester, and AFC Wimbledon. As Chap. 3 discusses, this movement has also led to fans following clubs in the lower leagues and outwardly rejecting associations with global football brands.

As well as examples from the UK, there has been quite widespread resistance to the neo-liberal nature of modern football, with Numerato (2015) suggesting it has led to increasing reflexivity among fans. One feature of this is the globally networked Against Modern Football social movement that is comprised of various actors and methods of protest at the local and global level to raise their discontent and seek to enforce change (see Gonda 2013; Hill et al. 2016; Turner 2017; Webber 2017; Doidge 2015). This is often visible through the use of flags, banners, boycotts, campaigns, workshops, political lobbying, petitions, as well as match day demonstrations. Across Europe, resistance to the commodification of football is often the responsibility of the sets of fans who call themselves 'ultras' who offer alternative patterns of contemporary consumption through the maintenance of a culture of traditional fandom (Pilz and Wölki-Schumacher 2010; Testa and Armstrong 2010; Doidge 2015). Doidge and Lieser (2017) refer to the global spread of the ultras movement from its initial origin in Italy through Europe and across the world (e.g., see the special edition on the ultras movement in the journal *Sport in Society*, 2017). While the local dimension of ultras remains important, Doidge and Lieser state how this is intersected at a global level through the global media, social media, as well as the increased engagement and interaction between the varied fan movements. Leftist ultras groups are explored in Chaps. 3 and 7.

In this respect, the internet became a significant feature within active fan culture 'as it allowed for content and information to be circulated, consumed, interpreted and reproduced at a global level with no restrictions on time, place or space' (Cleland 2015a: 115). The availability of the internet through computers, tablets, and smartphones has led to the emergence of a transnational 'network society' (Castells 2000) given the increasing opportunities to engage in synchronous or asynchronous communication at any time of the day in any part of the world via message boards, Twitter, Facebook, e-zines, and blogs. What these virtual fan communities have resulted in according to Millward (2008: 299) is 'a site for both the construction of (collective and individual) identities and "information age" sports fan democracy' as fans are now able to exchange views, opinions, and thoughts, and these can be shared across the world to influence fans of other teams and vice versa. As will be outlined in the case of Swansea City (Chap. 5), initial online conversations about the ownership of clubs can become more formal when supporters perceive there to be a significant threat to a club's future. Dunning (1999: 126) argued that 'fans are, individually, the least powerful person in the football figuration'. If supporters operated alone he would be correct. Any potential relational power of their collective actions might come from their mobilizing into a critical mass. Connections may emerge through different means and formats in the collective actions of football fans, but, as Crossley (2011: 206) states, they clearly 'matter'.

With the proliferation of opportunities to share information online, face-to-face interactions are still important. As argued earlier, football has a wide range of spaces to meet and interact. From pubs, supporters' clubs, and stadiums, fans regularly meet to share the emotional experience of the game. Chapters 3 and 7 reinforce the importance of face-to-face meetings. In the non-league there is greater opportunity to meet and this helps contribute to more durable relationships. Fan congresses, like those outlined at the start of this chapter, also provide a space to meet fans from a wide range of different clubs. They also have speakers and workshops where ideas and strategies can be shared, while also providing access to a much wider network of fans.

Summary: Connected Fans in Collective Actions in the Social Worlds of Football

We are clear in that we follow Crossley and Edwards (2016) in adopting no fixed method to the relational sociological approach of football fans collective actions. Indeed, our sole concern is that they capture the connections between social actors. In Chaps. 3, 4, 5, and 7, data is principally collected through qualitative fieldwork, interviews, and observations. Chapters 3 and 7 in particular were gathered through ethnographic work in the respective groups. This provides an opportunity to view the interactions in context and see how, why, and where fans interact. However, in

Chap. 6 we utilize SNA using Twitter scrapes around key phrases. This merits discussion. SNA starts with the premise that social life is created primarily and most importantly by relations and the patterns formed by these relations. Borgatti and Halgin (2011) elaborate on this position noting that a network consists of a set of actors and a set of ties (of a specified type). The pattern of these ties generates a structure and the actors occupy positions within the structure (Borgatti and Halgin 2011). In SNA the twin notions of structure and position play fundamental roles (González-Bailón and Wang 2016). Furthermore, an added component relates to network flow, that is, what flows between actors that create these ties. The threefold nature of structure, position, and flow within networks are important elements in a relational thinking towards social movements, yet the majority of studies lack an SNA approach, which for González-Bailón and Wang (2016) is strange as SNA theory and method are well placed to offer sound analytical insight into social movement structures and coordination. In addition online networks can readily be captured and explored and visualized using SNA. Borgatti and Halgin (2011) and Borgatti and Lopez-Kidwell (2011) document the theoretical framework for SNA, contrasting two fundamental network models that frame structure, position, and flow. These two models are 'the network flow' model and the later named 'network bond model', both of which are important for the networked interpretation of the protest movements on ticket prices, which we will show in highlighting the structured dimension of relational sociology in Chap. 6. However it is important that we lay out an explanation of these models. Network flow is a model built upon how information and other resources travel from actor to actor along paths consisting of ties interlocked through shared endpoints (Knoke 2012; Borgatti and Halgin 2011; Borgatti and Lopez-Kidwell 2011). In contrast, the bond model is indicative of bonds between actors, and the network tie serves as a bond that aligns and co-ordinates action, enabling groups of nodes to act as a single node, often with greater capabilities (Borgatti and Halgin 2011). Borgatti and Halgin (2011) note that this bonding function serves as the basis of coordination and is the analogue of the flow function in the flow model. Knoke (2012) notes that these two generic models underlie most SNA frameworks and can be jointly applied to uncover fundamental mechanisms to answer research questions about how network properties produce relational outcomes.

This book is divided into eight chapters (including this Introduction) and comprises of five distinct case studies. The next chapter, Chap. 2, builds upon the conceptual material discussed across this chapter to devise substantive touchstones that are useful in developing a cultural relational sociology that explores collective actions and, specifically, the collective action of football fans. Chapter 3 looks at connections and friendships, a key point in any relational sociology, formed between non-league football fans in England. Chapter 4 charts the ongoing protests of supporters of Coventry City who saw their team move to play home matches in Northampton, a neighbouring town, in the 2013/14 season. While the relocation of sports teams might not be unusual in North America, it is unconventional in European football and sparked a protest in which coalitions between fans and local journalists were formed. Chapter 5 discusses the theme of supporter ownership at Swansea City in which fans have a place on the club's board of directors and a say in governance issues. Chapter 6 profiles how supporters of various clubs have mobilized in order to lobby for the price of admission to football fans to be reduced. Although 'outcomes' are difficult to measure, this action has helped to usher in a maximum 'away ticket' price for visiting supporters of £30 at Premier League matches. Chapter 7 moves beyond the UK focus to discuss activist networks on a European scale of fans who pool their resources and know how to fight discrimination in football across the continent. Chapter 8 draws together the arguments we present in the case studies and the development of cultural relational sociology and concludes by offering that connections are central to social life, in all its social worlds, including within football fans' collective actions.

CHAPTER 2

The Touchstones for Understanding Football Fans' Collective Actions: A Primer in Cultural Relational Sociology

INTRODUCTION

In Chap. 1 we outlined the concepts and dimensions of a cultural relational sociology that is influenced by Crossley (2011) and could be applied to a range of socialities, including football fans' collective actions. However, despite discussing these, we did not provide the touchstones for analysis in the areas specific to collective action and football fandom. In this chapter, we critically draw upon literature and ideas located in the collective action/social movement and sociology of sport canons to provide these touchstones. In doing so, we draw upon seven areas: (i) the structures of and roles in collective action; (ii) affect, emotion, and collective effervescence; (iii) communication, cooperation, and conventions; (iv) mobilizing resources; (v) tactics; (vi) recruitment to collective action and 'outcomes' of mobilization; and (vii) the spaces and places of organization and action. By completing this, we both set up our analytical areas but also establish them for relational analysis by other sociologists of collective action/social movements, sport, and culture more broadly. We begin by looking at the positions, roles, and divisions of labour in collective actions.

© The Author(s) 2018
J. Cleland et al., *Collective Action and Football Fandom*,
Palgrave Studies in Relational Sociology,
https://doi.org/10.1007/978-3-319-73141-4_2

STRUCTURES OF COLLECTIVE ACTION: POSITIONS, ROLES, AND DIVISIONS OF LABOUR

As shown in the previous chapter, football fans constitute one of the largest and most frequent forms of collective action in the world (see also Hughson and Free 2006; King 2001; Pearson 2012). Yet football fans are also a heterogeneous group with a wide variety of people engaged in fandom in general and activism in particular. While this is not dissimilar to other forms of social movement, football is an important site of inquiry as political mobilization occurs around a form of consumption: football. Collections and syntheses of literature have showed no uniformity in the way social movements and collective actions are structured and organized (Chesters and Welsh 2010; Crossley 2002; Della Porta and Diani 2006 [1999]; Edwards 2014). At the core of these debates are the relationships between individuals in movements with the most contrasting positions broadly coming from 'social movement organizations' ('SMOs' see Zald and Ash 1966) and 'new social movements' ('NSMs' see Melucci 1996a). In the former of these categories, a social movement might range from being comprised of multiple organizations that may (or may not) work together in the pursuit of shared outcomes or may be a lone SMO (Carroll and Ratner 2001), while examples of the latter category may take a more fluid or 'networked' structure. For instance, Castells (2015 [2012]) argues that NSMs might be 'rhizomatic', that is, literally grass roots in their emergence, growth, and organization, defying traditional demographic boundaries or measurement procedures in manners that link a broad network of parties.

Campbell (2005) notes that SMOs have formal structures with appointed (and sometimes salaried) roles. Organizations like Football Supporters Europe, Supporters Direct, Kick It Out, and the Football Supporters' Federation have distinct roles and constitutions. Freeman (1973) argued that the role of an organizer in the formation of the movement has been underplayed in the literature. She suggests that this individual may not be the 'leader' and yet 'such an individual or cadre must often operate behind the scenes' (Freeman 1973: 806), while Chomsky (2003: 188–189) argues that the *real* agents in social movement are the grassroots organizers who engage people in movements rather than the 'Great Men' [sic] leaders, who are not necessarily (or even ordinarily) the same people who organize protest and provide the platforms for collective mobilization. For Castells, however, rhizomatic NSMs tend not to have explicit leaders. While broadly following Castells, Hill et al. (2016) use the example of the British 'Stand Against Modern Football' (hereafter Stand AMF) movement, who campaigns against various commercial tenets of football, to point that NSMs may not generally have 'formal' leaders but may still have a number of 'soft' leaders within their ranks who might be those who hold positions of social, political, and/or cultural influence and who might, for instance, have experience of dealing with media agencies, perhaps even having personal/professional relationships with people in 'formal' positions of influence (journalists, politicians, etc.), to be able to communicate the aims and tactics of their collective action. The key differences between the two forms of leadership may include levels of formality and temporality in the role—that is, 'soft' leaders might be more likely to assume their roles momentarily—and as specifically suited to the immediate task in hand due to knowledge and networks of connections, rather than as a long-term or semi-permanent venture.

Indeed Aronowitz (2003: 163–165) and Della Porta and Diani (2006 [1999]: 30; 50–51) have both pointed out that in social movements that have 'formal' or 'soft' leaders, those who have influential roles are likely to hail from the 'new middle classes' and/or have developed high levels of 'cultural capital' (Bourdieu 1986, 2004 [1990]). In a similar way, Florida's (2002) concept of the 'creative class', which describes those 'people in design, education, arts, music and entertainment, whose economic function is to create new ideas, new technology and/or creative content' and whose professions normally require higher levels of formal education but usually not set in Fordist working practices (Florida 2002: 8), could be used to describe those who formally, or informally, lead social movements. Beyond the 'leadership' of movements, uncountable other formal and informal roles in the division of labour might exist, depending upon the structure and nature of the collective action (Opp 2009).

While some of these roles are concrete, Castells (2015 [2012]) points out that others are less so. The two roles he is specifically talking about are 'programmers' and 'switchers'. To elaborate, he argues that the networked practices and goals of social institutions are shared and reproduced across multiple 'nodal materialities', including people, objects, organizations, corporations, and cities. These logics must be *programmed*, or assigned, substantiated, and distributed through communication structures. Although programs are irreducible to supporting communicative structures, Castells contends that networks and the social logics that they carry may be transformed—or 'reprogrammed'—through communicative activities set about through the collaborative actions of individuals who are, deliberately or accidentally, 'programmers' of collective action.

Programing new logics requires communicative work to ensure a program is endorsed across nodes that constitute a societal network. Castells describes this work as accomplished by 'switchers' whose power lies in their ability, 'to connect and ensure the cooperation of different networks by sharing common goals and combining resources' (Castells 2013 [2009]: 45). In the wider society, Castells (2013 [2009]: 429) declares Rupert Murdoch to be 'the most deliberate switcher', because of his capacity to link cultural, political, and financial networks through his media empire. In the context of football, he 'programmed' elite professional structures in England to produce the highly mediatized 'Premier League' in 1992 (David et al. 2015). Social movements as both SMOs and NSMs have switchers too—switching together previously disparate groups in protest by forming new coalitions, such as the emergence of 'no to modern football' collectives (see Chap. 3) and the trans-European networks that fight anti-discrimination in football (see Chap. 7). In this respect, the main difference, between the two types of collective action, might be a greater level of formality, such as contracts and official agreements, which are far more likely for SMOs (Carthy 2015). By working across geographical locations, without any identifiable formal leaders, and with an ability to mobilize a diverse collection of people, fluid and rhizomatic NSMs such as Occupy, the Indignadas, and MoveOn.org (Carthy 2015; Castells 2015 [2012]) are difficult to predict the actions of and on what terms protests will mobilize next, the individuals who will be involved, and how these individuals will respond to management and policing. SMO leaders, however, are more likely to have fostered working relationships with the police and maybe even the organizations they are collectively acting against, which may favour negotiations between the parties (Martin 2015; Minkoff and McCarthy 2005) as some of the 'soft leaders' in Stand AMF had pre-existing connections to those in the Premier League and the Football League (which administers the three professional leagues below the Premier League) in Hill et al.'s (2016) research. Beyond these differences, the formalized structures of SMOs lend themselves to official 'memberships' (Zald and Ash 1966), whereas NSMs generally consist of less formal and loosely organized social networks of 'supporters' (Buechler 1995).

Affect, Emotion, and Collective Effervescence

Most football fans will acknowledge that football is an emotional experience. One of the things that draws people to football is the atmosphere. This collective emotional experience links many people under the shared experience of singing, clapping, and cheering in unison. Fans openly talk of their love for their club and hate of their rivals. The oft-quoted Bill Shankly stated that football was more important than 'life or death'. Many fans have been married or had their ashes scattered at the football stadium of their clubs. Although it is a form of consumption, football engenders this emotional connection. People do not generally have their ashes scattered in a Tesco supermarket. Often football is the only time men and women are seen crying in public when teams experience relegation or a final loss. On a more mundane level, fans connect with one another through friendships that are fostered through regular conversations and meetings in and around the game (Giulianotti 1995; Jones 2000; Doidge 2015).

Emile Durkheim argued 'society' to be powerful, offering the capacity to affect feelings and make an individual feel powerful if she/he is connected to others through collaboration and support. Indeed, through studying Aboriginal rituals, he offered that such bonds can lift individuals to exaltation. He pointed out that periods of assembly are more excitable through individual's association and interaction with each other, calling this 'collective effervescence'. Relationships and the 'things' individuals do in those relationships give to the type of excitement undertaken in crowds, parties, football matches (Bromberger 1995), and protests (Jasper 1997, 1998), but with which people are less likely to exhibit when they are on their own. Excitement, for Durkheim, is created by joint ceremonials.

Durkheim therefore suggested that participation in collective activities can bring about exaltation which, through rituals and rites, can make individuals feel as if they are lifted out of themselves and made into new beings. Such rights and rituals can bring about intense emotions which are experienced as coming from external to the individual. This affect is collective effervescence and is generated by social relations although it may be transferred onto an external object that becomes sacred through symbolizing such at 'society' and the elevated emotions associated to it. Thus, Durkheim's account of collective effervescence is valuable as it captures the idea of social 'force' at its birth, when embodied humans feel themselves and are transformed through an emotional structuring of sensory and sensual beings. For social movements, as Collins (1990) states, 'Emotions are the "glue" of solidarity—and what mobilizes conflict'. Moreover, emotion is important in 'moving' the 'movement' of a collective (Crossley 2005).

Emotions are generally thought to be subjective, cognitive experiences that are characterized by biological, psychological, and physiological expressions and reactions (Barbalet 2001; Katz 1999; Prinz 2004; TenHouten 1996) that are understood as situational, interactional, and temporally situated (Denzin 1984; Kemper 1978; Shott 1979). The role of the emotions in protests was evident in some of the earliest theorizations of collective behaviour, such as in the work of Le Bon (2008 [1895]) and Blumer (1951), but it was alluded to rather than meaningfully analysed and generally 'denigrated' in the belief that 'one could be "gripped" or "seized"' by them (Chesters and Welsh 2011: 71). Emotions were, above all else, assumed to be 'irrational' (Chesters and Welsh 2011: 71), and this belief continued through rational action, resource mobilization, and political process trends in the theorization of collective action. Some branches of NSM have broken from the negative connotations of emotionally directed human behaviour, but interest in the area is tangential to a broader understanding of the collective identities associated with mobilizations (Castells 2015 [2012]; Melucci 1996a; Opp 2009: 275–303; Touraine 1981). These are experienced in relation to others in the collective and are therefore inherently relational (see Spencer et al. 2012).

As discussed in Chap. 1, emotions are inherently relational; they emerge from social interaction. Football and social movements provide ample opportunities for individuals to interact and build a collective effervescence. The reemergence of emotion as a central component of social theory can be traced to the work of Randall Collins (1970). Subsequently, Collins (2004) draws on the work of Durkheim, in partnership with Goffman's microsociological work, to develop interaction ritual theory. Goffman's interaction rituals highlight the small repetitive actions that underpin everyday interaction. They are rituals because 'this activity, however informal and secular, represents a way in which the individual must guard and design the symbolic implications of his [or her] acts while in the presence of an object that has a special value for him [or her] (Goffman 1967: 57). As social actors manage their presentation of self in relation to their 'others', they engage in patterns of interaction they deem appropriate for the situation. These patterns of behaviour have to be performed and reperformed for there to build an emotional rapport with others. As Collins (2004: 105) argues:

> Interaction ritual theory gives the most fine-grained picture of how emotions are transformed in the process of interaction: rituals begin with emotional ingredients (which may be emotions of all sorts); they intensify emotions into the shared excitement that Durkheim calls "collective effervescence"; and they produce other sorts of emotions as outcomes (especially moral solidarity, but also sometimes aggressive emotions such as anger).

Collins (2004) identifies four ritual ingredients that are required to lay the foundation of an interaction ritual: group assembly, barrier to outsiders, mutual focus of attention, and shared mood. The repetitive aspects of these factors produce collective effervescence, an emotional energy that bonds the participants. This can be within dyadic relationships, as well as larger groups. It also produces group solidarity and standards of morality, as well as creating the symbols of this social relationship.

A key breakthrough in the turn to emotions as a focus social movement research came from Jasper (1997) in his comparative study of protests associated with both proanimal rights groups (emerging from Jasper and Nelkin 1992) and anti-nuclear power groups (see Jasper 1990). In doing so, he shows that emotions are a part of a culture that allows humans to adapt to the world around them, process information, and interact with others (Jasper 1997, 1998). Jasper (1997) states that social life is filled with all range of emotions, which often cannot be separated from cognitive beliefs and moral values. Although there may be a range of stimuli that develop the emotions that stir people into protesting, Jasper (1997) argues that attachments to a 'place', grounded in the need for ontological security, and the 'threat' of losing some dimension of that 'place' can motivate a collective to work together to mobilize as a protest. Jasper paid attention to the development of 'moral shocks'—which are kinds of visceral unease that capture people's attention and encourage them to articulate their moral intuitions (Jasper 1997, 1998)—in the development of his theory. Indeed Jasper (1997: 113–115) argued that:

> If researchers paid attention to them, I think they would discover a variety of emotions in protest. First, individuals have emotional allegiances and experiences that help propel them into protest. Fear, dread and an accompanying sense of threat are key motives. Grief could also play a role, either

following the loss of a loved one or as a more general sense of cultural loss. An alternation between shame and anger drives much political conflict [...] as shame often triggers aggression. Anger and outrage will almost always play a part, as will pre-existing negative and positive affects towards symbols, places, individuals and groups.

Those researchers who have 'paid attention' to emotions that develop across a social movement have offered similar suggestions: 'frustration, anger, alienation and anomie' (Jasper 1998: 397); 'loyalty, joy, hope, fear, contempt, sadness, distrust, empathy, compassion, altruism, outrage, gratitude and happiness' (Flam and King 2007: 2–3); and 'positive feelings of love, loyalty, pride, joy and enthusiasm and negative feelings of hatred, sympathy, fear, anger, sorrow, sadness, jealousy, shame and dejection' (Yang 2006: 1389). Jasper (1997: 114) offers 30 'emotions potentially relevant to protest': affect, anger, compassion/sympathy/pity, cynicism/depression, enthusiasm/pride, envy/resentment, fear/dread, grief/loss/sorrow, hatred/hostility/loathing, joy/hope, love, outrage/indignation, resignation, shame, suspicion/paranoia, and trust/loyalty. These emotions are potentially useful for spotting which develop, when and in relation to what others. However, these emotions—by Jasper's own admission—are far from exhaustive and do not tell us anything but the vaguest terms about how they develop. Castells (2015 [2012]) tries to shed some light when he argues that in the twenty-first century, the internet, enabled by the communicative architecture of social media forms, plays a role in changing a collective's emotional state. With reference to the collective actions of social movements, he argues that protestors will talk around the issues that evoke their anger, but through these lines of communication, they metaphorically hold hands together, and when that happens their initial outrage turns into hope for the future. Thus, the internet offers the potential to facilitate geographically disparate communality between individuals which evokes the collective effervescence to change individual and collective emotions in their communicative relationships. Emotions are thus relational even if they might be mediated online.

Communication, Cooperation, and Conventions

The emotional bond fans have with each other and their club fosters a connection to a broader group. Blumer (1969: 94) argued that social reality was in a continuous process of (re)creation through coordinated 'group action' which 'takes the form of fitting together individual lines of action'.

It is therefore interactive. Group action consists of fitting together individual actions, brought about by interpreting other social actors' actions in a coordinated way. It is therefore inherently relational, involving actors working together to achieve common goals. Diekmann and Lindenberg (2001) argue that individuals cooperate if they willingly act in a manner that contributes to the others' welfare. In collective action research, theories of cooperation are closely linked to rational action theory (Olson 1968). In this vein of research, an actor cooperates if and only if she/he chooses a course of action that will lead to a collectively rational outcome when other actors behave cooperatively as well. Coleman (1973) suggests networks—and specifically, intermediaries in networks—are important in the understanding of cooperation. He argues that intermediaries in networks may play at least three roles: first, as an 'advisor' who introduces interested parties to coordinate, facilitating interaction between others to create trust (which he parallels to 'social capital'); second as 'guarantor' who absorbs the risk in the event that such trust turns out to be misplaced; and third, as 'entrepreneur' who combines the resources of several actors to place them into the hands of others who are expected to realize gains. However, individuals' willingness to cooperate may depend on how people communicate through definition, description, and 'framing' of a situation (Goffman 1974; Oliver and Johnston 2000; Snow et al. 1986). Of note, Kahneman and Tversky (1984) found that individuals are keener on avoiding losses than on achieving gains. Thus, social movement may recruit more members to cooperate in their collective action if they communicate their cause as a defence of a common resource rather than the achievement of a new public good.

Becker (1974) argues that conventions are constituted from the agreements in the way of doing 'things'. He states that artistic conventions include all decisions that must be made with respect to works produced in a given art world, even though a particular convention may be revised for a given work. This means that conventions shape the materials that are used in the case of music, when musicians agree to base their music on the notes contained in a set of modes or on the diatonic, pentatonic, or chromatic scales with their associated harmonies, or in art when photographers use black, white, and shades of grey to portray physical dimensions of space, place, or person. Conventions are important because they facilitate prompt decision-making by referring to a conventional—or standardized—way of doing things through easing efficient coordination of those within a network. This point noted, as well as enabling action, conventions constrain it too (Becker 1974, 2008 [1982]). This is because they come in complex interdependent webs of people, products, and ways of doing things whereby one small change requires making changes to other activities. Thus, if a set of conventions becomes physically concretized in equipment, materials, training, or facilities, all might have to be changed if a convention is altered. However, Becker is keen to point out that although standardized and constraining, conventions are usually open and this might emerge through relational interaction.

Football can be consumed differently, through ranging modes and of varying importance to the individuals involved, but conventions exist in the differing practices of football fandom (David and Millward 2012; Giulianotti 2002; Weed 2007). For instance, Millward (2011) outlines that wearing a replica shirt and a 'jester hat', knowing when and what to sing (and when not to), and which public houses to visit give a fan the distinction of being seen by others as particular 'type' of supporter. In other words, they are shorthand conventions in the ways Becker (1974) outlines. Coordination and conventions are based upon communication channels in the 'world' of the network (Becker 1974, 1976, 2008 [1982]; Crossley 2011). There is a wealth of literature that explores group communication (see, for instance, Dominick 1987; Habermas 1986, 1989; Lull 1995; McQuail 1985; Scannell 2007; Silverstone 2006; Williams 2016 [1962]). Kádár (2013) uses a range of data including historical letters and asynchronous email exchanges to focus on 'the ritualized relational practices formed locally within the social unit of network' (p. 4) and approaching communicative rituals as 'social action triggered by interactional practices' (p. 3). In making these points, Kádár (2013) argues conformity to intra-network communicative expectations, which he calls 'conventions', are necessary for a collective to smoothly 'function' and develop its own linguistic rituals (which may include 'politeness', a set of lexical terms and/or discursive topics). These modes of communication help to build 'trust' among group members and help to 'network identity formation' in the group (Kádár 2013). This conception of identity emerging from the network runs parallel to similar ideas offered by Jenkins (2014) and Melucci (1996a) in which social identity is inherently relational in so far as it is articulated and expressed against 'others'. In the context of football fandom, Clark (2006) points out that such social identities are often performed against rivals—clearly demarking the in-group ('we') as distinct from the out-group ('they'). Kádár (2013) suggests there are two rituals of communication that form network identities. First, there are contrastive identities which are inherently relational as they are intentionally adopted practices that are distinctive of a particular group set against contrasting out-groups, and second, there are non-contrastive identities to be the 'practices that form a network identity without positioning the network against others' (Kádár 2013: 67).

A large strand of the collective action of social movements literature views 'communication' as the way in which the mobilizing group expresses itself to the wider public through the media (Rosie and Gorringe 2009; Rucht 2005; Ryan 1991; Swank 2000). This form of communication may involve delineated brokerage roles for some in the network of protestors with media outlets (González-Bailón and Wang 2013, 2016). However, through the explanation of 'informational capital', Castells (2013 [2009], 2015 [2012]) talks about 'mass self-communication' media such as Twitter, YouTube, and blogs. In contrast to established, vertical modes of information dissemination—the traditional power-bases of communication corporations—these modes of communication encourage horizontal networks, 'self-generated in content, self-directed in emission, and self-selected by many who communicate with many' (Castells 2013 [2009]: 70). Castells particularly sees horizontal networks as loosening the hold of established structures by allowing 'individuals and organizations to generate their own messages and content and distribute it in cyberspace, largely bypassing the control of corporations and bureaucracies' that have traditionally controlled flows of information in society (Castells 2013 [2009]: xx). In bypassing the established 'nodes' of communication—the channels and places that process and disseminate information coded with a distinct network logic—Castells (2000 [1996]) explains that information-age mobilizations are able to disentangle from paramount power as these open and fluid communications afford new forms of network coalitions to mobilize. The ability for new network connections to be made relies on the 'horizontal' affordances of social media such as Twitter (Murthy 2013), technologies that bypass traditional 'top-down' media communications, allowing countervailing ideas to circulate unfiltered by the interests of established programmers (Castells 2015 [2012]). Castells asserts that digital communication technologies can 'switch on' connections between previously unrelated groups, renewing potential for social change by connecting coalitions of grassroots support with democratic processes. The invention of 'mass self-communication' is important in grassroots resistance (Castells 2013 [2009]; 2015 [2012]). 'Mass self-communicators' use the 'horizontal networks', which may be free of the established programming power-bases such as communication corporations, such as Myspace, YouTube, and Facebook, to countervail against the existing power relations (and the ideological forces they create), that is, the emergence of a new type of communication system that is 'self-generated in content, self-directed in emission, and self-selected by many who communicate with many' (Castells 2013 [2009]: 70). For Castells, the power of the internet lies in the formation of horizontal networks that connect people with similar interests and desires across traditional demographic and geographical divides. As such:

> [D]igital networking technologies allow individuals and organizations to generate their own messages and content and distribute it in cyberspace, largely bypassing the control of corporations and bureaucracies [and ...] A few technologically savvy youngsters with some ideas and a small amount of money can create companies that would challenge the restriction of free communication imposed by oligopolistic business. (Castells 2013 [2009]: xx)

Exploring how conventions and communication channels are made, and with whom, is therefore a key touchstone in a cultural relational sociology of football fandom and collective actions.

Mobilizing Resources: Generating Trust and Other 'Capital'

The emotional connection to the broader group motivates some fans to engage in political mobilization or develop a support for a particular football team. But individual fans have different personal networks and skills, so there are issues in coordinating mobilizations with the socio-cultural politics of football. Pierre Bourdieu (1986, 2004 [1990]) argued that individuals occupy multidimensional social spaces in which she/he is defined by forms of capital that are articulated through relationships with others. In doing so, he distinguished between three forms of 'capital'— 'economic', 'cultural', and 'social'—which are used to (re)produce inequality and may be either consciously acquired over time or passively 'inherited' from people, socialization, and surroundings.

Bourdieu (1977) does not pioneer on understandings of economic capital which are derived from a Marxist underpinning to look at how actions are given value in 'primitive' societies. For Bourdieu (1986), economic capital can be symbolic in the sense of money—the intrinsic coin or note denoting something more of social value—or material in the forms of the property and other objects with high use values being owned. Bourdieu first used the term 'cultural capital' to explain differences in future life paths and outcomes for children (see Bourdieu and Passeron 1990). He elaborated that cultural capital has three distinct forms (Bourdieu 1986). First, there is embodied cultural capital which is manifest in the mind and body, through—for instance—accents, ways of thinking, and even body shape. Second, objectified cultural capital includes the physical objects that are owned, including books, works of art, scientific instruments, and machines (Leguina et al. 2016). In one sense, this type of cultural capital is easily converted into economic capital by buying and selling such items, but in another, the sense of 'understanding' the item—such as a painting—is not paralleled to simple its ownership. Such cultural capital may be relational such as when an art dealer explains the significance of the painting to a buyer. Third, institutionalized cultural capital is that which symbolically denotes that an institutionally recognized level of cultural capital has been achieved. Academic qualifications might be a prime example of this which may then be converted into labour market gains for the individual, perhaps resulting in the generation of economic capital. Bourdieu (1986: 88) describes social capital as 'the aggregate of the actual or potential resources which are linked to possession of a durable network of more or less institutionalized relationships of mutual acquaintance and recognition'. Therefore, he views social capital as membership within a group, which provides each member of the group with the support of any mutually owned capital, specifically including the 'trust' of other people within the real or imagined community which may even advantage themselves, the social class, and their associated others (such as their children) (see Widdop et al. 2016). Ibrahim (2015) followed Crossley (1999, 2002, 2003) in developing a Bourdieusian approach to the collective actions of social movements, specifically focusing upon struggles and tensions in the British anti-capitalism movements. He argued that symbolic capital present in social and cultural forms was particularly useful in the movements since the actors involved sought rewards that did not produce monetary gain—with cultural capital including the knowledge and skills gained by workshops and social capital created by alliances formed through the 'switching' of networks together with individuals in other social and political groups. Effectively, Ibrahim guides readers to note that in the collective actions of social movements, various forms of social and cultural capital are traded and generated through interactions. Football fandom also entails the demonstration of cultural and social capital. This is seen clearly in the understanding of its cultures, given that there is no definitive way to read the 'signs' of the sport or individual clubs. Yet, such distinction is evident within the ways that one type of supporter assumes that she/he is more 'authentic' than other groups. Some 'traditional' supporter groups (see Millward 2011) view the sport and 'their' club in a particular way and—like the romantic tourist in Urry's work—'consider it as 'authentic', as real' while attempting to 'make everyone else sacralize [it] in the same sort of way' (Urry 1995: 138; see also 2005 [1990]). This is the product of a cultural capital of knowing the 'right' conventions of that fandom and the social capital of connections into those supporter groups. As such, an imagined geography emerges which might come to partially define authenticity among the group. This geography is largely based upon hailing from or laying some sort of cultural or biographical link to the town or city in which the supported football club is located. However, these boundaries are culturally constructed through networks of human relations given that outsiders from beyond the elastic boundaries are occasionally allowed to join the group of 'real' traditional fans.

Akin to Bourdieu, Castells views capital as largely synonymous with power. However, for him capital takes mobile informational forms as well as material and 'traditional' symbolic forms. Thus, Castells (2013 [2009]) adds 'network capital' to this mix. For him, network capital is the social capital that is specifically generated in the 'space of flows' of people, money, images, and information from across the world. As such, network capital is a result of cooperation via electronic networks and in turn fosters the habit of such cooperation. This cooperation includes sharing of information and the use of computer-mediated communications, the creation of specific products, and the achievement of set objectives. This form of capital is generally created by communities of interest, where membership is based on personal interest, skills, background/experience, and sharing of a common purpose. As network capital is generated in a 'space of flows', it is not bounded by physical location, thus opening up a wider array of possibilities for individuals to interact and behave as 'global citizens'.

Ibrahim's work can allow us to take this one theoretical step further. He reminds us that capital is only 'operationalized as resources' (Ibrahim 2015: 56). This brings, as Crossley (2015b) does in his work on punk and post-punk 'worlds', ideas from resource mobilization theory to the fore. It is offered in resource mobilization theory that core—often professional—groups in social organizations work together to bring money and supporters to the movement, as well as attracting the attention of the media and striking those alliances with those in power (McCarthy and Zald 2001). To do this, they mobilize resources which Freeman (1979) points out might be tangible (such as money, participants, organization, and communications infrastructure and leaders) or intangible (such as skills/knowledge and public support). Jasper (2006: 91) argues that resources are the tools, physical capabilities, money, and raw materials that are utilized in strategic interactions. He says that resources are related to material dimensions of life, even when they carry cultural messages and create affect. For Jasper, resources might be physical and/or symbolic, including the direct physical force of coercion and money (as the capacity to buy needed materials) which give them the clearest source of power to social actors and organizations in relationships with 'others'. However, Jasper (2006) also argues that resources might also include physical equipment, on the proviso they are accompanied by the cultural meanings and necessary ability to be able to use such equipment. Similarly, money only becomes utilized as a resource when the social actor/organization has the ability to spend that money on something that aids the mobilization. In this sense, the questions are raised about how these forms of capital, translated through social processes of interaction, might be generated through online as well as offline interactions and relationships involved in social movements and converted into resources and specifically how these relational processes might enable further collective actions to occur.

'Trust' is very important to these discussions. Trust refers to the actions of others (Luhmann 2017 [1979]) and, in many accounts, runs parallel to ideas of 'social capital' (Field 2008). Indeed, Crossley (2008b: 477) sees social capital as 'the manner in which networks and their emergent properties (e.g., trust and norms) can constitute a resource for their members' but cautions that such a basic insight has been developed in diverse ways. For instance, Bourdieu (1986) views high levels of social capital as having 'friends in high places' or 'old-boy networks'. It is not reducible to economic and cultural capital, but its acquisition runs parallel to them given that friends in particular social locations are acquired in social contexts (in the case of 'high-place' elite schools and/or golf clubs) which have economic and cultural entry barriers. In this book, we see connections between fan activists and media personnel and even politicians (see Chaps. 4 and 6, in particular).

Coleman (1973) argues that social capital is a property of social relations, rather than individuals. This means it is inherently relational but also that while it can be used, it cannot be exchanged. It only has a use value, no exchange value, or opportunities to make connections can be exchanged, but the social capital generated through that connection cannot be transferred to another social actor. Any 'sociology of trust' is thus a relational sociology, bound by social relations rather than individual actors. Sztompka (2003 [1999]: 25) states that in situations when social actors have to act in spite of uncertainty and risk, trusting in others becomes the crucial strategy for dealing with uncontrollable futures. This might emerge and be mobilized as social capital in the case of the various 'supporter trusts' that are referred to in this book but which is the central focus in Chap. 5.

TACTICS: 'TASTES', NARRATIVES, AND INNOVATIONS

Fan mobilizations coalesce around specific causes or symbolic targets, such as owners or charity work. Consequently, fans will discuss, debate, and decide upon a proposed course of action in order to succeed. Byrne (1997: 19) stated that 'if there is one characteristic which sets movements apart from other forms of political action, it lies in *what* [Byrne's emphasis] they do' arguing that such 'doing' is the range of tactics—or tools of action—a movement utilizes. Blumer (1951: 203) argued tactics to be an important dimension of collective action (or collective behaviour, in his terms) as it 'becomes more clearly organized'. He argued that tactics are context dependent but share three main aims of increasing the number of movement members, maintaining the number of movement supporters, and, most crucially, achieving the movement's aims and goals. Alinsky (1971) added to this list by stating a tactic might involve identifying a 'villainous' enemy who can be directly blamed for any perceived injustice. Thus, 'blame' becomes a tactic 'when some relation exists between the blamer and the blame' (Tilly 2008: 6).

Tilly (1978, 2008) used the term 'repertoire of contention' to refer to tactics. Under the social movement banner of 'contentious politics'—which was a new turn in political process theory Tilly developed with Sidney Tarrow and Doug McAdam—it suggests that repertoires are the product of interactions between social actors, and as one group (which could be a set of individuals or an SMO) finds a tactic or tool in protest to be successful, it will diffuse to other, similarly minded groups who will adapt and use it for their own means (see Tonkonoff 2017). Viewed in this way, the repertoire is a convention that shorthands a mobilization. However, viewed another way, Tilly argues that repertoires can be limiting too, as groups are more likely to revert to tried and trusted methods rather than seeking innovation. Jasper (1997: 97) adds to this by arguing that protestors might deploy a range of tactics that they value, enjoy, feel appropriate, and have skills in utilizing. These feelings might convince those in the mobilization that their tactics are the most appropriate in achieving the social movement's goals.

While Tilly demonstrates the limitations of 'repertoires of contention', he underplays the creative and innovative ways that emerge from the diverse range of people that constitute football fans. Fans have established new tactics to make their cases heard. For example, the choice of tactics might include: the creation of new associations with specific purposes (see Millward and Poulton's discussion of the emergence of F.C. United as a 'tactic' against the commercialization and leveraged financial ownership of Manchester United), coalitions with other, similarly minded organizations (see Hill et al.'s discussion of 'Stand AMF' as a coalition of disenfranchised supporters of various football clubs in the UK, and Numerato's account of similar groups in Italian football), public meetings (Tilly 1999: 253), media campaigns (see Cable 2016), vigils and rallies (Meyer and Whittier 1994), banners (Doidge 2015), petitions (Van Laer and Van Aelst 2010), boycotts (Friedman 1999), strikes (Casquette 2006), and pamphletting (Downey 1986).More recent examples might include internet campaigns and 'hactivism' (see Hands 2010; Schumann 2015) as new 'digital reper-toires' might emerge (Earl and Kimport 2011). These tactics are change-able over time and place (Shepard 2011) and might be made in the process of interact with other decision makers, such as opponents, the media, leg-islators, and potential allies. The process of deciding which repertoires of contention to adopt might also involve police in the relationship and interaction, by deciding what will be done, where it will take place, and even how many people could be arrested (Della Porta and Reiter 1998). As a result, Goodwin and Jasper (2014: 222) argue that 'any given action will probably be designed for several different audiences at the same time. An action that satisfies one may not please another', as different groups have different 'taste in tactics' (Jasper 1998).

Smithey (2009) points out tactical choices have often been presented as products of organizational structures, available resources, and opportuni-ties afforded by, or constraints emerging from, the physical environment.

However, this overlooks the interactive cultural dimensions of protest that make them, in Crossley's account of relational sociology, inherently relational. Jasper (2006: 117) argued that 'moral and emotional attachments influence our choice of tactics'; for instance, strength of views on (non) violence in protest might shape and/or divide groups and alliances from those with otherwise similar aims. He calls these judgements about what are group-defined 'acceptable' forms of contention 'taste in tactics'. In elaborating upon this point, Jasper (1998: 237) points out that Tilly has missed a key issue in his analysis of 'repertoires of contention'—namely, that tactics tend not to be value neutral or set against values protestors do not care deeply about. Rather, he argues tactics 'represent important routines, emotionally and morally salient' in those individuals who make up the collective actions lives. These 'tastes' may not be as pronounced as those who express a disregard for protest that risks becoming violent, it may merely emerge within the identities of those who are part of the mobilization: are they the type of individual to take part in 'direct action', or in 'radical actions', or in negotiation with the 'enemy'? These types of discussions are present in Nash's (2000) discussion of Independent Supporters' Associations that could not 'join' together with other clubs because of historical fan rivalries (see also Poulton 2013) or the Manchester United fans that agreed with the long-term protest of some of the club's supporters leaving the attachment of match attendance behind to set up F.C. United of Manchester but did not feel as if they could either undertake this action themselves (see Millward 2011). Those taking part in a collective action are constantly judging—'taste classifies, and it classifies the classifier. Social subjects, classified by their classifications, distinguish themselves by the distinctions they make' as Bourdieu (2004 [1990]: 6) argued—others within it and its associated groups. Jasper (1997: 240) argues that these feelings and dispositions towards particular types of tactics can cause internal rifts and conflicts in much the same way as differing goals might. This is currently evident in the disagreements some fans of the London-based football club Charlton Athletic are currently experiencing where there is widespread disquiet about the operational strategies that the club's owner, Roland Duchâtelet, has implemented, but there is disagreement among supporter groups over the tactics they should implement in order to challenge his actions. Jasper also points out that differing groups, composed of protestors with differing tastes, may decide to tolerate each other or even cooperate effectively even if distastes for each other continue if the strategy of the mobilization suits such collaboration. Tastes are important but so too is the urge to achieve the group aims, although—as Jasper notes—the two may be ultimately similar.

Narratives might be important in the faith the group shows in its tactics, as well as the maintenance of belief in the movement's aims and the continued identification of a 'villain'. As such, narratives became an important feature in Tilly's 'fundamentally relational' and cultural turn (Edwards 2014: 105). In particular Tilly (2008: 21) argues that stories are important to the relational analysis of social life for three reasons: first, they belong to relationships and therefore vary according to that relationship and roles, as he argues 'a mother gets a different story of a broken love affair than does a casual friend'; second, they simplify social processes to convey memorable images and sequences of what happened; and third, they include strong suggestions of responsibility therefore lending themselves to moral evaluations—making 'stories enormously valuable for evaluation after the fact' (Tilly 2008: 21). On this last point, Millward (2016a) pointed out that, when exposed to the 'counter-power' (see Castells 2015 [2012]) offered by newspaper and non-governmental organization allegations, the 'blockmodelled' (see Crossley 2011: 184–185) corporate actors that were together relationally 'responsible' for the (mis)treatment of some migrant workers on World Cup-related construction projects in Qatar. Each told a story that framed their response in terms of (a) regret that some workers had been treated in such ways but (b) a rejection of responsibility for the circumstances in which such treatment emerged. The stories told therefore became a form of tactical defence against allegations spread by the movements that opposed the (poor) treatment of many migrant works. For Polletta (2006: 4) narratives might also 'set the very terms of strategic action' by making some courses of action seem 'very reasonable, fitting, even possible, and others seem ineffectual, ill-considered or impossible'. In other words, the narrative actors tell about themselves, and their values and/or adversaries shape the choices of which tactics are chosen and which ones are not. These stories stretch beyond the 'tastes in tactics' (Jasper 1997) embedded within the collective action to assumptions about 'what has worked or failed in the past' (Polletta 2006: 170) without a thorough analysis of what tactics *actually* did work or fail previously.

Crossley (2011) argues that tactics form one of the conventions a group uses in its relational action, while Polletta (2006) offers that narratives play a role in establishing these tactical conventions (Polletta 2006). However, Crossley (2011) also argues that innovation might emerge when conventions are perceived by those involved in collective action to no longer work. Yet innovations and conventions are not binary opposites for three main reasons. First, Crossley (2011: 34) points out that 'conventions (and institutions) are simply sedimented innovations and improvisations of the past'. Second, innovations are important for the conventions in movements because—as Crossley (2015b) pointed out in the contexts of punk and post-punk—allied groups may attempt to usurp each other, even if that competition remains friendly. Third, Becker (2008 [1982]) shows that—in using the example of art—creative and innovative interaction will draw upon established conventions. McAdam (1983: 752) stated that in the quest to offset their relative powerlessness, challengers against established 'powerbrokers' (the Football Association and/or individual clubs in this book, rather than 'the state' as offered by McAdam) devise new techniques—or 'technical innovations'—in the quest to leverage power through the art of surprise. However, he is also keen to point out that these innovations only temporally afford members of a collective action bargaining leverage as alters—those who they are protesting against—'tactically adapt' to neutralize the new tactic (McAdam 1982, 1983). Tracing out the changing tactics—and the way in which these tactics are narrated and 'judged'—of social movement will tell us much about the relationships within and outside that collective action. Ultimately, protests are an internal interaction between individuals within the SMO and external to the group between the protestors and the institution being challenged.

Recruitment to Collective Action and 'Outcomes' of Mobilization

The tactical approach is just one part of what fan groups need to focus on. Recruiting new participants is a key aim of social movements. Football fandom is already a form of collective behaviour and consequently constitutes a ready-made network of fans. Mobilizations go through processes of recruitment, retention, and searching for—and potentially achieving—outcomes throughout their life cycle. Although the precise stages of the life cycle of collective action are difficult to generalize, Blumer (1951) tried to do so in his model of 'collective behaviour' suggesting that they have four 'typical stages of development' (p. 203). These are 'social unrest', 'popular excitement', 'formalization', and 'institutionalization'.

Millward and Poulton (2014) discussed these categories with an empirical analysis of the formation and continued running of F.C. United of Manchester (F.C. United), which emerged from the disenchantment of a sizable number of Manchester United fans with a range of different issues broadly related to the commercialization of elite English football in 2005, and found that Blumer's stages of development helped gain a theoretical foothold in the setup of the protest club but that it was difficult to order such stages as Blumer is tempted to do so. They suggest that in rigidly following a theoretical life-cycle structure to social movements, there is a risk of imposing a tautological approach to understanding collective action. However, we do know that collective actions have a 'beginning', even if we are less sure that they have a 'middle' and/or an 'end' in the sense of conventional narratives (Polletta 2006). For Jasper (1998) movements typically begin with 'moral shocks' of outrage, but Freeman (1973: 793) argues that most collective action has 'very inconspicuous beginnings' in which 'significant elements of their origin are usually forgotten or distorted by the time a trained observer seeks to trace them out'. Crossley (2015b) argues that collective actions (such as, in his example, punk and post-punk music scenes) might grow—often supported through independent printed outlets (such as fanzines) but more recently through the architecture of social networking technologies (Cable 2016; Gerbaudo 2012)—through word of mouth but might decline through an attrition of followers through either disengagement or achieving the movement's outcomes. Indeed, Klandermans (1997: 123) argues that 'movement decline results from the movement's inability to keep participants *and* its inability to attract new participants to replace those who leave'. Such processes in collective action often involve engagements with individuals, including protestors, outsiders, politicians, 'targets' and 'enemies', and other organizations in a relational map of mobilization. Consequently, this section plots out ideas that will be picked up in the analysis of the case examples on recruitment and outcomes of collective actions.

Whether or not individuals need 'rewards' for partaking in collective action is debatable. What a 'reward' might constitute is, of course, an open question ranging from material gain/the avoidance of material loss to connections into networks or, for instance, greater availability of places at 'good schools' for their children, or in the context of football fandom 'enjoyment' (which might come with the positive emotional connection with others), or 'team playing success' (with the grounds of what constitutes 'success' constructed through relational processes with other fans, the media, and employees of the football club). However, Olson (1968), analysing social movements from a rational action theory perspective, argues that they do, going so far as to suggest that those which offer no material incentives to their participants may experience problems in the recruitment and retention of participants. Klandermans (1997) disagreed with this proposition, suggesting that selective incentives do not usually encourage people to participate in social movements, although they might increase commitment. Hirsch (1990) argued that material 'rewards' were less important than ideological commitments to the cause and the belief that change has to be prompted by non-institutional means. Football fandom is not measured by material reward but by emotional connection to a broader collective: the club. McAdam (1982, 1986), while formulating the political process approach to collective action in studies of the African-American civil rights movement in the USA, found three important factors that shaped involvement in the movement. The first of these was 'ideological compatibility', signifying that although he thought 'the right attitude' alone was not enough to entice involvement insofar as lots of people outside of a mobilization might share the views of those inside it without ever becoming involved in any protest. Second, he suggested 'biographical availability' which is 'the absence of personal constraints that may increase the costs and risks of movement participation, such as full-time employment, marriage, and family responsibilities' has a large—and possibly the most significant—bearing on whether an interested individual may form part of a collective action (McAdam 1986: 70). Third, McAdam (1986) said an individual being part of a social network with ties to a social movement's 'recruiting agents' may positively influence his/her likelihood of becoming part of the collective action. For McAdam, the nature of these connections varied tremendously, and he was concerned with the imprecision of the term. From his case study, he deduced three types of contact: (i) pre-existing organizational affiliations, even if this had been connected to a different protest, (ii) personal ties with current individual activists who may have played an influential role in shaping opinions (such as parents, friends, university professors, etc.), and (iii) prior—but not necessarily consistent—activism with the organization on the issue that is the centre of the contestation.

Indeed, Goodwin and Jasper (2014: 53) offer that in recruiting members for collective action, 'direct personal contacts are important because they allow organizers and potential participants to 'align' their 'frames', to achieve a common definition of a social problem and a common prescription for solving it', while Snow, Zurcher, and Ekland-Olson (1980) went as far as suggesting that the best predictor of who will join is whether a person knows someone else already in the movement. More recently, Shepard (2015) argued that preceding friendship may encourage participation in collective action. He argues that such friendships generate affective capital such as fun and emotional support. Although he follows a well-established cluster of research that points out that recruitment and retention in movements *are distinctive* issues (Bunnage 2014; Fisher and McInerney 2012; Goodwin 1997; Kanter 1968; Klandermans 1997), he makes a clear point that 'friendships include social and emotional support, networks that support mobilization, and the capacity to effect social change' (Shepard 2015: 78). Football is a social activity where friends and acquaintances regularly attend together. They already constitute a network of emotionally engaged individuals (Brown 2008).

Crossley and Ibrahim (2012) explored recruitment in university student activist 'worlds' (borrowing from Becker 2008 [1982]). Of particular note for discussions about the role of networks in recruiting activists, they make four interconnected points. First, student activists will recruit other students into their protests. These recruitments will have often not been active in protest worlds but may have met the activists through either on their courses or in halls of residence. While some students expressed resistance to the overt idea of being recruited, many among Crossley and Ibrahim's (2012) samples reported attempting to draw non-activist friends into either specific actions or groups. Second, although networks were important to recruitment, Crossley and Ibrahim (2012) found that, alone, this was not enough to entice friends into bouts of collective action. Goodwin and Jasper (2014: 53) agree arguing that 'bigots don't join civil rights campaigns just because they are in the right network; leftists don't join right-wing movements because a "bloc" of their fellow parishioners do. The fact that not *everyone* with a set of beliefs or personality traits gets recruited does not mean that supportive ideas or other traits are not a necessary condition' (Goodwin and Jasper 2014: 53). Thus, Crossley and Ibrahim (2012) argue that recruitment also involved some aspect of symbolic work, such as when the aims of the protest were framed by trusted others—such as friends—to be analogous with the individual's own belief.

In short, Crossley and Ibrahim saw both framing and network approaches to social movements were important. Crossley and Ibrahim's (2012) theoretical eclecticism also encompassed NSM dimensions: they saw situational and identity definition with political networks as important, viewing conversational networks between activists as important in both sustaining identity and situational definitions and because affective pleasures of conversation and discussion were important incentives for remaining in the network rather than investing time and effort in other activities. For instance, they found one of their interviewees described his recruitment into student activist worlds on the basis of such conversations:

> It was the most interesting conversation I've had yet at university ... I thought there'd be lots of intellectuals in relation to university and there were not ... I was kind of like 'where's the conversation?' and I came to [meeting following Fresher's Fair] and people were talking about things that I already believed in ... I don't think I was looking for something political but just for like, like-minded people, and it turned out that like-minded people do, do this. (Crossley and Ibrahim 2012: 607)

Fourth, Crossley and Ibrahim (2012) found that network ties may also dissuade interested students from becoming part of the protest world as, for some of those, networks may become too tightly bound or rooted in deep friendship might may be off-putting to interested outsiders who may not feel they best 'fit' if they think 'cliques' may dominate a community (see also Adamic et al. 2003). Klandermans (2002) adds to the argument that networks play an important—but not all encompassing—role in recruitment into collective action; in doing so, he makes two points. First, he argues that an individual's biographical and lifetime of networks shape his/her likelihood of becoming part of a movement which 'does not come out of the blue' (2002: 89) and, second, he agrees with McAdam (1986) that activism may be a stage in the life course for believers and sympathizers.

In his analysis of the emergence of Manchester-based protest club, F.C. United, Poulton (2013) narrated the profile of the club's chief executive, Andy Walsh (see also Millward 2011; Millward and Poulton 2014; Poulton 2013), which would support Klanderman's argument. Walsh described himself as 'a socialist and I've been a socialist all my life' (Poulton 2013: 183) and had been an activist in issues relating to within and beyond football: in the late 1990s, he had rallied a group of Manchester United supporters who successfully fought against the football club's then-proposed sale to 'News Corp's' founding major shareholder, Rupert Murdoch (see Brown and Walsh 1999), and before then, he had been a leading figure in the anti-poll tax movement. By 2005, when F.C. United formed, despite being deeply embedded in the fan politics that surrounded the emergence of the club, Walsh considered whether his broader commitments away from football and politics could afford him the opportunity to participate—only after deep thought and conversations with family members, he decided he could gain involvement in the protest club. Further, although his research was not explicitly relational, Poulton (2013) found that Walsh and other Manchester United supporters who set up F.C. United recruited many of those within their social and political networks (Walsh had been member of the 'Militant' Labour Party group, and Poulton 2013: 183 found several F.C. United supporters who had originally met Walsh through that group).

Andy Walsh's initial reticence at becoming 'involved' prompts questions that can be read across the literature about what 'involvement' in collective action means. Clearly, the answers, and thus engagements, are variable. In their work on the impact of consumption on young people's identities, Miles et al. (1998) showed how 'retro'-style training shoes were popular because they allowed individuals to connect with an 'indie' sub-culture without the need to reorder the majority of the rest of their fashion tastes, consumer habits, or leisure time. In other words, the appeal of such shoes was that they facilitated access to a chosen lifestyle without a deep involvement in other areas of the individual's identity; thus physical and cultural 'involvement' was minimal. On the other hand, Hebdige (1979) argued that to be part of the 'punk' sub-culture involved a deep commitment involving the internalization of a set of attitudes, a distinctive way of dress that was quite different to that of the mainstream culture, and the styling of hair into a brightly coloured Mohawk. 'Involvement' and 'immersion' into sub-cultures vary wildly. The same could be argued for involvement in collective action—for some, such as those Manchester United fans who wished to express their dissatisfaction at the 'leveraged' debt that was loaded on to 'their' football club in early 2010 that simply wore a 'Green and Gold' scarf in protest (see Millward 2011), while ultras at AS Roma sustained a fan strike and refused to enter the stadium until the removal of a 'safety' fence that had been installed in the Curva Nord. Others go further, such as the Red Brigade left-wing paramilitary in Italy who were prepared to kidnap and assassinate opponents for their cause (see Della Porta 1995). Involvement in collective action includes a wide range of actions through networks of association with others.

'Outcomes' and the criteria for 'success' of collective actions are similarly difficult to define (Giugni 1998). Indeed, Kriesi et al. (1995) pointed out that success, impact, and outcome of collective actions may not even mean the same thing, given that 'impact' or 'outcome' might be more consequential or 'neutral' than a targeted notion of 'success'. Therefore, they are particularly concerned with 'a crucial unresolved problem: the link between a movement's action and an observed outcome. What allows us to say that a certain political change is the result of the action of a social movement or of a challenging group? Would it have occurred anyway?' (Kriesi et al. 1995: 211–212). Scott (1990) suggested that scholarly analysis of the 'effects' of social movements, such as survival as an integral entity, transformation of social relations, is inadequate. Rather he suggests that 'success' might take the form of integrating previously excluded issues and groups—such as football and its fans—into the 'normal' political debates. Since he argues that collective actions typically bring about change, or attempt to bring it about, by opposing specific forms of social closure and exclusion rather than challenging society as a whole 'success' might play a role in the end of the movement as its purpose for existence is removed.

Perhaps the most influential work on social movement 'success' was provided by William Gamson in *The Strategy of Social Protest* (1990 [1975]). This book included a desk-based historical analysis of the experiences of 53 voluntary protest groups in America that formed between 1800 and 1945, exploring the strategies that each used and the organizational characteristics that influenced the 'success' of their challenges. Although he did not label his approach to be 'relational', he argued that a challenge may occur if there are, first, individuals that have cross-cutting solidarities (and a strong identification with those groups) that overlap and cut across each other and, second, access to an arena in which dissatisfied voices can be heard and, thus, where connections can be made. Above all else he suggested:

> Success is an elusive idea. What of the group whose leaders are honored or rewarded while their supposed beneficiaries linger in the same cheerless state as before? Is such a group more or less successful than another challenger whose leaders are vilified and imprisoned even as their program is eagerly implemented by their oppressor? Is a group a failure if it collapses with no legacy save inspiration to a generation that will soon take up the same cause with more tangible results? And what do we conclude about a

group that accomplishes exactly what it set out to achieve but then finds its victory empty of real meaning for its presumed beneficiaries. (Gamson 1990 [1975]: 26)

Gamson's (1990 [1975]) questions arguably raise more counter-questions than they facilitate answers, but he broadly frames the aims of movements as seeking to bring about group acceptance or to advance group goals. Tarrow and Tilly (2007: 454) criticize him in this regard, suggesting that he overlooks that some movements seek personal development for members and others attempt to affirm collective identities. Kriesi et al. (1995: 209–213) engaged with Gamson's ideas to suggest that outcomes should be thought about as multileveled and having different impacts on different 'targets' in relation to others in society. For instance, they argued that some 'impacts' are internal to the collective action, affecting the group rather than necessarily those outside of it. They offer that this type of impact/outcome should not be thought about as necessarily weaker than external varieties as it can shape (a) the formation and maintenance of individual and collective identities of group members, therefore altering their judgments within the group or (b) the organizational structures under which an operation or movement is ordered. However, they also argued that a mobilization might have 'external' outcomes and impacts which can be conceptualized in four categories: procedural, substantive, structural, and sensitizing types. In the first of these, Kriesi et al. (1995) paralleled a procedural impact to Gamson's (1990 [1975]) discussion of a movement's 'legitimacy' and 'acceptance' from the authorities it lobbies against as a successful outcome. They saw procedural impacts as challengers networking with authoritative agents in the system by the challengers through establishing consultation procedures, undertaking negotiations, or by a general inclusion of the challengers. In the second category, Kriesi et al. (1995) continued to draw upon Gamson's (1990 [1975]) idea that a challenging group can gain 'new advantages' by arguing that substantive impacts can be either opposed to formulation of any potential new disadvantages ('reactive') or, alternatively, seeking the opening up of new advantages ('proactive'). In the third category (structural impacts), Kriesi et al. (1995) offer the possibility that a mobilization can open up a political opportunity structure, therefore determining their own chances of achieving its 'success'. They argue that this type of impact potentially has 'institutional structures' (i.e., a change in the form of the political institutions which in their most radical form could be revolutionary outcomes; see

Tilly 1978, 1999) and/or 'alliance structures', which are political realignments or splits in the government. Finally, Kriesi et al. (1995) suggest that 'sensitizing impacts' might be outcomes. These are the possibilities that a movement may sensitize actors in ways conducive to the movement's aims and may include a new feeling of injustice for potential recruits, a heightening of existing members' emotions, or a reshaping of protestors' preexisting views.

Gamson (1990 [1975]) argues that the conditions under which protests are most likely to 'succeed' are when they are under hierarchical organization and are making only modest claims. These protests 'work' best when they are peaceful and do not seek to displace individuals in elite positions. This is problematic for football fans that are seeking to remove unpopular owners. Giugni (1998) broadly agreed with these arguments but added the caveat that one challenger's victory is another's defeat. Diani (2003) offered an interesting approach to the 'success' of a movement by treating the formation of network ties as outcomes, arguing that movement-developed social capital is important in developing movement 'cultures', which Blumer (1951) suggested to be important for the endurance of collective action. Castells (2015 [2012]) also saw the scope of collective action aims and, as discussed earlier in this chapter, the structure of a mobilization rather differently to Gamson and Giugni. We will not return to his arguments on the rhizomatic structure of networked movements in this section, but he tends to agree with the 'sensitizing impacts' Kriesi et al. (1995) offer. To elaborate, Castells (2015 [2012]) argues that anger underlies mobilizations but that fear tends to repress them. He further suggested that collective gatherings and effervescence in online and offline spaces might overcome this fear as people 'stand' and communicate with each other; as such this might be an outcome of a protest. Indeed, in these spaces, collective anger may heighten as actors share and identify with each other—even if group members may not agree on everything (or even anything) other than shared emotions of anger (Castells 2015 [2012]). However, Castells (2015 [2012]) offers that overcoming repressors may see mobilizations develop and these give rise to feelings of enthusiasm and hope that things can be different, even if a uniform vision of what a 'better world' would look like is not necessarily shared across the network. Mathers (2014: 1064) is unconvinced, arguing that 'Occupy' and the other networked movements Castells studied have had a 'relative lack of success in delivering radical economic and social reforms' and presenting that Castells had valued 'the expressive above the instrumental element of the movements'. While it is a truism that some fan movements declare their collective actions to be 'successful' while others shy away from these claims (see Brimson 2006), the judgements of what constitutes 'success' are relationally constructed through interactions between fans and supporter groups with media personnel.

These debates do not offer any answers to what Kriesi et al. (1995: 207) refer to as 'the most fundamental obstacle to research on social movement outcomes—the problem of causality, that is, the difficulty of assessing the extent to which the movement has contributed to producing a certain effect' (see also Bosi and Uba 2009). For instance, in the example of Liverpool F.C. fans protesting against the business organization and—similar to protests at Manchester United—leveraged debt placed on the club between 2008 and 2010, the football club's owners sold it. A collection of fans from the club mobilized under the banner of Spirit of Shankly (see also Chap. 6) and claimed that they had forced the sale of the club's business rights 'through the magnificent efforts of the supporters' in their collective action (*Spirit of Shankly* 2010). Yet such claims of fans forcing 'victory' need to be questioned. It seems fair to argue that the actions of supporter movements made clear that many fans wished for the owners' removal from the club, but, despite face-to-face meetings and protest/ leafleting marches, they had little desire to sell their shareholding in the club until it became apparent that the loans that had been taken out to buy the economic rights of the club would not be renewed in October 2010, owing to 'post-credit crunch' financial climate (Millward 2011). That fans collectively mobilized and the financial owners sold the football club does not mean a model of causality where the financial owners sold the club because of fan protest should be assumed. In this case, it seems likely that it was the coming together of a network of pressure groups around the world that played a role in the sale of the club along with the impacts of the global economic crisis (Millward 2012); thus causality of collective action is not linear.

SPACES AND PLACES OF ORGANIZATION AND ACTION

Football has a range of pre-existing spaces where fans can meet, discuss tactics, and determine outcomes. Crossley (2008a, 2009, 2015b) points out that music worlds, as collections of individuals working together and potentially also competing with each other in the production of music, need spaces and places in which their collective action can take place.

Donati (2010) argues that spaces in society are quite literally the relationships—as transactions, interactions, social ties, and conversations—that take place. Places are only the past and present relationships that take place in them. In his work on punk and post-punk movements, Crossley (2008a, 2009, 2015b) points to Liverpool, Sheffield, and, especially, Manchester and London as the places in which these worlds emerge. In their work on the 'Britpop' music scenes, Millward et al. (2017) similarly saw the North London borough of Camden as a place where Britpop was practiced, produced, and mediatized. Meanwhile, Becker (2008 [1982]) argues that art worlds, as collections of individuals working together and potentially also competing with each other in the production of art, need spaces and places in which their collective action can take place. Space and place are important. Becker particularly spoke about these networks operating in San Francisco, while Thornton (2008: xi) described 'the contemporary art world as a loose network of overlapping subcultures [that] span[s] the globe but cluster in art capitals like New York, London, Los Angeles and Berlin'. Leach and Haunss (2009) also draw upon Berlin to discuss the emergence of 'social movement scenes' to discuss protest in Kreuzberg, Prenzlauer Berg, Mitte, and Friedrichshain districts of the city. They argue that 'scenes' have geographical dimensions that are expressed in their formation in recognized locations such as 'meeting places like clubs, parks, street corners and so on' where they can be physically experienced and membership enacted (Leach and Haunss 2009: 260).

Space and place are intrinsically important in the consumption of the sport. These places might include hostelries and public houses supporters inhabit (Dixon 2013, 2014; David and Millward 2012), the headquarters of supporters' clubs (Doidge 2015), and the stadium (King 2010; Schulke 2010), including the topophilia of specific spaces in the football ground (Bale 1993, 2000; Giulianotti 1999) even if some of these connections to specific spaces might be imagined to be more temporally enduring than they actually are (King 2002 [1998]). Some of these spaces can be temporary, such as fan congresses, as Chap. 7 demonstrates. Once again, we are reminded that space and place are important to relational practices.

In all of these cases, the spaces and places could be described as 'foci' (Becker 2008 [1982]; Crossley 2008a, 2009, 2015b). Becker (2008 [1982]) argued that 'foci' are important to networks of cooperation and innovation, suggesting them to be the interactive symbolic spaces made up of conventions and resources in which the collections of people that create the action congregate. It is in these foci that actors come together and build shared ideas and interests which, in turn, strengthen personal ties, that is, place matters (see Widdop and Cutts 2012; Cutts and Widdop 2016; Fieldhouse et al. 2014). The ideas and actions produced through previous relationships in that space may influence the development of ideas in the present and future in that space, giving such relationships a potential to bridge temporality. Marren's (2016) work on Labor movements in 1980s Liverpool found that participants recalled drawing inspiration from the radical history of the city. In the context of football, Doidge (2013) found how Livorno fans' attitudes reflected the relations that made and remade the urban fabric of the city, while Poulton (2013) found that those Manchester United fans who established and followed F.C. United did so in the alternative traditions and politics they associated with that city. These histories, traditions, and politics did not simply emerge though—the taken-for-granted assumption was that they were created by individuals and their interactions with other individuals and associations (which are the product of previous networks of people). Put simply, in these cases the imagined and real histories of place are the product of human relations.

The rituals of football provide a number of spaces where fans can meet and interact. These can be stadiums, supporters' clubs, bars, or online. These spaces can be considered 'working utopias' (Crossley 1999). They provide foci where members can visit in order to 'top up' their beliefs in the movements' aims and give the 'illusio', or the avoidance of disillusionment, that is needed for continued action. It is in the 'foci' of a movement that working utopias—set up and maintained through the actions of collectives—provide the sites where the movement's culture is reformed/reproduced and that 'people visit them in order to learn how to practice differently; how to perceive, think and act' in relation to other members of the community (Crossley 1999: 817). Crossley is clear that working utopias are places which people visit and as a result convert their tastes to match the culture of the group which might consequently change their world views and ways of acting. However, these places only have these seemingly transformative capacities because of the interactions, transactions, social ties, and conversations (see Donati 2010) that have taken place within them and the interactions that have seen those actions selectively remembered (see Taylor and Whittier 1992). In making these points, Crossley (1999) views past and present working utopias as spaces that shape collective action in six ways. These ways have distinct echoes in the relational practices that emerge within the consumption of football and we now discuss these ways.

First, those who visit working utopias use the material and sets of 'knowledge' generated through interactions in such spaces as a means to attempt to persuade others away from the space as to their specific views. In the context of football, Petersen-Wagner (2016, 2017) points out that in places ranging from public houses, football stadiums, and even social media spaces, supporters might try to convert others to 'convert' to either their football team or learn their codes of behaviour in carrying out that support. What is more, Dixon (2013: 48–50) suggests that these socializations may arise so early in some football fans' lives through interactions with family members that they claim their affiliations and modes of support to be 'natural'.

Second, communion in working utopias gives rise to commonly shared feelings of affect such as '"excitement", "stimulation", "enthusiasm", "evangelism", feeling "right" and having "heads blown" … [thus] tapping into a deeper level of belief' (Crossley 1999: 815). Once more, in the context of football support, King (1997b, 2002 [1998]) recounts how some football supporters describe their emotional bonds to a club as 'love' although these bonds are broadly held towards each other with the club merely symbolizing that relationship. In this relationship, the space of the football ground is important because it holds both imagined and real memories (see also Brown 2008). Indeed, on this point, Bromberger (1995: 295) argues stadium spaces are places where 'the joy of being united together against the opposition at least temporarily anaesthetizes any awareness of individual differences'. This is not to suggest that the mode of fandom is restricted to live match attendance at stadiums and these bonds can be felt between individuals in alternative physical and virtual venues (Crawford 2004).

Third, Crossley argues (1999: 822) that working utopias are 'places of pilgrimage, they become meeting grounds for key movement activists and intellectuals, and thus sites of debate and discussion. They lure like-minded activists, concentrating them in situations where they can and will exchange ideas'. On this point, it is interesting to note that Taylor (1987) in his new left realist account of 'football hooliganism' noted that in the 1980s the British government were keen to put in place symbolic and administrative barriers (such as identity cards) that would make attending football matches more difficult. He argued that a reason for this was the desire to minimize opportunities where frustrated unemployed and underemployed young people might meet, discuss, and debate issues that pervaded their lives.

Fourth, within working utopias as 'places of pilgrimage', people in 'different national movements, with different approaches, policies, and tactics were able to exchange views, learning from each other even when they could not agree and borrowing from each other, thus enhancing their discursive and tactical repertoires' (Crossley 1999: 822). This is a thread picked up in Chaps. 6 and 7, but the literature on football fandom shows that although there may be sympathies between some supporters of some clubs that are not normally defined as rivals (Armstrong 1998; Giulianotti 2002; King 2002 [1998]; Doidge 2015), cross-club collaborations— perhaps in the form of joint action—are rare with little known (see Hill et al. 2016; Numerato 2015; Webber 2017). However, Chaps. 6 and 7 detail cross-club mobilizations that meet up in physical places and communicate in electronic spaces enabling us to shed light on if and how tactics and approaches might be shared between football fan activists.

Fifth, working utopias have concrete dimensions in so far as they are physical places where social capital—a central movement resource—is generated and networks connect (Crossley 1999: 823). This draws interesting parallels to Castells' (2013 [2009]) argument about the fluid 'spaces of autonomy' that collective actions may have that span online and urban domains. He argues that though 'movements usually begin on the internet social networks, they are not identified as movements until they occupy urban space. [...] The space of the movement consists of an interaction between the space of flows on the internet and in wireless communication networks, and the space of places of the occupied sites and of symbolic buildings targeted by protest actions' (Castells 2013 [2009]: xxxix). An essential counter-part to the work that occurs in online space (the forging of new connections between previously disparate groups and the extended deliberation of concerning issues) is the work that occurs in urban space. Castells (2015 [2012]) argues that as occupying this space produces three important effects. First, being together in urban space enhances the collective emotional experiences: marching and chanting in unison across symbolic urban spaces produces affective 'glue' between individuals who become emotionally 'attuned' to each other. Second, urban protests materialize discontent in ways that are difficult to ignore by established programmers of societal values, such as the established media. Third, the urban materialization of protest is used to reinvigorate online activity. Mass self-communication and digital technologies continue to be used in urban space, folding the highly symbolic occupation of urban space back into the online space of Twitter through the use of designated hashtags. We pick up on this theme with the use of the hashtags to connect people using '#twentysplenty' and '#walkouton77' in Chap. 6 to map out networks of communication with respect to protests in relation to match admission ticket prices. The interplay between urban and online space helps to organize the protest in real time, while also providing a sense of connection for those unable to attend. Thus, Castells adds a social media dimension that connects with offline interactions that Crossley discusses when he makes his sixth point about working utopias, namely, that they also encompass symbolic aspects too: they would not be able to fuel movement illusion if they did not offer a cultural hold on the imagination of activists, yet a key factor in the power of these dimensions existing is their interaction as Crossley (1999: 826) argues a working utopia is 'so appealing to the imagination precisely because of their real existence beyond and outside of the imagination, because they were 'real' and therefore symbolized the realistic nature of movement aspirations'. In the context of football fandom these points are important as Pearson (2012: 175–176) found that although the use of communicative spaces such as internet message boards offered the potential to strengthen bonds between supporters, some fans who used the communicative tools were not seen to be authentic members of the community until they had been engaged with 'real life' (as offline interaction). Further still, in their analysis of the 'Stand AMF' protests, Hill et al. (2016) found that many supporter activists did not believe themselves to be part of any movements until they were, in Crossley's (1999: 826) terms in reference to the anti-psychiatry movement, 'able to visit and partake in them'. As such, the relationships between people in online and offline interactions, and how these modes of interaction come together, is important in a cultural relational sociology of football fandom and collective action.

Conclusions: Cutting a Cultural Relational Sociological Path for Football Fans' Collective Actions

As outlined in Chap. 1, the cultural relational sociology approach we advance is heavily influenced by Crossley's (2011) ideas. The approach Crossley offers is open to adjoining ideas, theories, and methods on the basis that they privilege connections between social actors and, sometimes, social artefacts (although he falls short of adopting the actor network approaches of Callon and Latour) in social spaces. However, this approach is not complete and needs the type of empirical and conceptual elaboration he offers in his work on punk and post-punk movements (Crossley 2015b). This book adds further flesh to the skeleton of this work by exploring supporters' collective actions in the social worlds of football fandom.

To do this, the cultural relational sociology approach needs 'touchstones' and areas for analysis through which the existing literature on collective action, social movements, and football fandom can be appraised and through which we can begin our empirical analysis. Cutting through the literature in these areas to draw out the usefulness of cultural relational sociology is a necessarily messy task. In doing so, we turned to seven areas that might be useful for guiding future—as well as this book's—investigation in this area but by which we do not intend to be exhaustive or prescriptive. These were (i) the structures of and roles in collective action; (ii) affect, emotion, and collective effervescence; (iii) communication, cooperation, and conventions; (iv) mobilizing resources; (v) tactics; (vi) recruitment to collective action and 'outcomes' of mobilization; and (vii) the spaces and places of organization and action. It is not intended that each of the empirical cases will take a number of these areas but that they will cut across the analysis and, along with the concepts and dimensions of cultural relational sociology that we outlined in Chap. 1, will be picked up and reflected upon in Chap. 7.

CHAPTER 3

Friendships, Community Ties, and Non-league Fandom: Opting 'Out' from the Commercialization of the Premier League and 'In' to Leftist Political Scenes

INTRODUCTION

This chapter explores the themes of friendships and connections that forge in urban space as the basis for adjoining different collective actors, in this case particularly focusing on the networks of supporters at two non-league football clubs in southeast England. Friendships are integral to cultural relational sociological understandings of connections at all levels of society for at least three key reasons. First, while the classification of 'friendship' has elastic meanings, it constitutes a tie in a relationship and is a likely product of previous interactions (Jamieson 1999). Second, friends are more likely to share similar tastes, through either the formation of these tastes through interaction or being attracted to each other through principles of 'homophily' where 'birds of a feather flock together' (Borgatti et al. 2012). And third Crossley (2011: 149) points out that actors can find the social, economic, and cultural resources they require for their practices if the connecting path is shorter. For instance, people are more likely to hear about an initiative of collective action if they have a friend involved in it rather than a friend of a friend of a friend or an uncle's next-door neighbour. As first discussed in Chap. 2, friendships may also be at the core of collective action, for at least three important reasons. First, Shepard (2015) argued that preceding friendship may encourage participation in collective action, perhaps through such associations generating affective capital such as fun and emotional support (see also Jasper 1997,

© The Author(s) 2018
J. Cleland et al., *Collective Action and Football Fandom*,
Palgrave Studies in Relational Sociology,
https://doi.org/10.1007/978-3-319-73141-4_3

1998). Second, friendships and the generation of ties between activists may reduce attrition from collective action (Bunnage 2014; Fisher and McInerney 2012; Goodwin 1997; Kanter 1968; Klandermans 1997). In other words, if a person has friends partaking in that action, she/he is more likely to continue his/her involvements. Third, friendship ties may shape the networks' reception to particular forms of movement approach: it is important in shaping 'tastes in tactics' (Jasper 1997, 1998). In other words, if a friend suggests a type of action that should be undertaken in the pursuit of a collective goal, it is more likely to be accepted as 'legitimate', 'plausible', and 'effective' by those around him/her. On top of this, also football fandom can be undertaken as an individual pursuit it is often framed (and potentially experienced) such that the act of its consumptions is more enjoyable in the company of friends and family members (Brown 2008; David and Millward 2012). Both popular cultural fandom and collective action provide the opportunities to tell storied dimensions of social worlds in a way that includes friends and facilitates the formation of new friendships.

This chapter's ethnographic fieldwork comes from two non-league football clubs, Whitehawk F.C. (hereafter Whitehawk) and Dulwich Hamlet F.C. (hereafter Dulwich Hamlet). Although we outline the organization of men's non-league football later in the chapter, it is important to give some context to these two clubs. Whitehawk and Dulwich Hamlet are both semi-professional football clubs. This means that their players are paid a small salary/sum of money for each appearance they make but they are also able to have full-time occupations. Whitehawk is in Brighton—a leftist, cosmopolitan city on the south coast of England (Sanders et al. 2014)—and the gentrified East Dulwich is part of the London Borough of Southwark. Both have experienced a growth in attendances in the last few seasons and 3000 people attended Dulwich Hamlet's final game of 2014/15 season (Forster 2015). Inside their grounds, unlike in the Football League and Premier League, supporters can drink alcohol in sight of the pitch, which appeals to some fans. Whitehawk is a members' club, owned by a coalition of fans but with financial support coming from directors Peter ('Ned') McDonnell, Mark ('Ted') Ratcliffe, John Summers, and (formerly) Chris Gargan, who formed part of a new board in July 2009 and since then has experienced on the pitch success. Although Brighton is an affluent city, the Whitehawk housing estate is not. Fans are drawn from across the city, with many drawn to the leftist culture surrounding the fan group, which includes anti-homophobic, anti-sexist, and anti-racist values and a belief that attending football matches should be affordable for all fans, while many of these self-identify as 'Whitehawk Ultras' (see Chap. 1 for a discussion of 'ultra'-type supporters in the existing literature).

Dulwich Hamlet have deliberately kept match tickets at an affordable level of £10 per game and attracts a diverse crowd of supporters disillusioned with the commercialism of the Premier League and the 'sanitization' of its atmospheres. Many Dulwich Hamlet fans call themselves 'The Rabble' with one of them, Jack Spearman, quoted in *The Guardian* as describing the club as having 'a [political] leftwing element to it, but only because if you're not leftwing, you're wrong' (quoted in Forster 2015). Accordingly, The Rabble have party politicized humour associated to the club: Forster (2015) claims that the opposition team's goalkeeper might be intended to be insulted by calling him a 'Lib Dem' (Liberal Democrat) and making anti-UKIP (United Kingdom Independence Party) Dulwich Hamlet stickers. The club carry forward this ethos, playing a non-competitive friendly against Stonewall F.C., an LGBT rights charity in 2014/15 season, while they regularly organize initiatives to supporting local food banks.[1] Despite this, influential fan Robert Molloy-Vaughan argues that: 'There are a lot of apolitical people who come here because it's affordable. The happy end is that they find out the football is great, it's more open and creative, which you can see on the terrace' (quoted in Forster 2015). The friendship ties emerging from the club may, however, politicize some supporters into leftist politics.

In order to show how these relationships of 'friendship' develop and prosper in non-league football, this chapter divides into five main sections. First, we outline the background and structure of non-league football in England to bring forward the importance of urban locales to the scene. Second, we draw upon ethnographic material to give an overview of non-league football being an urban site for making friendships and connections. Third, the chapter moves outward to discuss the making and remaking of non-league football fan culture before, fourth, discussing the importance of face-to-face interactions in shaping this culture and connection, which will then be considered before linking to wider fan networks and campaigns. Fifth, we move to discuss football club's community work as a manifestation of connections between it and its locale as well as between the networks of networks of supporters.

The Organization of Non-league Men's Football

Given the chapter's focus on non-league men's football in England, it is necessary to provide some context of this under-researched area. This term refers to those teams playing in competitions outside of the Premier League and Football League. Its roots are in reference to those teams who did not play in the Football League. Historically, the Football League administered the league competition of men's professional football (Russell 1997; King 2002 [1998]; Goldblatt 2007). Meanwhile, the Football Association (FA) administered the FA Cup competition, the men's national team, and latterly the women's national team and Women's Super League. The FA also administers non-league football which sits outside the Premier League and Football League.

England has a National League System that encompasses the leagues directly underneath the Premier League and Football League. It comprises 7 levels containing 57 leagues across 84 divisions (the FA n.d.), on a 7-step format, administered by the FA. Step 1 is the National League. Formally known as the Football Conference (from 1986 to 2015), clubs at this level are fully professional. This represents level 5 of the league pyramid (with the Premier League constituting Level 1 down to League 2 at Level 4). There are two promotion places to Football League Two. Relegation is to Step 2, which comprises of the National League North and National League South. Four clubs are relegated from the National League, with two clubs each promoted from the North and South. Participation depends on where the teams are based. Teams based in the border counties, between Suffolk, Cambridgeshire, Bedfordshire, Oxfordshire, and Gloucestershire, could take part in either the southern or northern league depending on the numbers already participating. These clubs are predominantly semi-professional.

The National League System gets increasingly regional from Steps 3 to 7. There are three regional leagues at Steps 3–4, under the National Leagues. These comprise the Northern Premier League, Southern League, and Isthmian League. Geographically, the Northern Premier League covers teams in the North of England and Midlands, while the Southern League predominantly has teams from the South West, South Wales, and central southern counties. The Isthmian League represents teams from the South East and London. Step 3 has the Premier League of each of these regional leagues, and Step 4 has a further regional subdivision. These leagues are levels 7 and 8 in the League pyramid. Steps 5 and 6 are also regional leagues but organized over a smaller geographic area. Examples include the Combined Counties League, which covers Greater London, Surrey, and parts of Hampshire and Berkshire, and the Hellenic League that covers Oxfordshire, Gloucestershire, Berkshire, and Herefordshire. Step 7 is regional, with leagues such as the South West Peninsula League that covers Devon and Cornwall, or covering single counties, such as the West Yorkshire League, or cities, as with the Manchester Football League.

Despite the prevalence of non-league and amateur men's football, there is little academic research into fans and clubs. While there is research on amateur football, this predominantly focuses on players and specifically in relation to the experiences of black and minority ethnic, gay, or female players within amateur football (Caudwell 1999; Burdsey 2009; Bradbury 2013; Themen and Van Hooff 2017); this does not include the experiences of fans. F.C. United of Manchester is one non-league football club that has received a lot of attention (Brown 2008; Millward and Poulton 2014). Yet this reflects the specific culture that has emerged at a club that was created with an explicit approach and culture in mind. While many of the principles that led to the formation of F.C. United are applicable to fans of other non-league clubs, there are distinct and diverse patterns of relationships that exist within other clubs, particularly around those in London and Sussex.

There is a long history of local football clubs acting as markers of 'local identity' (Holt 1989; Mason 1988; Russell 1997; King 2002 [1998], 2003; Doidge 2015). Throughout the nineteenth and early twentieth centuries, rapid urbanization and industrialization led to new forms of social engagement. Sport, in particular, provided a regular and local form of engagement in the local community. King (2003: 171) highlights that:

> Before the commercialization of football in the 1990s, fans looked upon themselves not as customers but as members of their club which they supported through active participation. The season ticket was not regarded as an onerous expense but rather as a subscription fee which was sustained an institution of which the fans were active members. The club was ultimately supported not financially but by fans' regular and vociferous attendance at games. The ticket price was a maintenance fee for use of an institution of which a fan was a member. Fans contributed to the very public goof from which they benefited. The rapid increase of ticket prices in the 1990s has transformed this membership model radically.

While King (2002 [1998], 2003) argued that the economic transformation of the 1990s has profoundly altered the engagement of fans with their clubs, this is predominantly true of fans of professional clubs. At the non-league level, fans feel more intimately linked to their club because of the greater range and intensity of relationships held within the fan base and out into the wider fan and local communities.

Taylor (1992) has demonstrated that there has been a long-standing relationship between fans and their club. The supporters' clubs held fundraising events, parties, fetes, and lotteries in order to raise funds and acted as a financial source for clubs. For example, the fans of Plymouth Argyle raised money for a new covered 'Popular' stand in the 1930s. Meanwhile, Luton Town supporters' club built new premises inside the new stand alongside 'two bars, a cafeteria, snack bar, games room, and a "wash and brush up" facility for "those members arriving on the ground from work"' (Taylor 1992: 27). These practices continue at non-league level, with fans crowdfunding renovations and new facilities. In the summer of 2016, Whitehawk fans raised money to redecorate the dressing rooms at their Enclosed Ground. The following season, they began raising funds for disabled toilet facilities. Similarly, funds were raised for new murals at the ground in 2016 and 2017. Online fundraising sites like *Crowdfunder* significantly help non-league fans raise money for their clubs.

Despite Putnam (2000) arguing that local forms of congregation are declining, football showcases a continued engagement with local politics and mobilization (Millward and Poulton 2014; Millward 2012; Doidge 2015). Non-league football highlights this voluntary form of engagement. Every Saturday across the country thousands of women and men prepare football grounds ready for matches. These volunteers staff clubhouses and turnstiles, design and sell match day programmes, wash kits, and undertake administrative activities in order for their clubs to host matches. Consequently, non-league football provides an excellent way of understanding localized forms of social engagement. Without the passion, dedication, and relationships that these voluntary activities engender, then football would no longer be a viable organized activity.

NON-LEAGUE FOOTBALL AS CONNECTIONS AND FRIENDSHIPS IN THE LOCALES OF URBAN SPACE

Our ethnographic material picks up a freezing cold January day, early in 2017. Often fixtures at this time of the year are postponed due to unplayable pitches, but this FA Trophy match was kicking off as scheduled. The previous season Dulwich Hamlet had visited Whitehawk in the FA Cup, and the Brighton-based side was victorious and went through to the first round for the first time in its history. The match was characterized by the friendliness and support of both sets of fans. This was symbolized by the after-match drinks in the *Hand in Hand* public house. The small hostelry was full of people wearing red-and-white and pink-and-blue scarves. So many fans turned up that dozens spilled out onto the pavement. All shared craft beers, conversation, and laughter—and fans looked forward to another match. For the return fixture, the same pub acted as a meeting place before and after the match, and fans of both teams walked up to the ground together. At one moment, a Dulwich Hamlet fan looked lost as he tried to find his way to the obscure location of Whitehawk's Enclosed Ground. Whitehawk fans noticed his predicament and walked up to the ground with him, chatting amiably about the two teams. At the ground, fans of both clubs mingled in the clubhouse and renewed acquaintances. Independent of this match, some Whitehawk fans had visited Dulwich Hamlet's home ground of Champion Hill when visiting London, while some Dulwich Hamlet fans had previously joined Whitehawk fans in watching their defeat in the Sussex Senior Cup to Crawley Town the previous week. Despite the home side suffering a 4-1 loss, both sets of fans continued as before, heading to the pub and maintaining friendships. These continued at the end of the season when a number of Whitehawk fans joined their friends from Dulwich at the latter's playoff final match against Sussex rivals Bognor Regis.

While this ethnographic observation takes place between two sets of fans who consider themselves friends, this is not necessarily unique. The culture of non-league men's football often encourages a friendly approach to fandom. At Whitehawk's final game of the 2016/17 season, Poole Town fans decided to join Whitehawk Ultras because it was 'the most noise they've heard at football'. They were welcomed and joined in the songs, before chatting to people in the bar afterwards. One fan stated 'this is why non-league is the fucking best. You can talk to other fans, have a pint and make friends' (field notes, April 2017). It is rare that grounds are divided into distinct ends for home and away fans. As a result, fans have many opportunities to interact before, during, and after the match. There is a tradition of non-league fans changing ends at half time so that they are always standing behind the goal that they are attacking. The start of matches usually brings a congregation of bodies waiting until the coin toss that determines the direction of attack. The anticipation for kick-off gives fans an opportunity to interact and discuss the team selection and prospects for the match. Once kick-off is underway, the fans make their way to their respective ends and pass on good wishes to their opponents. This is not to say that there are no rivalries at non-league level—local rivalries persist at all levels of football—but these interactions maintain the generally friendly culture.

Non-league football provides an opportunity to explore the relational aspects of football fandom. Because it is less determined by hostile rivalries, divisions, and a ruthless pursuit of victory, fans feel comfortable talking to each other and sharing ideas. For many, this is linked to a broader rejection of the moneyed Premier League and the 'Against Modern Football' movement (see Hill et al. 2016). This is not necessarily an active campaign against the Premier League, commercialism, or broader changes that symbolize 'modern football'. These fans are not consistently calling for changes to football or harking back to the nostalgia of the past (although these occasionally crop up in conversations). The very performance of their form of fandom is their act of resistance. As will be shown below, by supporting their clubs through ultras culture, friendships, and community engagement, these fans are enacting a form of fandom. As Rancière (2004) argued, the process of art and performance is itself political. Through their performance, these fans are making a simple assertion that this is how football 'should be'.

Taylor (1971a, b) argued that from the 1960s, football supporters were feeling increasingly alienated from the football club. But this is markedly different at non-league football clubs like Dulwich Hamlet and Whitehawk as players occasionally socialize in the clubhouse after matches and this allows fans to have the opportunity to interact with them. After a friendly match with Charlton Athletic before the 2017/18 season, fans and players interacted during a post-match barbeque organized specifically for the purpose of fostering relationships between players and fans. These relationships are particularly highlighted by Dulwich Hamlet's '12th Man' initiative. Run by Neil Cole and Shaun Dooley, the scheme has raised over £27,000 since 2012 through standing orders, collection buckets, and raffles. This money is donated to the club so that it can increase the playing budget, but only for specific, named players. Consequently, the player/s and fans know who is supported by the funds raised by the '12th Man'. The regionalized organization of non-league football also supports these regular interactions between fans. Geographically, fans can attend matches more easily as they are never more than two hours away from the matches. In the cases of Whitehawk and Dulwich Hamlet, this proximity means that fans can relatively easily attend each other's matches. This ensures regular and repetitive interaction that allows friendships to form.

Consequently, fans enjoy a variety of friendships with fans of other clubs. While fan groups may see themselves on friendly terms with fans of other clubs, these friendships are borne of interpersonal interactions between people. This pattern has been observed in Italy with a network of 'twinnings' (Doidge 2015) that align to what Dunning et al. (1986) call 'the "Bedouin syndrome"', where 'the friend of a friend is a friend; the friend of an enemy is an enemy'. At non-league level, rivalries are not negotiated on these lines, but friendships are cultivated in two distinct ways. First, through the acknowledgement that fans of both clubs are 'friendly'. The relationship that formed when Poole Town fans joined Whitehawk fans during their league clash exemplifies this. Conversations in the clubhouse and on Twitter and Facebook forums reiterated that Poole Town fans were 'class' (a slang word referring to a positive feeling or 'having class') and that Whitehawk fans should definitely make a trip down to Dorset the following season. Second, friendships are fostered when fan groups of clubs exhibit similar political outlooks. In London and the South East, these twinnings can be witnessed in the regular attendance of fans attending the matches of 'friendly clubs'. Alongside Whitehawk and Dulwich Hamlet, other football clubs such as Clapton, Eastbourne Town, and Lewes engage in 'friendships' on the grounds of shared political beliefs. Eastbourne Town has a small but growing group of politically aware fans called Pier Pressure (named after Eastbourne's famous Pier). They will often attend Whitehawk matches and share a combined dislike of Eastbourne Borough. Similarly, fan-owned Lewes are seen in friendly terms, mainly because they are a highly community-aware club and are fan owned. Consequently, it is not unusual to see scarves in a variety of club colours at matches involving these clubs. Even friendly matches between these clubs during the pre-season will engender a sense of anticipation and excitement.

This is not to argue that all fans of these progressive fan groups are on friendly terms. While many fans from Clapton will attend Whitehawk matches, this does not mean that they have a friendship with Dulwich Hamlet. This is where the 'Bedouin syndrome' does not apply. Ultimately, fans construct the image of how they want to present themselves (Giulianotti 1999; King 1997b; Robson 2004; Doidge 2015). Fans identifying as 'Clapton Ultras' are actively anti-fascist and more openly political in their chants and banners. In contrast, as shall be shown later, fans of Dulwich Hamlet have engaged in a range of community work. This has attracted media attention and the large increase in popularity. This has led to the subsequent label of 'hipsters' being ascribed to Dulwich Hamlet (see Forster 2015 who labelled them such in the national media). This is a marked contrast to how Clapton Ultras see themselves. This does not mean that there are no individual fans who have friendships at both clubs. Moreover, there have not been matches between the two clubs, and this is an important aspect of friendships at non-league level.

Non-league Fan Culture

For Mische (2003), relations in networks are what people do in interaction. The shared understandings for what people do and encounter can be broadly thought of as 'culture' (Geertz 1973). 'Authenticity' in fandom might be a flawed concept (Crawford 2004; Millward 2011), but many football supporters will argue that one of the criteria for being a 'true' football fan is to have one club for a whole life. This is because this culture is made and remade through the relations of actors in networks that orient this to be a 'truth'. As King (1997b) highlighted in relation to masculine football fans from Manchester, these are social constructions contingent on the dominant view of the group. In contrast, non-league fans often support their local non-league team as well as the team they grew up supporting.

Saturday afternoons in the clubhouse will have a variety of fans checking the scores of their other team. In some cases, these will be teams that are geographically proximate, such as Eastleigh and Southampton or Blythe Spartans and Newcastle United. In other cases, this might be down to political changes affecting their team. This can be illustrated by a critical scene in the 2009 film *Looking for Eric*. One Manchester United fan decries Spleen, a fan of F.C. United, for deserting the Old Trafford side. He reiterated the masculine construction that 'You can change your wife, your politics, your religion, but never, never can you change your favourite football team'. They then laughed at Spleen when he showed an interest in Manchester United scoring. This scene illustrated the conflicted loyalties of fans of non-league clubs when challenging the masculinist assumptions of fidelity to one club alone. In some cases, particularly of some of the clubs mentioned below, such as Clapton, Dulwich Hamlet, and Whitehawk, fans have migrated to new cities and still want to watch football; consequently, they have started supporting their local team, but with a political approach.

There is strong evidence that non-league men's football is experiencing a growth in popularity. As Merkel (2012: 364) states, 'One of the most convincing indicators of football's popularity is matches' attendance figures. Fans often react promptly and unequivocally to changes'. While Merkel was arguing that declining attendances were an indication of the quality of German football, rising attendances are also indicative of wider changes. Non-league football has seen rising match attendances over the last 20 years (*European Football Statistics* n.d.). Undoubtedly, this is due to the relegation of some clubs who traditionally are considered to be long-standing league sides, such as Darlington, Tranmere Rovers, Torquay United, and Luton Town. It also reflects the growth in popularity of protest clubs in England, such as F.C. United of Manchester and AFC Wimbledon. Despite these factors, there is also evidence that attendances are increasing across the leagues. The attendance for the match between Bognor Regis Town and Havant and Waterlooville in the Ryman Isthmian League on 18 April 2017 was given as 3455. This is greater than some Serie B, Ligue 2, and Liga 2 attendances. Elsewhere, Dulwich Hamlet averages over 1300 spectators at home. This is not reflected across every club, but many teams at Steps 3–4 will average around 400 for home matches. Cumulatively, these represent a sizable part of local populations regularly attending matches at 3 pm on Saturday afternoons.

An indication of the growing popularity of non-league football can be seen in the way that specific campaigns and media have arisen. 'Non-League Day' has emerged and grown in popularity. This campaign was initiated by James Doe in 2010 and now boasts official backing by the Premier League and Football League. Non-League Day uses international breaks to encourage fans to find their local non-league clubs. On Twitter, pages like Non League Crowds (@NonLeagueCrowd) provide details of non-league matches and their attendances. The popularity of non-league can also be witnessed in the launch of *The Non-League Paper* in 1999. This weekly newspaper provides match reports and features across the nine steps of the National League System. The significant niche occupied by this paper was witnessed by the fact that it has reasserted its place despite being subsumed in *The Football League Paper* but going alone since 2007.

Part of the reason for the growth in popularity at non-league clubs, particularly at Clapton, Whitehawk, and Dulwich Hamlet is the adoption of an ultras style of fandom. As discussed in Chap. 1, ultras cover a wide range of fan practices but can be characterized by a passionate dedication to the team (Testa and Armstrong 2010; Doidge 2015; Doidge and Lieser 2017). In *The Elementary Forms of the Religious Life* (1915), Durkheim observed how Australian tribes transcended their mundane nomadic lives when they collectively joined in religious rituals. These rituals produced a 'collective effervescence' that was an emotional sense of belonging to others in the group. Through regular, ritualistic interaction with others, the individual developed a sense of belonging to others. The smaller crowds with their greater opportunities to meet friends and acquaintances, combined with passionate atmosphere, help to create a collective effervescence that bonds the fans in attendance. The emotional energy generated by the crowd itself is a powerful factor in keeping the fans together and forging their collective sense of self.

The performance of the ultras style manifests in a number of specific ways. Through this performance the fans enact their approach to fandom. It incorporates the chanting and singing that is characteristic of football fans around the world. Clapton Ultras are the closest to an ultras group in that they have a capo who orchestrates the chants. Songs among Whitehawk Ultras and the Rabble at Dulwich Hamlet are more organic, with chants originating from various sections in the crowd. Although these are still heavily gendered, with men initiating most of the chants, female ultras at Whitehawk do originate chants, which is encouraging but still rare. The ultras style differentiates from an English approach by having visual elements. Flags, banners, and, in some cases, pyrotechnics help create a more aesthetic image of the fan identity. For example, Hawks Ultras regularly wave the rainbow flag to demonstrate their anti-homophobia and reflects their location in Brighton, while Clapton Ultras wave anti-fascist flags. The atmosphere is complemented with musical instruments. Drums are central to this, particularly among Whitehawk Ultras. The atmosphere at Whitehawk will often be complemented with horns and even an air-raid siren. Fans of Eastbourne Town's Pier Pressure also bring drums, horns, and even a saxophone to perform tunes from Madness or Pigbag. All of these help produce the collective effervescence that makes the atmosphere appealing to the fans who attend.

The performance of the ultras is enhanced through the active involvement of the fans themselves. Hills (2002) highlights how fans engage in 'performative consumption'; they literally produce the artefacts that they consume. This is in sharp contrast to the commercial juggernaut of global Premier League teams who protect their brands and licencing aggressively. Non-league clubs are reliant on the dedication of fans who volunteer their time to keep the team going. At Whitehawk and Dulwich Hamlet, fans run the club shops and produce and sell merchandise for the club. Notably, the 'bar scarf' that simply depicts the colours of the team is the most popular item at matches. These scarves do not have the team logo or any legend upon them. As Brown (2008) argues, this reflects the implicit rejection of 'modern football'. Through fashion and style of dress, fans enact their rejection of commercialism (King 1997b). Other fans produce their own range of scarves, T-shirts, and banners to showcase the combined love of their club and political outlook. Whitehawk and Clapton scarves and flags will include anti-fascist logos, while Dulwich Hamlet has a range of flags, including one in the club colours of pink and blue declaring 'Refugees Welcome'. This DIY culture simultaneously reflects the intense involvement of fans in their fandom but also provides opportunities to share and interact with other fans, both within the stadium and across clubs.

These developments have come from fans attending matches across Europe and in Germany in particular. King (2000) has observed how greater European travel has resulted in a restructuring of identity in football fans. Regular European interaction has shifted the focus from the national to the local. At clubs like Whitehawk, Clapton, and Dulwich Hamlet, the European influence is powerful. Not only do their fan bases boast an international contingent, these fans bring their own fan culture with them. The smaller crowds mean that a critical mass can have a wider influence. This helps explain how certain markers of ultras culture are appearing in the non-league. Drums, pyrotechnics, and flags have all been incorporated. The fans and culture surrounding St Pauli in Hamburg have a broad influence on the development of fan culture among the socially orientated fan bases of non-league clubs. For example, fans at both Whitehawk and Dulwich Hamlet shake their keys when their team has a corner. This 'key moment' has been explicitly borrowed from St Pauli and helps produce more noise when the team are attacking.

The German influence on non-league fan culture can be witnessed in friendships held with other clubs. Dulwich Hamlet has a friendship with Hamburg-based Altona. This came about through face-to-face interaction between two fans. Mishi Morath, a long-standing fan of Dulwich, was visiting Altona and chatted with the editor of the All to nah fanzine, Jan Stover. They realized that both clubs were formed in 1893 and had actually played a friendly in 1926. Through sharing fanzines and stories, friendships were formed. But as Mishi said, 'meeting face-to-face is the important factor. We would play each other regularly and we would become friends' (field notes, 25 March 2017). The Dulwich Hamlet Supporters Team would travel and play matches with other supporters' teams, such as Queens Park in Glasgow and Red Star Paris. This allowed fans to build networks of relations with other teams. The strong relationship with Altona has now been translated to the first team. In July 2015, Altona travelled to Dulwich to play a pre-season friendly, and the return will be held in Hamburg in 2018 to celebrate the 125th anniversary of the two clubs. Fans are crowdfunding the trip so the team can travel. Altona have even adopted the pink and blue colours of Dulwich as their away strip. Similarly, Whitehawk have a friendship with Tennis Borussia (TeBe) from Berlin. This originated through fans attending a match and striking up a personal friendship. A Whitehawk scarf is proudly displayed in the Fanladen of TeBe. Since then, other relationships have formed with Whitehawk fans visiting TeBe and vice versa. Football Supporters Europe also facilitates these friendships as they provide another space where Whitehawk and TeBe fans have renewed their acquaintances.

The German (and to a lesser extent Polish) influence has also seen the emergence of stickers as a marker of fan activity. These stickers express support for the club or make political statements or show solidarity with friends. One Dulwich Hamlet sticker, for example, has the number 1893. The number '1' is surrounded by blue and the '8' with pink. This is followed by the '9' being surrounded by black and the '3' with red. These colours reflect the club colours of Dulwich Hamlet (pink and blue) and Altona (red and black). Above the date is the legend 'Friendship. Freundschaft' to advocate the friendship between the two clubs. Likewise, Whitehawk Ultras and Pier Pressure of Eastbourne Town coproduced a sticker that had a circle divided into quadrants with the badges of Whitehawk and Eastbourne Town, juxtaposed with the anti-fascist symbol and a pint of beer. Surrounding this circle, the legend declared the underlying politics of the two groups: 'Anti-homophobic. Anti-sexist. Anti-racist.'

Stickers also act as material gifts that can be exchanged between fans. Mauss (1967) argued that gifts were not value-free, and in reality they enacted a social relationship. Stickers are a physical reflection of these relationships. Fans will share the stickers of their clubs with friendly fans. Not only do these symbolize the friendship, but they also help to reinforce the enduring nature of the relationship. Stands at Clapton's Old Spotted Dog Ground or the Enclosed Ground of Whitehawk will be adorned with stickers. These will display the political thoughts of fans, as well as the friendships. Whether this is a Clapton anti-fascist sticker, a Whitehawk 'Football For All', or supportive stickers declaring 'Refugees Welcome' or 'Football Fans Against The Sun', they reinforce the political leanings of the fans as well as declaring who are friendly clubs.

These stickers are produced by the fans themselves and draw on the creativity and ingenuity of dedicated fans. They reflect the DIY attitude of non-league football and also explicitly and implicitly rebel against the notion of 'modern football'. Pier Pressure and Hawks Ultras have replicated Panini stickers for their star players, and one Dulwich Hamlet sticker depicted two Subbuteo players painted in the colours of Altona and Dulwich. These styles exhibit a nostalgia for football before the economic transformation of the 1990s. One Hawks Ultras sticker clearly states: 'Whitehawk against modern football. Love the game, hate the business'. This statement surrounds an 'old-style' leather ball with laces to reiterate the 'traditional' approach supported by the fans, visualizing the values that are made and remade in the supporters of the club's interactions. As Doidge (2015) argues, this harking back to a non-existent golden age of football often overlooks the misogynistic and racist culture surrounding football in the 1970s and 1980s. Yet, other stickers of the Hawks Ultras reiterate their anti-discrimination approach and desire for 'Football for All'. This reinforces the complex nature of football fandom and how symbols can be read in a variety of ways.

THE IMPORTANCE OF FACE-TO-FACE INTERACTION

As Mishi Morath stated, face-to-face meetings were instrumental in building long-standing friendships. Many of these relationships developed long before social media and formed through fan trips. While social media facilitates these sustained interactions, the shared interest in football and the community aspects of football are central. Football provides a sense of sociability (Doidge 2015). Simmel (1950) observed that many people connect through the mundane pleasure of shared interests. While football also provides the collective effervescence of congregation as well as the emotional energy of the atmosphere and result, many fans enjoy being around people like themselves. As Walter Thompson, community lead for Dulwich Hamlet Supporters' Trust, mentioned: 'You only have it at grass-roots level where you can see your friends … they don't know what you do as a job, but they share a love of football, and have a mutual identity through a shared love of the local club' (personal interview, 28 April 2017). For fans of Dulwich Hamlet and Whitehawk, the shared interests of social causes and enjoyable fandom help bring people together.

It is important to note the gendered aspect of sociability. Some women prefer affective relationships over those based on a shared interest (Allan 1989), while traditional gender roles still exert an influence with many women prioritizing romantic and family relationships over leisure sociability (Sandfield and Percy 2003). Football, however, is increasingly becoming a sociable space for women, as well as men (Themen and Van Hooff 2017). In this way, friendships can be formed based on the shared interest in football and encourages an active involvement in the community activities. This is reflected in the relatively high proportion of female members involved in the Trust movement (Dunn 2017). This is particularly important for clubs like Whitehawk and Dulwich who openly express a sentiment of non-sexism at matches. For example, Whitehawk includes anti-sexism in its collection of chants, and Dulwich Hamlet celebrated International Women's Day by commissioning a special purple kit, which was auctioned after the match, with the proceeds of both the auction and the match day going to two charities supporting women (Catalyst and the World Association for Girl Guides and Girl Scouts). Trust member Walter Johnson interviewed many women associated with football to showcase the wide range of opportunities for women within the game (*Dulwich Hamlet Supporters' Trust* 2017). As Dunn (2017) identified, however, this does not preclude the continuance of sexist comments towards female fans and colleagues. Consequently, these are important initiatives to challenge the stereotypes and make football welcome for all.

In the case of Dulwich Hamlet and Whitehawk fans outlined at the start of this chapter, the geographical proximity between South London and Brighton facilitates an easier interaction. This is also assisted by the regional league structure of non-league football. Even though Whitehawk was in the National League South and Dulwich Hamlet in the Ryman Isthmian League one step below, fans of both clubs can still meet fairly regularly.

Dulwich Hamlet has to play elsewhere in Sussex, including Lewes, Bognor Regis, and Worthing. This often requires a change of trains at Brighton, so Dulwich fans can meet Whitehawk fans after their respective matches. Dulwich Hamlet's playoff final match away at Bognor Regis in May 2017 provided an opportunity for fans of Whitehawk to travel down the coast and support Dulwich against their hated Sussex rivals. Even though they may not be playing each other, they still have fairly regular opportunities to meet and interact, both at football matches and in pubs after matches. It is this regular interaction that permits relationships to be born and sustained. Furthermore, the notion that Dulwich Hamlet and Whitehawk fans are friends encourages further interactions. It is far easier to engage in a conversation with a fan of a club one has never met, when there is a broader understanding that the fans of the clubs are on friendly terms.

The combination of growing attendances and specific localized cultures is leading to new fan relationships forming. Fans are not hermetically sealed units that eschew any interaction with other fans. As we mentioned earlier, many are quite happy and willing to converse with fans of other clubs. Within clubs like Dulwich Hamlet and Whitehawk, there are a range of people who actively sustain their friendships and acquaintances at the other club. This can simply be through engagement on social media, notably tweeting messages of support, as Whitehawk fan John Ayling did to 'our friends at Dulwich H fc ... you're your friends at Whitehawk' (tweet, 27 April 2017). Occasionally, this can include visual images of match attendance which reinforce the importance of face-to-face sociable interactions. As Mishi Morath stated, these help create the bond between different clubs. These fans provide important bridges between the various networks. These bridges are important as they dramatically increase the network of people that fans can access. As Granovetter (1973) highlighted, the strength of networks rests in the 'weak ties'. They are not the ties of close friends, colleagues, or family but the broader network of 'friends of friends'.

The 'strength of weak ties' enables the exchange of ideas and initiatives between fan groups. The next section will outline how fan culture is enacted through community initiatives, some of which are shared by different fan groups. But one specific aspect of non-league fan culture also enables fans to access broader networks. In some cases, at non-league level, fans will also follow a different team in the professional leagues. Consequently, individual fans will have access to a much wider network. When the owners of Whitehawk filed a desire to change the club's name to Brighton City, there was a quick mobilization against the changes. Some fans of Whitehawk had grown up in Hull and supported the Yorkshire club. As a result, they knew Hull City fans who had successfully challenged Assem Allam's desire to change the Yorkshire club's name to Hull City Tigers. These personal connections enabled fans to access strategies and resources that had been successfully used elsewhere. This also helped motivate and energize the fans and give them confidence in their protests. Wider networks provide material resources for support, as well as emotional bonds of solidarity and inspiration.

COMMUNITY WORK: NEW FORMS OF FAN ENGAGEMENT

Many of these new forms of fan engagement are characterized by partnerships with social enterprises outside of the football club. Non-league fandom at clubs like Dulwich Hamlet and Whitehawk are not necessarily actively challenging 'modern football' through protests and campaigns. As with the ultras style and their friendships, these fans are asserting a style of fandom through their fandom. This approach is implicitly challenging the globalized commercial approach of the Premier League by operating within the local community. King (2000) has identified the twin processes of transnational football; fans are becoming simultaneously more local and more global. This can also be seen in the Supporters' Trust movement where trusts have actively sought ownership and involvement from the local community, not just from football fans (Dunn 2017).

The social activities of the non-league clubs outlined in this chapter actively seek to work with the local community. Significantly, this is not just 'people like us', but with an explicit commitment to reaching out to all sections of the community, particularly the most marginalized. For certain clubs, like F.C. United and Lewes, the formation of a new club with fan ownership becomes a clear opportunity to enact a new manifesto and agree upon the future direction of the club. For clubs like Clapton, Whitehawk, and Dulwich Hamlet, the fan base has grown significantly over the last five years so requires more negotiation as the groups evolve and new fans join. Although there can be conflict between fans (Nash 2000; Brown 2008), the general acceptance that these groups are positive and friendly ensures positive outcomes.

What can be seen from the various partnerships of these non-league fans is a wider commitment to the local and global community. This involves being inclusive of all fans, regardless of their economic status, gender, ethnicity, or sexuality. For example, Whitehawk fans held a Refugees Welcome Day and have organized collections of food for the Whitehawk food bank. This community engagement has been sustained with regular collections, as well as providing space in the fanzine, *The Din*, for the food bank to explain to fans why it was a vital service locally. Each month the fanzine showcases a 'charity of the month' for fans to find out about. Similarly, Clapton Ultras engage in social activities in their local area of Newham. They regularly organize collections of food and toiletries for the Refugee and Migrant Project in Newham. Fans have also worked with local residents to clear fly-tipping from the empty Old Spotted Dog pub near the ground and raised funds for 'Paris', Newham's only LGBTQ youth group, and Newham Action on Domestic Violence. Elsewhere, Lewes was also prominent supporters of the 'No More Page 3' campaign to remove photos of topless women from *The Sun* newspaper.

Supporters' Trusts enable a more structured approach to community engagement. For instance, Lewes engage in a range of community activities, particularly around football provision, including older players and those with mental health issues (Lewes F.C. n.d.). This structured approach is replicated at Dulwich Hamlet. As well as their successful event around International Women's Day in 2017, Dulwich Hamlet have also held an annual charity match to raise funds and awareness for specific causes. In February 2015, Dulwich were the first team to organize a friendly against Stonewall F.C., England's top-ranking gay football team who play in the Middlesex County League (Step 7 of the National League System). Fans were able to organize the Stonewall game through relationships they had with the club and manager. Earlier that season, the club became one of the first clubs to adopt rainbow laces to campaign against homophobia in football. Reinforcing the argument that non-league fans are enacting a specific form of activist fandom through their activities, Mishi Morath observes that 'Other football clubs say they're against things, but in many cases it is just lip service. We're not just saying 'we're against homophobia,' we're trying to welcome gay fans to Dulwich. That sums up the ethos of the club, we try to go that bit further' (Abiade 2015).

Each match is accompanied by official charity partners. Proceeds from the Stonewall match were donated to the Elton John AIDS Foundation. A year after the Stonewall match, the Supporters' Trust helped organize a match against F.C. Assyria (who also play in the Middlesex County League). This match raised money for the Southwark Refugee Forum and British Red Cross Syria appeal. This followed on from a series of appeals and collections for refugees throughout the season (as will be discussed later). In 2017, Dulwich Hamlet continued their annual charity event with a match against Centrepoint XI to raise money and awareness for homelessness. This was followed by a sponsored walk to Dulwich Hamlet's match against Wingate and Finchley in North London. This raised money for Shelter and for the funds to travel to a pre-season friendly in Hamburg against Altona. Similarly, the auction of club shirts for International Women's Day raised money for girl guides and Catalyst who support people in abusive relationships. Fundraising is a continuous activity and ultimately becomes the embodiment of the values of the club. This is outlined by Alex Atack, vice-chair of the Supporters' Trust:

> Our ethos as a club is to welcome all and this has resulted in a large number of women attending matches and being part of the Rabble. Therefore, we see it as aligned with our values to celebrate the empowerment of women and help raise awareness in the hope that it may encourage support from others where such diversity is not prevalent. The campaign was exceptionally well received by our fans who supported it on the day by wearing their own purple shirts, and then subsequently through taking part in both the silent auction and raffle to win one of the match worn shirts, raising nearly £2000.

By acting in this way, the fans of Dulwich Hamlet demonstrate the form of fandom that they want to see. Valuing and celebrating diversity can come from regular social engagement and charity campaigns.

Charity and social engagement is not restricted to one-off matches but is part of a sustained engagement with the local community and specific campaigns. The Supporters' Trust permits a more formal structure. In this way Dulwich Hamlet have established an official charity partner with Football Beyond Borders for the 2016/17 season. This educational charity uses football as a way to engage young people across London. In return, Football Beyond Borders have their logo displayed on the shorts of the official men's kit. These official partnerships replicate similar partnerships undertaken by professional clubs, leagues, and FAs. While some aspects of non-league football fandom are involved with challenging 'modern football' and the focus on money and income generation, this is not simply a binary opposition to any form of organization associated with professional clubs. At Dulwich Hamlet, dedicated non-competitive 'friendly' matches are used as opportunities to raise awareness and funds for community groups, rather than for commercial gain. Nonetheless, non-league football retains commercial influence. Clubs still have shirt sponsors and commercial sponsors around the pitch. Finances are often more important at non-league level as the costs associated with participation in the league are more fragile. Yet the engagement of fans permits a wider range of flexibility in social activism.

Most significantly, these partnerships are facilitated through personal relationships. Many of these initiatives have emerged due to connections that existed outside of football. These partnerships reiterate that the networks of football fans are not bounded by acquaintances within the fan base but extend outwards into a wide range of groups and organizations in the wider community. For non-league clubs, these are more locally focused as the clubs see themselves as part of the local community. For example, personal connections between the trust, club, and the voluntary organization Dulwich2Dunkirk ensured that the club became a hub for donations and activities supporting refugees. Dulwich Hamlet Supporters' Trust community lead David Rogers helped coordinate collections of clothing, food, and other important items at the stadium (*Dulwich Hamlet Supporters' Trust* 2017). Local connections also facilitated another appeal for refugees. On 17 December 2016, Dulwich2Dunkirk, the Trust, and club asked fans to bring unused bikes to the stadium for The Bike Project, who are based in Denmark Hill near East Dulwich. The Bike Project collect old and unused bikes, teach refugees to repair them, and donate them to refugees to improve their mobility in the city.

These activities help promote the club to a much wider community than traditional football fans. As Southwark Councillor Jasmine Ali, who was involved in organizing the charity match between Dulwich Hamlet and Assyria to raise awareness and funds for Syrian refugees, stated, 'They [Dulwich fans] are seen to be making football anti-racist and anti-homophobic. I'm not really a football fan but I'll be bringing my children to a game soon!' (Millar 2016). The welcoming and inclusive focus of these fans groups helps open up football to those who may not see themselves as football fans or feel that they are able to go to league football clubs. This is affirmed by Dulwich Supporters' Trust board member, Walter Thompson, 'These are big statements that say Dulwich Hamlet is a place where all can feel welcome and that is why it draws more fans. A lot are drawn to those values' (personal interview, 28 April 2017). Community work is a clear performance of the values of the fans who devote their time to their club and community. They are showing that, through their networks of networks of association and the relations and interactions within these, they have constructed a value as to what a local football club 'should be' and that future networks of friends in their interactions will keep it as such. This holds the benefit to the club of opening up its networks to attract other potential fans who share these values.

CONCLUSIONS: COLLECTIVE ACTION, FRIENDSHIP, AND URBAN SPACES

As outlined in Chaps. 1 and 2, even apolitical forms of football fandom are forms of collective action (see Melucci 1996a)—with fans as social actors attending, singing, cheering, clapping, and even 'just' feeling together. These forms of fandom are not any less 'real' than those that are political (in any variant or position in the political spectrum) and are exhibited among some supporters outlined in this chapter. However, non-league football has developed a new form of activist fan culture over the last five years. This has coincided with a growing interest in forms of fandom that are flagged as explicitly 'local' and connected to specific urban locales (King 1997b; Giulianotti and Robertson 2004). This connects to consumer practices within and outside football. In the latter, there has been a growth among young, affluent, and often leftist-orientated actors to buy into consumer products that are 'locally sourced': locally grown vegetables, locally sourced meat, locally farmed fish, locally produced handcrafts, locally brewed beer (Schrank and Running 2018; Thurnell-Read 2016). Locally produced football is an extension of this ethos as a matter of 'taste' produced within the networks of interactions and relationships (Crossley 2011) of fans. Within football, some of these derive from a reaction to the economic transformation of English elite level men's tournaments that see the Premier League broadcast to 2012 countries across the world. As the Premier League attracts increasing revenue from global television deals and investors, some fans prefer to focus on supporting their local team. Some fans have deliberately been drawn to football clubs that buy into a political leftist view of football fandom, using the leisure pursuit to build networks that actively engage in anti-discrimination activities and community work. Because these are engaged in politically homophilic relationships, they are more readily welcoming to each other when they attend matches. The relatively small crowds and lack of segregation at non-league grounds enable these fans to mix before, during, and after the match. This allows relationships to form. The fact that non-league football is organized regionally also permits the easier and more regular interaction between fans. Friendly groups and individual can attend each other's matches relatively easily as well as meeting in pubs when their respective teams play close by. These face-to-face interactions are fundamental in maintaining relationships and help the flow of information and ideas across the network.

Friendship underpins all of this as the relationships bind groups of supporters into their own collective actions and attract them to join with networks of others on the non-league circuit. For those so inclined, who are flocked together for the very reason that they are so inclined (Borgatti and Halgin 2011), word about a new political initiative that may (or may not) be connected to a football club spreads quickly because the supporters are bound together in friendship ties. In other words, the paths to spread word about such programmes are shorter (Crossley 2011: 149). Supporters stay engaged in these socio-political projects because they are bound through not just a shared belief in any potential outcomes or a mutual bond with the team or the non-league scene but for the very reason that they have become—or were before—friends (Shepard 2015). Similarly, they continue to attend football matches through periods in which they generally agree that entertainment has been poor and results have been underwhelming because in doing so, they meet up with their friends—even if these friendships do not stretch beyond engagements on match days or games between the football clubs. Friendship that is forged in urban locales underscores this type of relational collective action in football.

NOTE

1. 'Food banks' are non-profit, charitable organization that distributes food to those who have difficulty purchasing enough food to avoid hunger. They were introduced to the UK in the light of the recessions caused by the global economic crisis that emerged in 2008.

CHAPTER 4

'Bringing City Home': Coventry City, Sisu Capital, and the Ricoh Arena

INTRODUCTION

Bale (1991, 2000) points out that many supporters feel a strong attachment to the topographical spaces in which they situate themselves in football stadia. King (2002 [1998], 1997b) argues that some of these attachments come from a partial and even invented history of family associations to—and through—those specific spaces. They are, using Crossley (2008a, 2009, 2011, 2015a, b), a foci of football fans' collective actions where conventions in their supporter codes are (re)made and—given the symbolic dimensions of such spaces triggering memories of relationships with other fans (who may be friends or family members)—concrete representations of past and present human interaction (King 2010). Place—in the spaces and symbolism of a football ground—can facilitate the development of a collective identity for even those who imagine themselves to 'belong' in them (Melucci 1996a, b). Identification with an urban locale is also related to support for a football club. The story of Coventry City and its fans' collective actions in mobilizations provides a case in point of these relational forces in action. Formed in 1883 under the original name of Singers Football Club (becoming Coventry City in 1898), the club moved to a new ground (Highfield Road) in 1899 that was to remain the club's home for 106 years. In doing so, it became a key physical manifestation of the way supporters remembered their interactions and relationships with each other.

© The Author(s) 2018
J. Cleland et al., *Collective Action and Football Fandom*,
Palgrave Studies in Relational Sociology,
https://doi.org/10.1007/978-3-319-73141-4_4

Although the period just after the Second World War was one of a downward spiral for the club, it steadily began to gain promotion through the leagues, culminating in 1967 with promotion into the old Division One (now the Premier League). Despite numerous battles with relegation over the years, the club managed to remain in the top division of English football (including winning the FA Cup in 1987) for 34 years. It was during this period (in 1997) that the then chairperson, Bryan Richardson, stated how the club had outgrown Highfield Road, and he set in motion a multimillion-pound project with the support of Coventry City Council to build a proposed 40,000 all-seater stadia with a retractable roof and a sliding pitch (the initial intention was for the ground to be one of the venues for England's bid to host the 2006 World Cup) on a former gasworks site in the city. The local authority granted permission to build the new stadium in 1998, but as costs began to increase it was decided by the club's board to sell Highfield Road for a fee of around £4 million to the property development company George Wimpey and rent it back until the new ground was built. Added to the financial concern was the decision by the Co-op Bank to reduce lending to many football teams, including Coventry City, and this resulted in plans for the new stadium being redrawn (Gilbert 2016).

At the end of 2000/01 season, Coventry City were relegated from the Premier League to the Football League's Division One, which was then the name for the second tier in English football (later relegations into the third tier, then renamed League One at the end of the 2011/12 season, and into the fourth level, League Two at the end of the 2016/17 season, also occurred). Materially, relegation meant changes to business operations at the club as it reduced sponsorship revenues, negatively affecting attendances which immediately dropped from an average over 20,000 paying spectators to just over 15,000 in 2001/02 (these numbers further dropped in subsequent years—in 2016/17 this number had reduced to under 10,000 people) and crucially lost the share of £400 million per year of domestic television broadcast revenues paid to the Premier League which was to be split between the 20 teams in the division (Millward 2017).[1] Indeed, it is from this point that the chapter examines the social relations between fans, the media, and the club that Crossley (2011) refers to, particularly around collective action, interaction, tactics, networks, and protest and how these emerge through disharmony and a lack of trust, which for Burkitt (1997, 2014) are not expressions of inner processes but are the products of social relationships between human actors. It also analyses the power in these relationships and the extent to which 'success' has been defined *and* achieved through collective action at Coventry City.

DISHARMONY AND DEBT

The role of a chairperson is not standardized at all football clubs (Millward 2011; Senaux 2008; Waddington et al. 2001) but is broadly understood to the be the figurehead in the social world of the board, connecting the business, commercial, and administration dynamics with those of the manager and, from there, the playing team. Indeed, Watkins' (2000) non-academic account shows his former role as AFC Bournemouth chairperson involved planning and running the day-to-day financial realities of the club, such as ensuring decisions are made when required, keeping order, and creating consensus among members of the board while also ensuring the club as a whole makes and sticks to its outlined objectives and policies and serving as a spokesperson for the club to those outside of it (including supporters). In this role, he outlined that the chairperson brokers relationships between the club's owner, the team manager, and maybe even members of the media. The latter of these potentially influence the stories that come out of a football club. In effect, the chairperson connects various dimensions of a football club making him/her central to its networks of operation.

By the point of relegation from the Premier League, Coventry City had run up a level of debt at £60 million, and the local evening newspaper (the *Coventry Evening Telegraph*) ran a number of stories outlining how the chairperson at the time, Bryan Richardson, had negotiated with the 'club' (which included himself) a remuneration package worth £588,045—a 170 per cent increase from the previous year. As the financial cost of relegation from the Premier League was being felt, a vociferous protest from supporters at both matches and through the local press developed. A consequence of this was that in January 2002, Richardson was replaced by Mike McGinnity as chairperson on a non-payment basis as part of the club's cost-cutting strategy.

One of the most important tasks McGinnity immediately faced was to develop a realistic business plan, and the results of this came when he reduced the debt from £60 million to just over £20 million. The need for this strict business plan was seen as crucial to the club's future because during the 2001/02 season for each £1 the club generated, £1.11 was being spent on the wages of the club's employees—specifically the football players (Deloitte and Touche 2003). Although football clubs are cultural institutions as well as businesses, this 111 per cent wages to turnover ratio was not sustainable for Coventry City and, if either costs were not cut or revenue grown, would have endangered its existence.

In 2002, negotiations between Coventry City Football Club and Coventry City Council saw Arena Coventry Limited (ACL) created as a joint enterprise. This company was to become responsible for managing the yet-to-be-built Arena. Although the club initially invested an estimated £2 million in the stadium project by 2003, the financial impact of relegation meant that an application for a loan of £21 million to complete the project was rejected. Fearing the end of the project, the council stepped in and, via Yorkshire Bank, loaned ACL the £21 million. The financial burden the club was under was emphasized when they decided to sell their shares in ACL to the locally based Alan Edwards Higgs Charity for £6.5 million in 2003 (who, like the council, became 50 per cent owners of ACL), with the proviso that they could buy back these shares in the future. As part of this sale, the club sacrificed its right to non-match day income for events held at the Arena as well as match day revenue gained from food, drink, and car parking.

Following the emergence of Supporters' Trusts across the UK at the beginning of the twenty-first century (Nash 2000, 2001), the Sky Blue Trust originated from a public meeting held at the Coventry City Supporters Club on 24 April 2003. One of its first tasks was to present a 4600 signature petition at an emergency council meeting held on 16 October 2003 in relation to the 'Build It' campaign for the Arena. To try and create a united voice, the Sky Blue Trust merged with the Association of Coventry City Supporters Clubs and Groups and initially had a positive relationship with the board of the club that led the Trust to seek ways to enhance supporter representation on the club's board of directors. As discussed in Chap. 2, Kádár (2013) argues conformity to intra-network communicative expectations, which he calls 'conventions', are necessary for a collective to smoothly 'function' and develop its own linguistic rituals. However, the board of directors and football supporters often have conventionally different aims and communicate differently. Nevertheless, dialogue between the club and the Trust was initially positive with a case in point being the Trust's proposal to form a Joint Council (later termed the Supporters Consultative Group) in order for supporters to be consulted at board level and improve communication channels between the club and its supporters. Indeed, the first meeting was held on 28 October 2005, and this form of communication remained in place until December 2016 when it was disbanded.

The first home game at the newly named Ricoh Arena was on 20 August 2005 against Queens Park Rangers. Given the financial situation, the club did not contribute to the eventual cost of £116 million and subsequently became a tenant in a facility that was originally going to be built for them. By 2007, with financial difficulty showing no signs of abating, the club was actively seeking new ownership. In this situation, a football club's boards of directors will often employ a broker to match them with a potential buyer (see Millward 2011), but it is unclear if such an individual was employed by Coventry City at this point. Therefore, with the threat of administration looming and after a failed takeover by a consortium called The Manhattan Group, a bid by Mayfair-based hedge fund Sisu was accepted under the condition that all of the 55,000 shares in the club had to be handed over. Joy Seppala (founder, chief executive officer, and director), Dermot Coleman (founder, partner, and director), and Onyechchinaedu Igwe (board member) are three 'key executives for Sisu Capital Limited'. The group had been linked to buyouts at Derby County and Southampton football clubs at the time but only bought into Coventry City. Shortly before that time period, in a story disconnected to football, Seppala was described in *The Sunday Times* as:

> [C]hief executive of Sisu Capital, [who] does not look like 'one of London's most ballsy traders'. A smartly dressed 44-year-old Finnish-American blonde, she likes to describe herself as an investor. But, according to rivals, appearances are deceptive. Seppala is a force to be reckoned with. 'She has balls of steel', said one. Seppala has a reputation for playing hardball in the distressed-debt market -demanding that companies and administrators 'stand and deliver' what she believes her investors are due. From an anonymous building in London's Mayfair, Seppala and her 15 staff run an $800m (£460m) hedge fund that specializes in investing in troubled companies. It looks for firms whose debts are undervalued and trading at a large discount to their face value. (Fletcher and Drillsma-Milgrom 2005: 7)

Of significance to the focus of this chapter was the appointment of Tim Fisher, who has held various board level positions but at the time of writing is currently chairperson. With the involvement of Tim Fisher and a continued climate of driving down costs to protect their investment, Sisu began discussions with ACL in early 2012 about reducing the £1.3 million annual rent. One tactic they adopted was to stop paying the rent in what was later argued through the courts to distress ACL who relied on this money to make regular payments to Yorkshire Bank to reduce the £21 million loan that had been taken out to fund the purchase of a lease to operate the Arena from the council (Gilbert 2016). Sisu argued that they had continued to make ongoing pay as you play payments to ACL during 2012—payments which eventually totalled around £230,000 for the 12 months the club was not paying the agreed rent (Gilbert 2016).

Despite a heads of terms agreement being recorded on 18 June 2012, the deal did not materialize, with Gilbert (2016) referring to an internal memorandum from Chris West, the head of legal and finance at Coventry City Council, being sent to Martin Reeves, the council's chief executive in August 2012 that outlined council opposition to any deal being struck. By December 2012, ACL claimed it was owed £1.1 million in rent and led to a statutory demand that gave Sisu 21 days to settle the debt or face a winding-up order. At the same time Gilbert (2016) reported on how the council were having discussions with Yorkshire Bank about buying out ACL's loan—a deal eventually that saw ACL owe the money directly to the council. This consequently led to a judicial review where Sisu argued it prevented any chance of them owning a stake in the Ricoh Arena through buying out the Alan Edwards Higgs Charity stake. However, the presiding judge dismissed this argument, insisting that talks between the Alan Edwards Higgs Charity and Sisu had fallen away months before the council struck a deal with ACL and Yorkshire Bank.

Further developments occurred on 13 March 2013 when ACL applied for an administration order at the High Court after failing to reach an agreement with Sisu over more than £1.3 million in unpaid rent. Sisu was made up of initially submerged networks (Melucci 1989) of subsidiary companies and on 21 March 2013, one of these, Arvo—the club's single biggest creditor—placed CCFC Limited into administration and a subsequent 10 point penalty from the Football League. After a hostile process played out through the local media, Sisu remained owners, but after ACL and Her Majesty's Revenue and Customs voted against the Company Voluntary Agreement which would decide how much each creditor received from the debt recovery process, the club was again forced to endure a further 10 point penalty from the Football League ahead of the 2013/14 season.

NORTHAMPTON AND THE EMERGENCE OF COLLECTIVE ACTION

In May 2013, with the dispute showing no signs of abating, Tim Fisher announced that the club would be leaving the city to play its home matches while they sought to secure land and build a new stadium by 2016. Discussions took place with Walsall, but Coventry City moved to play matches at Northampton Town's ground, Sixfields. Given the decision to play home matches 35 miles away from the Ricoh Arena, it is easy to see how this would increase the likelihood of networks forming together in collective action and how the actors within it are 'shaped by how they are affected by it'. The actions of another '"call out a response" from me' (Crossley 2011: 30). Although a number of fan mobilization groups emerged, including 'get Cov Back to the Ricoh' and 'Keep Cov in Cov', an immediate response came from the *Coventry Evening Telegraph* who voiced the concerns shared by many custodians of Coventry by creating the 'City Must Stay' campaign, which more than 14,000 people eventually signed. When asked how he saw his involvement in the move to Northampton, the political reporter at the *Coventry Evening Telegraph*, Simon Gilbert, stated:

> I saw my role as giving supporters a voice—a way of being able to vent their frustrations at the situation. As a local media outlet and a pillar of the local community we saw it as a responsibility to make people aware what was potentially going to be something that was completely unacceptable was about to happen. The owners were about to take the club out of the city which gave it its name. From our point of view, very early on we said that cannot be allowed to happen and we must do what we can to try and stop it. (Personal communication, November 2016)

Although Castells (2013) suggests that information-age mobilizations could bypass the messages and content of corporations such as the traditional media to create their own messages in cyberspace, it was found at Coventry City that the local media (particularly the *Coventry Evening Telegraph*) played a significant part in the collective protest that was taking place. Instead, networks of mobilizations emerged through the role played by the traditional media in highlighting the resistance taking place at Coventry City. Reflecting on patterns of communication between fans and the paper during this period of collective action, Simon Gilbert stated:

'Our voice is just one among many. We can shape people's opinions, we can influence the way people think but people aren't machines, they can come to their own conclusions.' Addressing this, on 20 July 2013, was the first serious attempt at collective action by the Sky Blues Trust when an estimated 5000 Coventry City fans marched towards the city centre in protest at the decision by the owners to take the club out of the city. Referring to the march, the chairperson of the Sky Blues Trust, Moz Baker (elected in October 2016), stated:

> We never actually called an official boycott of Sixfields. I think that is important to say. It was just something that evolved. The strength of feeling was such that this was wrong, our club was being moved out of the city which gave it its name to go 35 miles down the road to Northampton was clearly wrong on every level possible. So something needed doing to try and stop it. So we thought about a protest or march, but no-one knew what sort of support it was going to get. We were hoping for a few hundred but the estimates from the police were that it was actually several thousand and there was a real strength of feeling in the first protest. A real coming together of people. Not just people who come together on a regular basis, but people who lived in the city and realized how important the club was to its community. (Personal communication, November 2016)

Reference to 'strength of feeling', a 'real coming together of people', 'protest', and 'community' by Moz Baker above outline how social life is filled with emotions. With particular resonance to the situation at Coventry City during 2013, we can draw on Jasper (1997) as to how emotional attachment to a 'place' and a sense of 'cultural loss' such as a 'threat' towards it can lead to collective action as a form of protest. The place of emotions and the opportunities created for individuals to interact is what Durkheim calls 'collective effervescence' (an emotional energy that bonds participants) or what Collins (2004) refers to as interaction ritual theory (how emotions are transformed in the process of interaction through the production of emotional outcomes such as moral solidarity, as well as anger). In the case of football culture, space and place (such as public houses, the stadium, and other specific places) are an important feature of football fandom, even as we suggest in Chap. 2 how some of them are imagined to be more temporal than real.

Despite widespread local coverage however, the club continued to ignore such protests and was supported by the Football League who agreed that the club could ground share for three years, with an option of an extra two in return for paying a £1 million bond that acted as an assurance that they would return to Coventry. The club started the 2013/14 season at Northampton with the first 'home' game taking place on Sunday 11 August against Bristol City that attracted a crowd of 2204, with only 908 Coventry City fans recorded to be in attendance. This sense of protest was underlined by a charity match of Sky Blues legends taking place at the Ricoh Arena at the same time attracting over 7000 fans (Gilbert 2016). Indeed, it was to be a season of protests, with the average attendance of 2364 the fourth lowest in the whole Football League, only beating Accrington Stanley, Dagenham and Redbridge, and Morecambe, all of whom competed in the league below. It also reflected a 78 per cent drop in the average attendance from the 2012/13 season of 10,938. These figures reflected the 'Not One Penny More' stance taken by a large number of supporters to starve the club of any income from attending matches at 'home'. Other fans took up a season-long position on a hill at Sixfields that allowed them to avoid paying an entrance fee but still able to view approximately two-thirds of the pitch. This became known as 'Jimmy's Hill', in recognition of his work in positioning the club among England's elite in the 1960s. Individual matches also provided an opportunity to protest on a national and global level including the 4th round FA Cup tie against Arsenal at the Emirates that was being broadcast live on television. In the 35th minute of the match (representing the distance between the Ricoh Arena in Coventry and the Sixfields stadium in Northampton), Coventry fans and some Arsenal fan held aloft signs with the word 'why?' to represent their feelings. Outside of the glare of international broadcasters were city-wide visual tactics that included tying sky blue ribbons to prominent buildings across the city, including club's training ground, Coventry Cathedral, and Coventry City Council as well as major routes into the city. This visual protest was not just confined to the city of Coventry however, with ribbons also tied to the headquarters of the Football League and Sisu in London.

Kieran Crowley, who was appointed as a club journalist in September 2011 and became head of communications at the club in the summer of 2013 (the time when the club were preparing to move to Northampton), was also interviewed. This was a position he remained in until he left the club in May 2016. Addressing the period at Northampton and the subsequent reaction he had to deal with, Crowley refers to the strength of feeling, emotion, and isolation that the move created:

It was a very tough period. Your head is telling you this isn't right, but looking back I was Ok with the move because we had such a closet mentality because we felt were being attacked from all sides, the fans, the council had done numerous things to the club, ACL. I just thought we had it make it work. We were paying £1.3 million in rent. If that contract was still in place the club would not be in existence … it was us against the world. I look back on that period and think how was what we did right? At the time I did. It probably made the job slightly easier for me, but everything you put out the time was vilified. It was hated. … There was no way of using the local paper to our advantage so that just leaves you with the official website and fans just refused to believe what we said. (Personal communication, November 2016)

Choosing Tactics: Webs of Media and Social Media Connections

A variety of tactics are used by various individuals and groups over the course of the move to Northampton. Reflecting on what action he took, the football reporter at the *Coventry Evening Telegraph*, Andy Turner, stated:

It did affect me personally because it affected my family. My dad was a season ticket holder in his 70s who used to go to every home game and he stopped going. He was disenfranchised. With him not going it meant my son wasn't going. I just thought it was so wrong and that's just the personal side. It was a microcosm of all the bigger issue which affected all fans. It was deplorable and despicable what they did. I channeled that through my comment pieces. I was quite aggressive in my writing and I would take every opportunity to have a dig at the club because it was so wrong and I felt so strongly and passionately about what they were doing. With other issues you try and take a step back and be objective, but with that it was difficult to do. (Personal communication, November 2016)

For Burkitt (2014) emotions are inherently relational, emerging through human relationships. Andy Turner was 'affected' because familial connections (he mentions his father) were negatively affected. These relationships and associated emotions created the 'moral shock' (Jasper 1998) to integrate into the emerging sets of protest and shape public opinion through the communication space of the media. Given the move by traditional media into online space, an increasing feature is to make articles and stories that would have initially been for the print version only available online and promoted through various social media sites. This is tactic being readily adopted by the traditional media to get readers immediately reacting and engaging with published story rather than wait for the print copy to become available. The importance of social media bringing everyone together supporters the views of Castells (2015 [2012]), who illustrates how the internet plays an important contemporary role in changing the emotional state of a collective, who can metaphorically hold hands together with no geographical barriers. Referring to the potential of social media as an available and effective tactic that can be utilized during campaigns, Simon Gilbert stated:

> Social media is a huge part of driving any campaigns these days. It has got to be the quickest and most effective way of getting a message to people. We came up with the graphics that people could share, we came up with the hashtags and we made sure we spoke to the right people online. ... When it comes to campaigns and galvanizing support, the ability to do things instantaneously, to get the news away and get high profile figures sharing the news, you would not get that in any other way. (Personal communication, November 2016).

While Castells believes that fear represses collective actions, collective effervescence in online and offline space challenges fear as people stand and communicate with each other in a shared sense of collective identity and shared emotion of anger. According to Ryan (1991), an important element for mobilizing a group is media communication. Increasingly this is through hashtags on Twitter as it allows a group to widen the cause and appeal to a wider collective, such as in the case of Coventry City bringing the club back to the Ricoh Arena (Castells 2013 [2009]). As suggested by Crossley (2015a, b), social media techniques played a prominent role in collective action at Coventry City. In the summer of 2014, the *Coventry Evening Telegraph* made another concerted effort to build collective actions within supporters by creating the #BringCityHome slogan that encouraged fans to use social media and the newspaper to engage in this form of protest. This was matched by a second march organized by the Sky Blues Trust, which was attended by more fans than the march the year before. Referring to how protests evolved once the decision was made to play in Northampton, Moz Baker stated:

The whole season at Sixfields was dreadful. We did various protests on the hill, we did the big protest at the Emirates. The following summer when we were still there so although we were skeptical we decided we should do another one, but the turnout was good because the feeling was probably stronger the second time around. Whether it made an impact who knows but we have been told by various sources that it did have an impact because of the galvanizing nature of support the protests got. At the end of the day I think there is something to be said for fan power. Sitting on your hands does not get you anywhere. You have to raise your head above the parapet and make yourself heard. People will say you are trouble makers and you should just support the team, but sometimes you have to look at the bigger picture. (Personal communication, November 2016)

While recognizing the importance of online space, the views above from Moz Baker reflect those of Castells (2015 [2012]) who indicates how the action taking place in urban space is also an essential component of collective action. The three important effects of occupying urban space that he refers to were prominent in the collective action taking place at Coventry City: (1) being together enhances the collective emotional experience—that is, marching and chanting in unison in a symbolic urban space (the two protests that congregated in the centre of Coventry in 2013 and 2014) produces an effective 'glue' who become emotionally 'attuned' to each other; (2) urban protests materialize discontent that is difficult to ignore by established programmers of societal values, such as the established media (the visual protests and general demise of the club has been recognized at a national level); and (3) it reinvigorates online activity mass self-communication and digital technologies which are used in urban space such as designated hashtags (as outlined by the examples including #BringCityHome).

Crossley (1999) problematizes the notion of 'social capital' but broadly sees it as a central movement resource through the recognition of pivotal personal contacts and certain individuals played a prominent role in the process of collective action. As well as using the *Coventry Evening Telegraph* and his personal Twitter account to relay ongoing developments, Simon Gilbert also adopted other tactics which would also play a significant role in the club returning to the Ricoh Arena. The first one was to personally visit the headquarters of the Football League in London with special editions of the newspaper with pictures of fans holding placards containing the 'hashtag' #BringCityHome on the day a meeting was taking place between officials from the club, ACL, Coventry City Council, and the Alan

Edward Higgs Charity to discuss the settlement of a £470,000 bill the club were forced to pay to ACL as a result of the administration of CCFC Ltd in 2013. Due to the hostility in which the administrative process was played out between the key parties, Gilbert also made contact with local MPs as well as the prominent Conservative MP, Damian Collins (in October 2016 he became elected Chair of the Culture, Media, and Sport Committee), to also apply governmental pressure on Sisu to pay, which they eventually did (Gilbert 2016). This subsequently paved the way for the return to the Ricoh Arena with the *Coventry Evening Telegraph* headline on Friday 22 August 2014 stating 'after 503 days, 59 games, two marches, 13,000 signatures, a judicial review, six campaigns and thousands of broken hearts, the Sky Blues are finally … COMING HOME'. Thus, on 5 September 2014, over 27,000 fans watched Coventry City defeat Gillingham 1-0. It was a highly emotional time for the fans, but it was also emotional for people employed at the club, with Kieran Crowley commenting:

> I will never forget that day when the deal was done. It was really emotional for the supporters to see their club come back to the city. The staff as well. They had been through it. It wasn't a normal football club situation. (Personal communication, November 2016)

The move back to the Ricoh Arena was part of an initial two-year deal, with an option for a further two years and a revised down annual rent charge of £100,000. However, a few weeks later it emerged that Coventry City Council had agreed a deal with the Premiership rugby club, Wasps, to purchase the council's stake in ACL for £2.77 million and subsequently pave the way for a quick completion of complete ownership of the Ricoh Arena by acquiring the other 50 per cent share from the Alan Edwards Higgs Charity for £2.77 million (Wasps also took on ACLs £14.4 million loan from the council). Illustrating what could be referred to as some form of collective fatigue at the time due to all of the emotion being put into the return to the Ricoh Arena, Simon Gilbert stated: 'It was surprising that there was not any organized opposition to the takeover of the Ricoh Arena by Wasps.' This decision certainly took a number of parties by surprise, and the quickness of the sale to Wasps from shares in the council and the Alan Edwards Higgs Charity allowed no real time for a further collective action to occur and try to force a change in this decision.

As Blumer (1951) argued, the tactics used in a collective action are an important element depending on the context in which they are being used. In the case of Coventry City it was trying to gain national and international exposure to the plight of fans as a result of a sense of powerlessness caused by a 'villainous' enemy (Alinsky 1971) in Sisu who could be blamed for the injustice impacting on them. One innovative tactic used was the throwing of plastic pigs onto the pitch by both sets of supporters during a league one game on 15 October 2016 against Charlton Athletic at the Valley. Referring to this, Moz Baker stated:

> We made contact about doing a joint protest and they were really up for it. They have got a lot of funding which we haven't got. They've got people backing them who are quite wealthy. They didn't want anything from us. (Personal communication, November 2016)

This intersects with Smithey's (2009) account of how tactical choices are often a product of resources and opportunities within the physical environment. Given both sets of fans were in open dispute with their current owners, here was an opportunity for both sets of supporters to collectively organize a protest that was witnessed across the world and gave them the coverage of their plight that they wanted. Thus, the interactive cultural dimension of two separate sets of supporters protesting in this way through an innovative tactic to leverage power through the element of surprise ties in nicely with relational sociology. Indeed, innovative tactics are important, particularly for lower league clubs who do not get the exposure that Premier League clubs receive from the global media seeking new stories to feed into a saturated market. This was raised by Moz Baker who stated:

> The test is to try and do something different but it is not easy because the way the media work is they want a fresh story. You have to keep reinventing stories and that is why the pig protest was fantastic but you can't do it again. I came away from Charlton thinking that went as good as it could do. (Personal communication, November 2016)

NETWORKS AND SOFT LEADERS IN THE COLLECTIVE ACTION OF FAN MOVEMENTS

In an analysis of networks and roles in collective action, McAdam (1982, 1983, 1986, 1988) refers to how activism in collection action might come about as a result of being in a stage of the life course. With regards to the life course of Moz Baker as a Coventry City fan and his role in the collective action:

I have been a fan since the 1970s but I got more involved in our last year in the Championship in 2012. I spoke with two of the guys who had set up the Trust in the early 2000s but it had never really got off the ground and in 2012 we resurrected it and that was the start of more and more fans getting involved. ... We could see what was happening and this was not going to happen in a good situation. We knew that relationships with ACL were breaking down and just generally the way the club was being run we felt we needed to stand up and represent supporters. That was before protests were being spoken about. Make sure fans were being represented and their views were being put forward. It was a situation that a lot of people could see happening. (Personal communication, November 2016)

As suggested earlier, it is important for any type of social movement to have social capital (Crossley 1999). While individuals like Simon Gilbert managed to acquire this, it is also important within a movement that each member has mutually owned capital, such as the trust of other members within the real or imagined community. Responding to the collective action that took place once the decision was made by the club to relocate to Northampton, Moz Baker stated:

Essentially when we resurrected it there wasn't a membership as such. We actually started from scratch. Because it was a trust we had to go through all of the legal ramifications through Supporters Direct who set it up. We just went out and promoted the idea. In town, we set up stalls, we went to the Town and Country festival. We went very public and went from a member-ship of 0 to 3,000. ... There is still a strong feeling out there, probably big-ger than when we started the Trust again in 2012. We get a steady number of people joining us all of the time, but it's not anything significant. (Personal communication, November 2016)

Although the Trust was operational before the move to Northampton, it was the 'moral shock' (Jasper 1998) of the move to Northampton that galvanized support. So what does 'involvement' in collective action mean? Following Millward's (2011) analysis of some Manchester United supporters protesting about the Glazer takeover just simply wearing a 'green and gold' scarf, for the vast majority of Coventry fans not paying any attendance money or deciding to sit on the hill at Northampton was their way of protesting. Thus, network capital (Lin 2002) was generated through Coventry City fans' collective action, whose situation captured a wider community interest who shared a common purpose of disputes with owners or were general football traditionalists who had an interest in football clubs and their history with fans. This was reflected in some opposition fans also refusing to attend Sixfields while Coventry played there.

As a key individual, the collective action undertaken by Simon Gilbert saw him engaging with fans, protestors, and politicians as 'targets' (Klandermans 1997) as well as tapping into the Coventry population (and wider) through his ability to generate coverage and exposure as a journalist. The outcome, he believes, was significant enough to force the club to return to the Ricoh Arena. So, did he see himself as a leader or a switcher who could link networks together with the resources he had at his disposal?

> I saw myself as a campaigning journalist. I saw myself as someone who could potentially help to right this wrong. No one person can have that much influence that they can claim that they are solely responsible. Of course it is a combination of factors, but my view of my role was to keep it in the public eye, to make life publicly uncomfortable for people who had the ability to make decisions that could rectify the problem by asking questions that supporters wanted answers and that means putting pressure on people who were unwilling to answer questions and if they weren't willing to answer questions from us then finding routes that would allow those questions to be answered and ultimately that meant the involvement of politicians which is really the only way you can get private organizations or corporate organizations to listen to what supporters are saying. … In some of the conversations I had during those very early days I did make private appeals for individuals to get together and sort this out, but the main linkage role I played was between the supporters and the decision makers. Supporters don't always have a direct line to the decision makers. I was their way of putting questions to people and providing the answers they were searching for. (Personal communication, November 2016)

Reflecting on the extent he was a leader as a result of his presence during the first and second organized protest in the centre of Coventry, where he was tasked with providing a speech to the crowd who had marched, Moz Baker stated:

> At the time I wasn't chair of the Sky Blue Trust, I was just a member of the board. Because I am comfortable with public speaking the board suggested

I got up there. It wasn't until I did the first one that I realized the weight of responsibility on my shoulders because people were coming up to me afterwards and saying well done and keep going and when you realize people are relying on you then you realize the weight of responsibility. I had some nights where I couldn't sleep because I was thinking 'what could we do?' because people were reliant on us to do something, but at the end of the day we can only do so much. I felt it was a situation I couldn't walk away from and I felt we all felt the same. (Personal communication, November 2016)

The development and reemergence of the Supporters' Trust at Coventry City follows what Castells (2015 [2012]) refers to as a 'rhizomatic' new social movement due to its grassroots emergence, growth, and organization. They also do not have explicit 'formal' leaders; instead they have soft leaders who hold positions of social, political, and/or cultural influence, such as dealing with the media and being able to communicate the aims and tactics of their collective action to supporters. Soft leaders tend to assume their role momentarily because they are suited to immediate task in hand due to their knowledge and networks rather than have ambitions of mid-term of long-term leadership. As suggested by Bourdieu (1986), they have developed a level of cultural capital that is beyond the leadership of types of formal and informal roles in the division of labour that might exist depending on structure and nature of collective action.

Coventry City's Supporter Mobilization as a Success?

Giugni (1998) is clear that the criteria for 'success' of collective actions are difficult to define. However, such criteria—whether 'official' and/or written or not—are the product of interactions between activists in relation to the actions of those people, issues, and policies they are agitated by. The idea of 'success' is inherently relational. The aim of the first collective action was to force a return by the club to the Ricoh Arena, meaning that it was regarded by Coventry City supporters as a 'success'. But how much did the visual campaigns and protests play in this return? Reflecting on this, Andy Turner stated: 'The Ricoh return is a good example of a campaign that you set out knowing you have a 99 per cent chance of winning because there is an appetite by the football club who were desperate to get back.' However, he also referred to the failed campaign to stop the club going to Northampton and the inability to, at the time of writing, put enough pressure on Sisu to sell the club:

As was proved in the Sixfields situation, sadly, I don't think they will get anywhere. It doesn't matter how much pressure they exerted, they voted with their feet, took to the streets 2–3 times and the club still didn't listen to them. They were their customers, they were screaming and shouting at them, do not do this or we won't go to Sixfields and they still went ahead and did it so that tells you a huge amount about the owners of the club. They will operate on their own terms and will not be dictated to by anybody—the local newspaper, by the national press or by their own customers, the fans. It's usually the other factors, the financial factors that drive the situation which is what happened with the return to the Ricoh Arena. (Personal communication, November 2016)

These views were echoed by Kieran Crowley who stated:

It became apparent early in the summer of 2014 that we needed to go back to the Ricoh Arena. The financial impact was vast. There was a hesitance at board level but [chief executive] Steve Waggott pushed it and eventually he was given permission to do the deal. The visual impact of the protest at Arsenal, the visual impact of the marches in Coventry had no impact. People in the club, not that they didn't care about the supporters, but they saw the protest as a product of a fans group which just wasn't representative. … The only thing that got the club back to Coventry was the financial impact. (Personal communication, November 2016)

Given this insider perspective at the time, it is clear that protest can take many forms and the decision by thousands of Coventry City fans to refuse to watch the club play home matches 35 miles away was a successful tactic. Although Kriesi et al. (1995) state that an outcome may not always be the result of collective action, such as the cases within football of the Spirit of Shankly (SoS) protest group at Liverpool (Millward 2011) and the frequent protests against Mike Ashley at Newcastle United (Cleland and Dixon 2015), but in the case at Coventry City, it was evident that the fact that no one actually went to Sixfields forced the club to try and repair broken relationships. Indeed, in one way it was helped by two new people at both the club (chief executive Steve Waggott) and at ACL (chairperson Chris Robinson) to strike a deal out of the spotlight of other individuals.

So, what now? It is difficult to adequately summarize the situation at Coventry City because it remains fluid. With the club continuing its downward spiral, the *Coventry Evening Telegraph* have instigated a 'Sell Up and Go' campaign against Sisu that has gained over 19,000 signatures. Responding to the reasons behind this, Andy Turner stated:

> The *Coventry Evening Telegraph* took a stance. They stepped off the fence, we've seen what the situation is, we've assessed everything and we've decided we are going to listen to our customers are saying, what our readers are saying, and we are going to act on that, we are going to get behind them. (Personal communication, November 2016)

Indeed, the Sky Blue Trust wants to enter into negotiations with Sisu, who thus far have refused to meet with them. Focusing on supporter representation at individual clubs, Nash (2000: 482) stated 'until fan groups penetrate those club decision-making processes, their value systems will remain largely abstract ... and so mostly irrelevant'. A case in point was this response from Moz Baker:

> When we eventually started up again one of our key objectives was to get some form of fan representation, fan ownership. This has been in the background for a bit because of Sixfields and the other stuff going on ... recently, we asked for a meeting to discuss the issue of fan ownership and what the possibilities were and we were told the club is not for sale. That still remains our aim, but the ball remains in Sisu's court and there's not a lot we can do, but that does not mean less keen on the idea and we have always thought that is the way the club should go. (Personal communication, November 2016)

The club want to relocate to a site in the centre of Coventry and become a tenant of Coventry Rugby Club and this is becoming an increasingly pressing matter as they are about to enter their final season as a tenant at the Ricoh Arena during the 2017/18 season. A recurring theme in the breakdown of talks with local stakeholders such as the owner of Coventry Rugby Club is a result of the continued litigation Sisu are seeking against various parties in the city. The first judicial review concerned Coventry City Council and ACL and the second one is due to again involve Coventry City Council but this time also Wasps. This was a result of the failure to capture the Alan Edwards Higgs Charity 50 per cent share in ACL and has subsequently led Sisu to instigate another judicial review into the deal between Wasps and the council which, at the time of writing, has not yet taken place. Much uncertainty remains as to the future of the club and highlights the importance of collective actions in what looks like a difficult future. As this chapter has indicated, however, financial protest had the biggest influence on the move back to the Ricoh Arena from Northampton, but with Sisu seemingly ignoring all others forms of collective action, the situation remains very much in their hands as to the future direction of the club.

Conclusions: Place, Identity, and Collective Action

Football supporters often feel a strong attachment to the topographical spaces in stadiums (Bale 1991, 2000) through their association of such physical spaces with the memories of interactions with others (King 1997b, 2002 [1998]). This identification with 'place' is also strong with the urban locale and has been the catalyst for fan action association at Brighton and Hove Albion (Carder 2006; North and Hodson 2011 [1997]), Charlton Athletic (Barnes 2006; Everitt 2014) and Wimbledon (Couper 2012; Joyce 2006), and here, Coventry City. The stirring of such emotions, generated collectively and through relational processes of interaction (Burkitt 1997, 2014; Castells 2004 [1997], 2015 [2012]; Jasper 1997, 1998), can be strong when 'belonging' is challenged (Melucci 1989, 1996a, b).

Thus, Melucci (1996a) centralized 'collective identity' in the collective action of mobilization. In the case of the protests of Coventry City fans, the 'we-ness' of supporters was felt before the protests began, but they drew upon people of key positions of influence, such as in the local media, to create messages to enable action. However, this action was not belonging to those such as Simon Gilbert but to the collective and the relationships within that network. In Melucci's (1989) sense, the collective action was not just the sum of individual actions involved in it but within a 'multipolar action system'. Together, they defined the aims of the movement and the parameters of 'success'. Although Coventry City now play home matches back in the city (widely drawn as a marker of 'success'), they will play 2017/18 season in the bottom division of the Football League, and the network of 'investors' involved with 'Sisu' remain as financial owners of the football club, even if supporters see the 'spirit' of the club belonging to them. These latter two points are not drawn as a success of the movement and see dissent continue. The story of Coventry City fans' protest is unlikely to be complete, but networks of agitated fans of the club and other clubs are likely to form the basis of future mobilizations.

NOTE

1. This figure is before lost overseas television revenue is worked into the equation.

CHAPTER 5

Supporters' Trusts as Collective Action: Swansea City in Focus

INTRODUCTION

This chapter discusses 'Supporters' Trusts' as a form of collective action in the relational social worlds of football, empirically detailing the story of Swansea City. This Supporters' Trust has often been held up as an exemplar of successful practice in the Supporters' Trust movement, even appearing as a *BBC* documentary 'A Jack to a King' (2014). Discussions about Supporters' Trusts inevitably prompt questions about how they relate to sociological ideas about 'trust', in both its senses as an emotion and social act. As initially discussed in Chap. 2, trust is an inherently relational concept—having 'use' but not 'exchange' values and borne out of human interactions. Sztompka (2003 [1999]: 25) argues that trusting in others becomes the crucial strategy for dealing with uncontrollable futures in situations where social actors have to act in spite of uncertainty and risk. Indeed, Martin (2007) points out that most Supporters' Trusts emerge and/or gain influence when a football club is facing a form of hardship, most likely of a financial form. Luhmann (2017 [1979]: 24) states that 'trust is only involved when the trusting expectation makes a difference to a decision'. Indeed, fans normally expect the Supporters' Trust to make some sort of positive difference to the running of the club or else there would be no need for that form of collective action (Kennedy and Kennedy 2007).

© The Author(s) 2018
J. Cleland et al., *Collective Action and Football Fandom*,
Palgrave Studies in Relational Sociology,
https://doi.org/10.1007/978-3-319-73141-4_5

Coleman (1973) argues that social actors must have the trust of others for cooperation within networks to exist. In making this point, he suggests that intermediaries in networks may play the role of 'advisor', introducing social actors to coordinate, which facilitates interaction and creates mutual 'trust' between social actors, as a 'guarantor' who absorbs the risk in the event that such trust in others turns out to be misplaced or as an 'entrepreneur' who is entrusted to invest multiple actors' resources to realize gains. The fan movements and, in particular, Supporters' Trusts typically contain all three of these roles: advisors, sometimes from external agencies such as the part UK government-funded Supporters Direct advising trusts on their operational needs and helping to facilitate the bringing together of interested social actors; the guarantor who becomes the figurehead in the specific Supporters' Trust and manages expectations or reassures fans that reasonable aims will be met; and the 'entrepreneur' who might take control of the combined resources to fulfil goals. In this sense, the entrepreneur might be a supporter who sits upon the football club's board of directors.

There is no shortage of literature on the Supporters' Trust movement in football (Dunn 2017; Lomax 2000; Martin 2007; Michie and Oughton 2005; Smith 2000; Turner 2017; Walters and Tacon 2010), but it is clear they exist in at least four 'ideal types' (Weber 2001 [1930]) that should not be conflated in any way other than to mean fan interest in the running of a football club. Elaborating on these four ideal types, first there are those Supporters' Trusts that own a club outright, perhaps using the Industrial and Provident Society model, where each shareholder (rather than shareholding) is only entitled to one vote. This model runs at the non-league F.C. United of Manchester and gives the collective action of supporters the full reign of running the football club (see Brown 2008; Kiernan and Porter 2014; Millward 2011; Porter 2015). Second, there are those Supporters' Trusts, such as those attached to F.C. United of Manchester's 'parent club' Manchester United (see Chap. 1) and Coventry City, as detailed in Chap. 4, that do not own a financial stake in the club—although in some circumstances individual Supporters' Trust members might do so. Instead, they exist as a voice of the fans through the media and involve personnel who are well connected to the journalists and local/national politicians. Third, some Supporters' Trusts own a controlling financial stake in the club, with the remainder made up of other 'investors'. This controlling interest might be modelled on the 50 per cent plus one share model that operates in Germany (Frink and Prinz 2006). Fourth, there are those Supporters' Trusts where the aim is to ensure a formal communication channel to fans, where the Trust has a formal seat on the board of directors. In the 1990s, Manchester City F.C. appointed fanzine editor Dave Wallace as a supporter representative to the board of directors. However, when the fanzine criticized the club's choice of new team manager, Alan Ball—who had experienced relegation at four different clubs—in 1995, the club made clear that Dave Wallace's duty was to present the board to the fans and his place was taken from him (Conn 2002 [1997]: 217). This type of representation is not the aim of Supporters' Trust who, instead, demand representation of supporters in the boardroom. Swansea City is the only Premier League club with a fan on its board of directors with the Supporters' Trust owning a fifth of the 'business' and operating in this way.

Located on the coast of South Wales, Swansea City was formed in 1912 and its home stadium was the Vetch Field for much of its history before moving to the Liberty Stadium in 2005. During the mid-1970s the club had to apply for reelection to the Football League, but success arrived under the management of John Toshack in the late 1970s and early 1980s before the club fell down the leagues again. The collective action of mobilization is not new to Swansea City as in the 1980s after a high court wound the club up, fans actively engaged in a successful campaign to save the club. However, it was the collective formation of a Supporters' Trust in 2001 and the subsequent part-ownership in the club that this chapter shall focus on. Of particular interest to the scope of this book is that the club was promoted to the Premier League in 2011 and is the first club in the history of the Premier League to have supporter ownership as part of an overall ownership structure. This chapter focuses on the emotions, tactics, and successful collective mobilization of supporters in late 2001 and early 2002, in particular the relationships between people in online and offline space and how these modes of interaction come together. It then considers some of the challenges now facing the relational idea of 'trust' in the Swansea City Supporters' Trust as a result of the takeover of a majority of the shares by a consortium led by Steve Kaplan and Jason Levien that was officially ratified by the Football Association in July 2016.

CONNECTIONS AND INTERACTIONS MATTER IN FOOTBALL
FAN COLLECTIVE ACTION

Cleland (2010) referred to the changing nature of fandom from the late 1980s, with fans becoming more active, rather than passive, in their involvement in football. Initially this started with the fanzine movement, but from the mid-1990s the internet helped many fan groups collectively share thoughts and ideas on a variety of topics, some of which concerned how their club was being governed by its owner(s). Indeed, in his book on the history of the Supporters' Trust at Swansea City, *From Graveyard to Ambition: The Official History of the Swansea City Supporters' Trust*, Phil Sumbler (2013) refers directly to this after he purchased a computer in 1997 and was directed to the Swanmail emailing list to read and share views with fellow fans from all over the world. Of particular note to his importance to this chapter was when he was handed the administrative responsibility of the message board jackarmy.net in the summer of 2001 (this was a 'fanzine'-like online message board and not officially connected to the football club) before he joined the board of the Swansea City Supporters' Trust in 2004, and a year later he was appointed chairman, a position he holds at the time of writing. In this sense, Phil Sumbler was the guarantor (Coleman 1973) of 'trust' in the movement, drawing upon the advice he believed to give 'best practice' offered by Supporters' Direct as the 'advisors' (Coleman 1973). McAdam (1986) illustrated that activism might occur at the appropriate stage in the life course for believers, and as a fan for over 35 years Sumbler felt that this was an opportunity to become more actively involved in the fan-club relationship.

One of the most pressing discussions that initially took place on jackarmy.net was a concern raised by supporters that the club was in financial trouble and there was an urgent need to preserve a professional football club in Swansea. Jasper (1998) outlines how social movements usually begin with a moral shock, and as more fans sought to join the Swanmail emailing list, Sumbler (2013) states how supporters at Northampton Town were often referred to as an important example, with its Supporters' Trust chair and Supporters Direct informant Brian Lomax as an 'advisor' in to how to rescue a club in financial difficulty (Coleman 1990). With the club in financial difficulty, a Northampton Town Supporters' Trust was formed in 1992 that resulted in the Trust raising enough money and subsequently accruing enough shares to have supporter representation on the board of directors. A new ground was built and it became a condition of the lease that this representation had to remain in place (Cleland 2015a). Although he states how club ownership was not initially high on the agenda for supporters discussing the club on jackarmy.net, Sumbler (2013) refers to an introduction within this online space with what would eventually be other important individuals in a shared network where discussion quickly turned to the management and ownership of the club. Castells (2015 [2012]) states the importance of the internet in changing a collective's emotional state as people use these sites to talk about issues and metaphorically hold hands together with no geographical barrier that can lead from outrage to hope for the future. As suggested by Crossley (2011: 30), 'actors are shaped by the interactions in which they are involved. Trajectories of interaction can transform the way in which they act, feel and think'.

Sumbler (2013) refers to a Supporters' Trust working group being set up at Swansea City in 2000, but due to success on the field at the time (the club was promoted in 1999/2000 to the old Division Two), apathy was in play with a significant number of passive supporters. However, he indicates how the foundations had been laid and only a year later the Swansea City Supporters' Trust was formed after a series of public meetings in July and August 2001 that culminated in an official launch on 27 August 2001. The creation of a Supporters' Trust was matched by other Supporters' Trusts being formed across the UK from the beginning of the twenty-first century as fans sought a greater voice in the decisions being made by individual clubs. In some cases, such as at Coventry City (Chap. 4), a Supporters' Trust was initially set up but faded away until the club moved to Northampton Town, but at Swansea City it was set up for the very survival of the club.

The reason behind this was that during 2001 the club was owned by Ninth Floor who subsequently sold the club to former commercial manager, Mike Lewis, who then sold the club to Tony Petty. Indeed, these fears were realized quicker than they thought when in October 2001 Mike Lewis sold the club to Tony Petty for £1, but this included the retention of the £801,098 debt owed to Ninth Floor. As the share fund among supporters grew, a meeting was arranged at Swansea Rugby Club that included Swansea City Supporters' Trust representatives Richard Lillicrap and Nigel Hamer where it was decided to offer Tony Petty £10,000 for fan ownership of the club. This offer was quickly rejected, as was an improved offer of £50,000 a few days later (Sumbler 2013). This represented the ill feeling towards Petty by the supporters, and when news that Ninth Floor was willing to sell the £801,098 debt for £100,000, the supporters sought ways in which this money could be generated to purchase the debt.

As outlined in Chap. 2, one aspect of relational collective action is the tactic of outlining a 'villainous' enemy (Alinsky 1971) through a mobilizing narrative who can be directly blamed for any perceived injustice (in this case Tony Petty). As Pearson (2012) suggests, while online space can create bonds between people, it is in the urban space that gives the group more credibility as it becomes more visible and authentic. Highlighting this, there were some collective gatherings and effervescence in online and offline space that encouraged some key people to take a stand and act upon the anger they felt towards the ownership of the club (as suggested by Castells 2015 [2012]). For example, a series of tactical protests were arranged including a march attended by around 2000 fans from Castle Square to the Vetch Field ahead of a game as well as a crisis meeting which television crews attended. Borrowing from Jasper (1997), emotional allegiances in football fandom that lead people to protest often involve an attachment to a place and when this is under a sense of threat that collective mobilization can take place.

Although generally subjective, emotions are inherently relational and emerge from social interaction (Burkitt 2014). As suggested by Durkheim, an individual can feel powerful if they are connected to others through collaboration and support as this can bring about intense individual emotions. The impact of this is collective effervescence (an emotional energy that bonds participants) that is generated by social relations and football fandom is a clear example of this in operation. According to Blumer (1951), group action is inherently relational as actors within it work together to achieve common goals to achieve a collective outcome. Of particular prominence at Swansea City was the role of fans who were accountants, financial advisers, solicitors, and businessmen who collectively engaged in a process to seek ways in which to save the club. According to Crossley (2011: 22), 'networks form and are formed around "social worlds" which centre upon specific shared or overlapping interests which bring actors together in collective action'. This also included those in the media, such as the journalist Chris Wathan who began at the *Western Mail* in 2002 and has covered the club ever since:

> Swansea City were used to struggles, used to failures. When they were faced with a threat that's when people were forced into taking responsibility they

might not have had before because it was a club at a local level it didn't feel removed it felt like there could be an influence. (Personal communication, February 2017)

SUCCESS, TACTICS, AND REWARDS

Sumbler (2013: 82) refers to the online and offline collective mobilizations as being crucial in gaining support from the wider fan base to the four main aims behind the creation of the Supporters' Trust at the club:

1. To maintain a professional Football League club in Swansea
2. To have an elected supporters' representative on the board of Swansea City Football Club
3. To raise sufficient funds to buy a stake in the club, in pursuance of the aims above
4. To bring the football club closer to its local community

With developments showing no signs of slowing down, a meeting was arranged with Tony Petty on 24 January 2002 where an offer of £20,000 was accepted. A further meeting took place on 6 February 2002 to discuss the Consortium Agreement, a signed agreement that led to the formation of Swansea City Football Club 2001 Limited (Sumbler 2013). Of particular relevance to relational sociology was the reluctance by any one individual to purchase the club on his/her own. For example, alongside the Supporters' Trust investing in the club were Martin Morgan, Huw Jenkins, Brian Katzen, John van Zweden, David Morgan, Mel Nurse, Robert Davies, and the Dineen family. The Trust was granted extra time to find the initial £50,000 investment but crucially there was an agreement that they could be represented by a Supporter Director (initially this was Leigh Dineen who was also the chair of the Swansea City Supporters' Trust as voted in by fellow members) on the newly formed board of directors.

As highlighted in Chap. 2, at the core of debates on social movements and collective action are the relationships between individuals. As a new social movement based on a fluid and networked structure, the emergence of the Supporters' Trust at Swansea City follows Castells' (2015 [2012]) description of new social movements as 'rhizomatic', for example, grassroots in their emergence, growth, and organization, and they tend not to have explicit leaders. Instead they have soft leaders who are elected into roles for a period of time and who hold positions of social, cultural, and/

or political influence. This includes dealing with the media and being able to communicate the aims and tactics of the collective action to its broader membership (Hill et al. 2016).

With regards to the importance of tactics in collective action, Blumer's (1951) three main tactical aims were prominent in the origin of the Supporters' Trust at Swansea City: (1) increase the number of members, (2) maintain the number of members, and (3) achieve its aims and goals. Highlighting the active nature of supporters in a perceived time where change is needed, Sumbler (2013) illustrates that in the first year the Supporters' Trust had 1400 members against an average attendance of 3000, but this dropped by 30 per cent in the second year as a more fan-friendly structure of ownership was in place. On this point, Crossley (2015a) outlines how mobilizations go through the process of recruitment and retention in the search for a desired outcome and when followers believe that the movement has achieved its aim then attrition is more likely. Thus, resource mobilization theory (Crossley 2015a) can be applied to the case study of the Supporters' Trust at Swansea City as members work together to bring money and supporters to the movement as well as attracting the media and striking an alliance with those in power (McCarthy and Zald 2001). One element of trying to maintain resources is that the Trust has a share fund which allows members to contribute towards when there is an opportunity to buy further shares in the club.

Even under partial Supporters' Trust ownership, the finances of the club remained fragile with Sumbler (2013) reporting on how shareholders were asked to make short-term loans that were converted into shares, and by doing this, the Swansea City Supporters' Trust shareholding was worth £100,000 after the move to the Liberty Stadium. Although this was not always popular with its members, to boost their shareholding the Trust took advantage of loan schemes that enhanced their shareholding. For example, Sumbler (2013) reports on how the Trust has invested £199,999 in the club and this represented a shareholding of 19.99 per cent, until a purchasing back of shares from Mel Nurse reduced the overall share capital and took their investment to a 21 per cent shareholding. Up until April 2016, the Supporters' Trust was the joint second biggest shareholder in the club with Brian Katzen and just behind Martin Morgan who owned 23.6 per cent. As suggested by Sumbler (2013: 121):

> One of the challenges that any supporters' trust has is to ensure that it remains at the forefront of thoughts of the supporters of the club in which

it has an interest. … When everything seems to be going well, as it has at the club for all of ten years, then it is a real battle for us as a Trust to get people to understand why they would want to be members and, even more importantly now, why we would need a strong Trust, when the club turns over somewhere in the region of £100 million per year. (Personal communication, February 2017)

Over the years the Trust has tried different tactics to boost the number of members. For example, in 2011/12 they offered free membership to season ticket holders with the aim of encouraging regular donations, and this resulted in 13,000 members. For the 2013/14 season, the Trust kept the idea of free membership to season ticket holders but gave voting rights to paid members. Reflecting on the current level of membership and how this relates to the wider fan base, Phil Sumbler stated:

Membership is currently around 1800. It continues to be a frustration for us because we have 14,000 to 15,000 season ticket holders, but I always think that's a slight misnomer when we look at numbers like that because I look at how many season ticket holders would we have if we were in League One because that is probably our hard core support. There's new fans that have only ever known the good times. The people who see the benefit of the Trust are those that have also seen the bad times like when we were rock bottom of the Football League and we have to pass a bucket round to pay players' wages. (Personal communication, February 2017)

From the outset of their involvement as coowners of the club, the Trust has used monthly newsletters to communicate with members, with Phil Sumbler outlining that the emergence of new media, particularly Facebook and Twitter, is crucial to spreading news about the Trust and to cater for the wider membership and other interested parties (of which there are many given the success behind the Trust at Swansea City):

We send an e-newsletter once a month to all of our members that we have emails for, so in excess of 800 emails. We have our website where we put the monthly Trust minutes on that are advertized across social media and fans' forums. We get the message out there as much as we can, but we are a group on volunteers, most of whom have other work and family commitments. In a perfect world we would probably update people more than we do. (Personal communication, February 2017)

Given that the Swansea City Supporters' Trust is a voluntary organization and was created when the club were in difficulty in the lower reaches of the Football League, it ties in with Hirsch (1990) that material 'rewards' are not as important as the commitment to the cause and belief behind the creation of this group. As a voluntary organization a lot of time is given by Trust members, most notably through the two-hour monthly meeting at the Liberty Stadium and the various ongoing sub-groups looking at Trust work that results in mid-month sub-group meetings in order to report back to the Swansea City Trust board.

NEW CHALLENGES IN TRUSTING THE SUPPORTERS' TRUST

Given the fluid nature of Premier League club ownership, particularly given the increasing number of overseas investors, Sumbler (2013: 144) was right to suggest how the Trust has 'to be prepared for many possibilities and our place in the Premier League makes one of those possibilities more likely'. Although Sumbler felt that having seven different shareholders would provide a safeguard with regards to potential investors, this was proven to be fallible when a number of them engaged in secret negotiations without notifying the Supporters' Trust about their intention to sell to an American consortium in April 2016 led by Steve Kaplan and Jason Levien. Speaking about how the takeover was handled by the other shareholders, Phil Sumbler stated:

> The Trust was brought in at a very late stage and we were told that there is a consortium looking to buy the club and this is what the deal is going to look like. Effectively you have been completely excluded from it. The bit that never sat well with the Trust board and will never sit well with the Trust members was that a large proportion of these discussions took place behind our backs and we find out about them when we are probably 75 per cent down the path of actually making the deal happen. It is the situation that if we were aware from day one we could have probably done a lot of work to try and seek the protection we wanted might have been able to have been built in or maybe we would have considered a partial sale ourselves. (Personal communication, February 2017)

The story about the imminent takeover was broken by Chris Wathan at the *Western Mail* and when asked about his emotions having to report this news to supporters, he responded:

I broke the story and I had a very negative response from certain sections of the fans that led to accusations that I was for the takeover. ... I am sure the Trust would have liked me to have done things differently. You just report what you see to be fair. You try and take some of the emotion out of it. There has been an acceptance on all sides that it wasn't handled the way it should have been ... the relationship with the Trust has been tested at times, they have told me their grievances and I have defended my corner, not the actions of others because that is not for to defend ... you make judgement calls and that's that. (Personal communication, February 2017)

Reflecting on the takeover and the role of the local media, Phil Sumbler stated:

As a Trust during the takeover we felt like the local media let us down because they didn't ask any questions in terms of what does this investment look like, what does it mean for the club, how much is going in, what is the transfer budget going to be. They just reported it as a great thing and £100 million pound worth of investment and there's never been a £100 million pound worth of investment. There has been a share sale in the region of £70 million and nothing else has gone into the club in terms of cold hard cash. It is as if they report what the club wants them to report rather than what they should be doing. (Personal communication, February 2017)

Huw Cooze was then the Supporters' Trust member on the football club's board of directors. He was, using Coleman's (1990) earlier outlined ideas, the entrepreneur in the movement as he symbolically (not materially) took the financial resources of the club to give him a guaranteed seat on the board. However, when news of the takeover broke, he began to lose the trust of those supporters who were uncomfortable at potential changes in the way Swansea City would be run, as Huw Cooze suggests:

It was a difficult period. We knew that change was afoot but we didn't know the detail. Before the current takeover about 18–24 months ago some other Americans came over and we met them, we did our due diligence and we felt that they weren't quite right for us, not for the club but for us personally at the Trust. So we decided not to sell at that point. This was the back end of 2014, but when this load of Americans came over we didn't know nothing about them. It was the beginning of March 2016 when we were told we are selling the club and we were not given our chance to do due diligence but we've subsequently done it. They're just hedge fund people who know how to get the money in. Time will tell. This is a personal opinion, but some of our fans think they are only here to asset strip, take money out, but I don't believe that. What I think is that they will be here for a few years and bigger players will then emerge but for that to happen the club has to be in the Premier League and be financially secure. (Personal communication, February 2017)

Not all of the other shareholders sold their shares completely (Huw Jenkins and Martin Morgan kept 5 per cent each), but with regards to how this would impact on future voting rights, Phil Sumbler commented:

Despite the fact that the Americans own around two-thirds of the club, the key point is that those who sold their shares also sold their voting rights so they own less than 75 per cent of the club but they control 75 per cent of the voting rights. (Personal communication, February 2017)

Thus, for the first time in its history the Trust had to be reactive rather than proactive and is now left with no substantial influence on votes and no security for their continued involvement. Hence, when asked about the Swansea City Supporters' Trust's relationship with the new owners, Phil Sumbler commented:

At the moment there's technically no difference. We looked at protection with the takeover but we are in no different position. We own 21 per cent of the club, other people own 79 per cent. The difference being that the other 79 per cent was owned by a mixture of half a dozen people, now most of that is owned by one particular group. Do we have less protection now than we did a year ago? We don't although it's probably a lot more at risk than it was 12 months ago. One of our challenges is to absolutely show our value and we have been heavily criticized as a Trust over the last 6 months for the fact that board members sold their shares and did not tell us about it. The argument being that we should have seen it, we should have known it was happening. Since it happened in April 2016 we spent the first few months trying gain protection for our shareholding or alternatively try and sell some of our shareholding but that never materialized. … I think both parties know we have an individual question mark that sits over our shareholding. (Personal communication, February 2017)

Given the influence of the Supporters' Trust at Swansea City, it is a different scenario to what Cleland and Dixon (2015) found with the tactics of Newcastle United fans who were unhappy at the ownership of Mike Ashley where the club's presence in the Premier League created a sense of passive apathy among the vast majority of fans and the active voice was subsequently lost. At Swansea City, however, the tactics they can adopt are different, and although they still have a number of passive fans, the support the Trust receives in club-specific message boards is extensive and they also can use the wider media to convey their message to the wider public given the important role that they play at the club. Addressing these two different circumstances, Smithey (2009) illustrates that the tactics a movement can adopt of often a product of the resources and opportunities within the environment. Responding to the tactics the Trust adopted during the early part of the American takeover, Phil Sumbler stated:

> We again used the local and national media. When the takeover was first reported in the press we came straight out and said we did not know anything about it, but we now need to sit down and discuss the plans with the new owners. Generally if there's a disagreement in the boardroom we try and let it stay in the boardroom. But if there's something obviously wrong and all of our members are saying something's not right then we have to come out and say we agree and the media gives us the mouthpiece to do this. (Personal communication, February 2017)

Although there have not been any urban protests against the current owners, one tactic was to use the high-profile journalist David Conn of *The Guardian* to complain in October 2016 that the new owners failed to 'circulate in advance proposed changes to the club's articles of association'. Conn also refers to the adoption of new articles of association in August 2016 that effectively creates a new constitution, 'including that all shareholders have to sell if Levien and Kaplan do', that the Trust strongly object to and has refused to sign; instead they continue to operate under the terms of the original 2002 shareholders' agreement. Indeed, this level of resistance was also raised by Phil Sumbler:

> When the American owners came in they said that one of the attractions to them was the supporter ownership that was in the middle of it. I think the bit that they are learning over time is just what that supporter involvement really looks like. It is not a token gesture from a group of supporters that arranges busy travel and raffles, it is an organization that plays a big role at the football club and the success we have had over the last 10 to 15 years.

> This is not solely down to us but we played a big part in it. We are not
> watching partners. (Personal communication, February 2017)

Of critical importance to collective movements is the process of communication as this helps to mobilize the group to the wider public (Rosie
and Gorringe 2009). On this point, Castells (2013 [2009]) refers to mass
self-communication, including YouTube and Twitter, but within football
fandom, this also includes fan message boards as they connect people with
similar interests and avoids the geographical ties that some traditional
media have historically suffered from (although this is increasingly being
alleviated due to traditional media also engaging in online space to disseminate articles and stories and their journalists also engaging on social
media to debate with supporters). Using the media is an important element in grassroots resistance as it allows individuals and organizations like
the Supporters' Trust to generate their own message. However, their
engagement with the media, particularly the local and traditional print
media (in the case of Swansea City this being the *Western Mail* and the
South Wales Evening Post), allows the message to be disseminated to the
wider public. As suggested by Castells (2013 [2009]), information-age
mobilizations are open to fluid communications and this allows new forms
of network coalitions to potentially emerge and mobilize.

'Switchers' are important to social networks. Castells (2013: 45) refers
to 'switchers' as those that 'connect and ensure the cooperation of different networks by sharing common goals and combining resources'. Unlike
the situation with the local journalist Simon Gilbert at Coventry City
however, Chris Wathan did not see his role as a switcher who could link
groups in protest to form new coalitions:

> Ultimately that is not my role. My job is to report the news and report the
> facts as we understand them. If that improves the relationship then fantastic
> and it is your job to see both sides and understand both sides. You don't
> necessarily have to agree with it but you do have to understand. That's the
> important job. You are the conduit of messages but you can't dictate what
> messages go out based on the worry about whether it upsets the club or
> fans. (Personal communication, February 2017)

Addressing Bourdieu's (1986) notion of how social capital can be
acquired through membership of a group, Cleland and Cashmore (2016)
explained that within the culture of football fandom, social and cultural

capital can be an effective way that allows individuals to secure particular profits through their participation. One individual who this could be applied to was Huw Cooze who filled the role of Supporter Director for ten years and therefore must have had enough power and consciously built enough social and cultural capital among the Supporters' Trust board and members for him to continue to do it for that length of time. Castells (2013 [2009]: 10) defines power as a 'relational capacity that enables a social actor to influence asymmetrically the decisions of other social actor(s) in ways that favor the empowered actor's will, interest and values'. Despite his role as acting as a bridge between supporters and the club however, Huw Cooze felt that his role was misunderstood by some of the fans he was trying to represent in and out of board meetings. The supporters' trust in him had been damaged:

> I do not think all of the fans really grasped it totally if I am honest. Some of them thought and probably still think that once you become part of the board of directors you are one of them. Some of the fans always thought it was a case of them and us. It was never that but you can't change people's perceptions. For these fans they just felt that you weren't looking out for them. (Personal communication, February 2017)

While Ibrahim (2015) outlines the presence of symbolic capital in social and cultural forms where actors do not seek monetary reward (such as the voluntary aspect of the Supporters' Trust board), it was revealed by the Supporters' Trust in October 2016 that Huw Cooze was, in fact, being paid for the role of Supporter Liaison Officer. A Supporter Liaison Officer role is a requirement of the Premier League to ensure better communication between the club and its fans (see Garcia and Welford 2015; Kossakowski 2017). 'Trust' in his role was further damaged. Responding to this revelation, Huw Cooze commented:

> I took a lot of stick off the fans when this was revealed. When we reached the Premier League in 2011, they were insistent that all clubs had to have a Supporter Liaison Officer. We didn't have one and we didn't know much about it and our chairman asked me to take it on. It was an extension of what I was doing but it meant a lot more hours. So I took that to the Trust board and we have two options, we let someone at the club take it on or we take it on and if we take it on at least we control it. I told them there was a salary involved and I got backed by the Trust board so we could keep

control of it. That was the only reason. And it went out to the fan base. We were probably naïve because we never told the fan base so it came out last year that we were looking at our governance and we felt it was right that we come clean on this. We didn't hide it, it was just a salary and at the time we did not think it was right to tell the fan base. Obviously with hindsight we should have so of course it kicked off. It went pear shaped for me because we have always been known as a volunteer organization and I can get what the fans are saying—as a volunteer you should not get paid. Once the fans found out I had to resign from the Supporters' Trust. (Personal communication, February 2017)

Reflecting on the chain of communication and changes that the resignation of Huw Cooze as Supporter Director has had on the Trust's relationship with the club, Phil Sumbler stated:

We thought this was a great opportunity to change the way that we work with the club so we now have a three-pronged attack to the day-to-day operations so we have got Stuart McDonald as supporter director, myself as chairman and Will Morris as vice-chairman and this is the three-pronged attack we have with the owners so it can be all three of us involved … it is also important to us to be in the board room on match days because we were marginalized in the sale and we don't want to be marginalized in the operations. (Personal communication, February 2017)

Addressing concerns about not being marginalized in the operations of the club, the Swansea City Supporters' Trust has retained a supporter director on the board of directors who is there to represent the fans' views and as well as an associate director on the board of directors. As raised earlier by McCarthy and Zald (2001), there are a range of ways that the Trust can go about to mobilize resources for its collective benefit and one of these is to strike an alliance with those in power. When asked how he saw the Trust's tactics moving forwards given the challenges it now faces, Phil Sumbler stated:

We have accepted that the American owners are here to make money and the way they are here to make money is to keep the club in the Premier League. The club would only ever be worth fraction of what it is worth in the Premier League. The way we look at it as a Trust is that we currently retain a shareholding of 21 per cent in a club they valued to be around £110 million. We could for arguments sake in five years own 15 per cent because the club is now worth £200 million, so therefore our shareholding would be worth more. There is a danger that we could be diluted in the future. We have agreed with the Americans that we will go back and talk with them in the summer about what our shareholding looks like because there might be a piece where they want to buy one-third of our shareholding and put £10 million in our bank at which point we might think that's not a bad deal and we will protect that. There is an argument should we sell it all and bank £25 million. But what does £25 million get you nowadays? Given the amount of money flowing into the Premier League, the Americans could double their investment in five years and we would be part of that. (Personal communication, February 2017)

In their analysis of collective mobilizations, Kriesi et al. (1995) identified internal and external outcomes. Internal includes those that affect the group such as the formation and maintenance of individual and collective identities of group members. With regards to external, these include engaging in consultation procedures and undertaking negotiations to seek inclusion with the potential to open up new advantages in seeking to gain some identified 'success' (such as what is about to happen with the current owners). Sumbler states how they do not have a target figure for their shareholding, but believes it should be over 10 per cent so that in the event of any takeover they cannot be forced to sell and can always have a director on the board as this is what they had worked so hard for over the last 15 years.

Conclusions: 'Success' and 'Trusting' in Supporters' Trust

As outlined in Chap. 2, space and place are of social and cultural importance in football fandom at clubs throughout the world. In the case of the emergence of a Supporters' Trust at Swansea City, it was the fear of losing a professional club due to financial difficulty that was a driving force in seeking supporter ownership of the club. Collins (2004) interaction ritual theory can be applied to the emergence of collective action at Swansea City as emotions were initially transformed in the process of everyday interaction in an online space where social relations were built before moving into urban space. Beginning with emotions such as fear and anger, this intensified into collective effervescence that produced a moral solidarity that sought to enforce change and preserve the status of the club as a cornerstone of the local community. The example of Swansea City also had resonance to Castells' (2013 [2009]: xxxix) description as to how 'movements usually begin on the internet social networks, but they are not identified as movements until they occupy urban space'.

This chapter has illustrated is the success behind a collective mobilization of supporters that can challenge the views of Kriesi et al. (1995: 207) who state: 'the most fundamental obstacle to research on social movement outcomes—the problem of causality, that is, the difficultly of assessing the extent to which the movement has contributed to producing a certain effect'. The aim for any movement is to advance its set goals, and building on Gamson's (1990 [1975]) work on success, the Trust were part of a change in organizational characteristics that influenced the 'success' the club has managed to achieve since 2002. While there remain a significant number of passive supporters at the club (in terms of membership numbers for the Supporters' Trust), given that the Trust has been a part-owner of the club for over 15 years indicates the important role it has played in using networks and collective mobilizations to guarantee a professional club in Swansea as well as contribute towards the club gaining promotions through the leagues to compete in the Premier League and in a European cup competition (in the 2013/14 season the club competed in the Europa League).

Furthermore, although Giugni (1998) stated that success for collective actions is often difficult to define, it was clear as to what the Supporters' Trust at Swansea City was established for. Without its involvement there was a real danger that the club would have potentially faced irreversible financial catastrophe. For 14 years, there was a relatively tranquil period with on-the-pitch success, but since April 2016 the Swansea City Supporters' Trust has faced a different kind of challenge with the takeover and questions being asked of the Supporters' Trust by members as to its knowledge of this and its future role as a significant shareholder. In the eyes of many fans, Huw Cooze lost their trust as their representative on the board of directors and was replaced. For many others, this was not enough to prevent a reduction in their trust in Phil Sumbler. These two individuals represented the entrepreneur and guarantor of their collective trust. With the current owners being majority shareholders and having the majority of voting rights, the Trust is employing different tactics to retain a collective presence in an overall ownership structure. One aspect of this, at the time of writing, is to meet with the owners to engage in discussions about the possibility of reducing its shareholding but maximizing its value if the club retains Premier League status. Given the unique circumstances in currently owning 21 per cent, any reduction could reflect the reality of collective mobilization at a Premier League club in a global world where investors have greater financial resources than the vast majority of supporters at their disposal.

CHAPTER 6

Ticket Prices Campaigns, Urban Space, and Twitter: Social Networks and Storied Connections

INTRODUCTION

In a typical transaction system a market comprises a set of buyers and sellers who interact within their relationships to exchange money for a good or a service. In football, clubs sell their goods or services (such as tickets to matches) to supporters, and the actions of both sets of agents jointly determine this ticketing price structure (Knoke 2012). In the neo-classical economic tradition of perfect competition, it is assumed that there is a complete absence of market power: the proportion of football fans involved in action is too small next to the wider body of seemingly apathetic supporters to affect price, even if they may benefit from match attendance ticket price cuts (see also Olson 1968). In its place, the intersection of buyers and sellers aggregate supply and demand curves determines both the quantities and prices that 'clear the market' (Knoke 2012).

Crossley (2011: 29) noted how social world, or fields, has temporal dimensions where what had previously happened in an interaction shapes what may happen later. However, the traditional neo-classical economic model overlooks this, assuming that information about previous transactional histories is unrelated to current price-setting exchange; therefore, markets are atomized institutions in which social, political, religious, cultural, and other connections are irrelevant. Free markets form the ideological bedrock of modern capitalist economies (Davies 2016). Taking the football market as an example, if clubs (producers) and consumers

© The Author(s) 2018
J. Cleland et al., *Collective Action and Football Fandom*,
Palgrave Studies in Relational Sociology,
https://doi.org/10.1007/978-3-319-73141-4_6

(supporters) can freely pursue their self-interests, without government intervention or constraint, they will collectively choose the most efficient allocation of ticket prices and in the wider sense maximize the utilities of networks and aggregations of social actors. As Smith (1937) notes, the self-regulatory dynamics of an unfettered market creates the best of all possible economic worlds (Knoke 2012). The relational sociology approaches outlined in Chaps. 1 and 2 rejects this assumption. Football clubs (consciously or unconsciously) and supporters are deeply embedded in social relations, as well as other institutions such as the media and politics. Actions are not isolated from each other, or for that matter from other institutional systems that deeply influence behaviour, but are continually shaped, constrained, and distorted by network structures.

This connectedness impacts on the economic and political issues of actors who are part of the multitudes of supporter collective actions, who mobilize around diverse issues such as the perceived injustice related to multifarious forms of social inequality, anti-government campaigns, and consumer exploitation. It is the connectedness of the protest movements that mobilize individuals and can facilitate change, be it falling of governments (Goodwin and Jasper 2014) to a reduction in consumer prices (Hendrix et al. 2009), and social media is a prominent tactic. Indeed, as discussed in Chap. 2, social media has played an increasingly important role in contemporary mobilizations across the world, from protests in Iran, Iceland, to the Egyptian revolution; online connectedness combined with offline networks (Castells 2013 [2009], 2015 [2012]) has been a key feature, and they impact upon economic and non-economic behaviour. As Chap. 2 outlines, Castells suggested that networked social movements that draw upon offline space might be 'leaderless', with actors involved able to connect and reconnect instantaneously rather than being held in bureaucratic and hierarchical structures. He argues that they are characterized by the hybrid of urban and online space. While this asserts the connectedness of collective action in the digital age, it is less successful in evidencing it to be the case. Using the tools of SNA with social media data, we explore protest campaigns against the level of ticket prices.

As such this chapter has two distinct parts, reflecting various dimensions of cultural relational sociology. First, as noted in Chap. 1, interactions have *phenomenological* and symbolic dimensions as actors reflexively read and respond to their own actions and those of others. In making this point, the affective dimension is important in making the movement 'move' (Crossley 2005). However, second, we recognize that network structures underpin and shape human behaviour, thus drawing upon the *structured* dimensions of cultural relational sociology. In this chapter we capture both these positions by exploring how football fans are embedded in networks of social relations that impact perceived value and ticket prices and as a movement constrain the normal market conditions which see rising prices when demand outstrips supply. Additionally, we provide a critical exploration of the social worlds of movements that operate in online and offline spaces, focusing on its structure and how information flows, relating it back to touchstones for cultural relational sociological analysis of collective action presented in Chap. 2. In doing so we focus on two inter-related fan movement protests, the FSF's 'Twenty's Plenty' and Liverpool fans' 'Walk Out on 77', the former a national protest movement against the cost of ticket prices in English Football, the latter a more localized protest relating to a specific club. While FSF was introduced in Chap. 1, it is worth reintroducing it as 'a democratic, non-partisan, non-profit making and non-party political organization' (FSF 2014) that represents over 500,000 members and has strong affiliations with various other fan organizations across England, such as those related to individual clubs and Supporters Direct, with whom it shares its annual 'Supporters' Summit' meeting (Burnham 2000; Hamil et al. 2001; Kennedy 2012; Kennedy and Kennedy 2012). We have attended each of these joint meetings since they were launched in 2013 and found that, although they change physical place, they serve as the movement 'foci' (see Crossley 2008a, 2009, 2015b) where groups of fans engaged in collective action at football clubs meet with their equivalents at others, while politicians such former Labour front bench minister Andy Burnham (who was also chair of Supporters Direct) to discuss the cultural politics of football in the UK. Thus as an officially recognized supporter body, several of FSFs key personnel have pre-existing working connections and are engaged in the 'submerged reality of movement networks' (Melucci 1989: 338) with senior members working with the Football Association, the Premier League, and the Football League, as well as some politicians and high-profile journalists, even if these connections are seemingly informal such as personal friendships. In this chapter, we principally explore the networks associated to these protests and campaigns on the social media platform Twitter, looking at how the people come together to build a network structure and what flows within. We begin by outlining the phenomenological story and backgrounds of these bouts of collective action before later moving on to explore the network structures of communication around two protests.

'Twenty's Plenty but Thirty's Dirty': Ticket Prices, Supporter Campaigns, and 'Success' Stories

The section heading relates to a campaign line which the FSF spread to combat the cost of away ticket prices in the Premier League. Each number was related to the number of pounds a ticket might cost, and the full phrase was: 'Fifty's shifty, forty's naughty, thirty's dirty—twenty's plenty. A fair deal for away fans please'. The levels of match admission prices were not new concerns to many football supporters: for instance, in 1971 Ian Taylor argued that football's commercialization—of which rising match admission prices was part—was alienating lots of supporters. Similarly, while King (1997b, 2002 [1998]) points out that many of the 'lads' he researched—a masculine group of Manchester United fans in the 1990s—found it difficult to keep up with increasing match-day ticket costs. At the launch of the new Premier League some fans shared concerns of being dislocated from the club they support and being priced out of attending matches (Millward 2011; Taylor 1992). These concerns became manifest in the idea that the rising financial costs meant newer, more affluent but less vociferous supporters who would weaken the vibrant atmosphere at matches. A typical form of this discourse is found in Manchester United fans' Red Issue around the time in the new elite league was launched:

> In years to come the joy of watching a simple game of football is going to take investment of huge proportions. How are supporters of tomorrow going to be indoctrinated in to going to Old Trafford if the cost of the game for a family of four is in excess of fifty pounds. (Veg. (1992) 'New Year Portion', *Red Issue* 4(6): 3)

In the material sense, the cost of match attendance grew relative to the broader inflation of other consumer products in the UK and elsewhere. From 2011, *BBC* published results from its (now annual) 'Cost of Football' survey. The initial results showed that, despite levels of seat occupancy levels of over 90 per cent in the Premier League, tickets at some clubs were very expensive: '[London based football club] Arsenal hav[ing] the most expensive ticket in domestic football at £100 for one of five Category A games [the highest profile matches] for the new season' (*BBC* 2011). Relationships are sometimes based upon contrasting differences as well as similarities entail, and such a contrast was regularly given to Germany's Bundesliga clubs where the ownership structures gave the collective fans' groups a controlling share of the legal ownership of the football club (see Kennedy and Kennedy 2012) and, crucially, in the vibrant standing sections of the crowd—outlawed in the UK in the aftermath of the Taylor Report (1990, see Bale 2000)—match admission ticket prices were considerably cheaper than in the UK. For example, FSF chair, Malcolm Clarke, reflected upon the *BBC*'s 2012 'Price of Football' results by stating:

There's a danger of alienation between fans and players at the top of the game. Younger fans in particular are being priced out and if they don't get the live football bug at a young age they might not become season ticket holders. If you compare prices to other countries like Germany there are huge disparities. Season tickets at Borussia Dortmund start from €225 [then approximately £183] which includes three Champions League games—that works out at about £8.90 per match and includes free public transport. In comparison the prices at many of our clubs are simply unacceptable. (Quoted in *FSF* 2012)

Spirit of Shankly (hereafter 'SoS'), a supporters' union of Liverpool football club fans, had made the quest to keep football match attendance 'affordable' for working-class fans one of their key aims since their formation in 2008 (see Millward 2012, 2016b; Monaghan 2014; Rookwood and Millward 2011; Williams 2012). Although the group had roots in other cultural movements that predated SoS, such as the 'Keep Flags Scouse' campaign (see Millward 2011), the 'moral shock' (Jasper 1997, 1998) which sparked the group into action and was the catalyst for recruitment and connection for some members was the 'leveraged debt' that was being placed on to the football club by its unpopular then-financial owners Tom Hicks and George Gillett. After SoS played an active role in Hicks and Gillett being forced to sell the club in 2010, relationships between members were sustained and grew but had turned their collectively generated aims towards lowering the cost of match attendance. Crossley (2011) points out that interactions and networks can be the product of pre-existing relationships and this is important to understanding how this action unfolded. In January 2013, Liverpool supporters were charged £62 to watch a match against Arsenal. This was before travel, food, drink, and other costs were worked out. This provided a further 'moral shock' for a televised Wednesday evening fixture. SoS' network of fans contained members who were savvy with media production knowledge and produced banners that adorned stadiums on match days in front of a television audience that stretched 212 countries across the world. The dissatisfaction gained a visual dimension that was beamed around the world. SoS began producing flyers and, as a tactic to raise awareness of rising ticket costs, distributed these to fans of Liverpool and other clubs to spread their message. One such flyer, passed to one of the authors when Liverpool visited Wigan Athletic in March 2013, is photographed in Fig. 6.1 (below):

The graphic flyer works out that, between 1989 and 2013, the average football ticket price had risen by 716 per cent. It then takes the typical price of a range of other goods in 1989 and multiplies this by the margin of ticket price increase to show how the cost of attending football matches had grown disproportionate to other consumer goods. The graphic gained traction among fans of other clubs and was discussed on social media channels and online forums as well as, no doubt, in physical spaces such as homes, public houses, and football grounds around the country. In doing so, although we do not know if it was a deliberate move or not, SoS were forging affective connections to supporters of other groups around the common concern of ticket prices, and these new relationships often cut across traditional fan rivalries.

Manchester City also visited Arsenal in January 2013 with their supporters also charged a match admission price of £62 for a match televised on Sky Sports in the UK and on many other channels around the world. This pricing policy and fans' response received significant media coverage, particularly in *The Guardian* newspaper where the 'political economy of football' journalist and Manchester City supporter David Conn worked. Many Manchester City supporters boycotted the match and 912 out of 3000 tickets were returned unsold to Arsenal. *The Guardian* interviewed Manchester City fan Richard Taylor in its coverage of the event. He said:

> Ticket costs are becoming a big problem for fans, especially at away games, and I thought that, by making a banner, we'd get the issue a bit of publicity. We took it into the ground and it seemed to create a bit of a stir; people were taking photographs of it. Then, within a couple of minutes, a steward walked over. He told me: 'I agree with what you're trying to say but I'm under strict orders from my boss to take it off you'. It used no offensive language and there had been no complaints about it, but the steward replied

Fig. 6.1 Personal photograph of SoS flyer illustrating the growth in the price of match attendance

that it was against ground regulations and if I didn't give it to him he'd have to get the police. [When he refused to surrender the banner] Suddenly two policemen were on one side of me and two on the other. They told me to hand it over or be escorted out of the ground and arrested [for a breach of the peace]. Part of me didn't want to give in but I didn't want to miss the game and, in the end, I decided it wasn't worth the hassle so I let the police take it away. A steward brought it back at the end but it's disgusting that we couldn't use it to challenge the ticket prices peacefully. It's disgraceful. In Germany it's very different, when we travelled to Dortmund [last month] to watch City in the Champions League our tickets were £24 and we had free travel from Düsseldorf. (Quoted in *The Guardian*, 14 January 2014)

To be sure, Richard Taylor was asked to hand his banner voicing displeasure to the security stewards or the police. When he initially refused the confiscation, he was threatened with ejection or arrest until he handed it over. Once again, the comparison with ticket prices in German football is given.

FSF launched its 'Twenty's Plenty' campaign later that month with the aim of capping the price of away tickets at £20. FSF premised that visiting supporters provided a vibrancy to the atmosphere, which is important to the mediatized product—and that the television revenues the Premier League generated were worth significantly more than what would be raised through away ticket sales. At the launch of the campaign, FSF deputy chair Martin O'Hara said:

Without away fans, the atmosphere at games dies and football loses a large part of what makes it so special. In the short term, clubs might make a few extra quid by squeezing away fans dry but long-term vision is required. Who wants to go to games without away fans, games without passion? We believe that an away ticket price cap of £20 would make football more affordable and halt the decline in away fan attendances. (Quoted on *BBC* 2013)

SoS launched its 'Football Without Fans Is Nothing' campaign at Liverpool's 'Static Gallery' on 9 May 2013 and followed it up one week later with a meeting held in The Horseshoe Inn public house, near London Bridge. The meetings were a clear attempt to reach out to other fan groups and organize a collaborative ticket price protest march outside the headquarters of the Football League and Premier League, at Gloucester Place in London on 19 June—the date when the fixtures for the following season would be released. Hill et al. (2016) cover the run-up and description of this event. However, at the launch meetings, SoS chair, Jay McKenna, whipped excitement up in the room by declaring:

Spirit of Shankly have started a campaign on ticket prices and we've wanted to a do a bit more on it because we believe it's too much. We believe not enough is being done to tackle how supporters are being priced out because it's been left to the clubs and to the sponsors and to the authorities to decide how this game is run. We are the mass movement of this game—we are the many and they are the few—and we've forgotten that and allowed them to break us down into they're Liverpool, and they're Everton and they're Manchester United. But we want to go over that, we want to push past it and say that 'if as one, if as football fans in general we want to work together we can achieve huge gains. And the first one of them is ticket prices […] We want as much contribution as possible from the floor—I could go on about this matter all night, as many of you can testify so … please do join in and contribute and share your thoughts and ideas on what should be done. Don't be afraid to say 'I think that'll do shit, basically' and tell us where we are going wrong or tell other clubs what you need them to do or what you're doing at your clubs or where the big issues lie. So tonight's attendees, just look at the list, we've got people who've signed in who are supporters from all the big clubs like Liverpool and AFC Wimbledon [as AFC Wimbledon fan Kevin Rye from Supporters Direct pointed at the sign in sheet], Manchester United and Everton also turned up and Tranmere [Rovers], Crewe [Alexander], Wigan [Athletic] and people from Melbourne and Toronto FC as well. (Field notes, 9 May 2013)

It was clear that as well as generating collective excitement and a belief that the level of ticket pricing could be challenged, Jay McKenna was holding out the opportunity to connect with other fan groups at clubs considered Liverpool's rivals. Effectively, rivalries were suspended in the name of the cause, and new networks of connections—and the sharing of skills/resources—were forged. Short statements of support were provided by Dave Kelly, representing the Everton supporters' group Blue Union (who stated: 'I think there's an enthusiasm out there that the fightback needs to start and it needs to start now', field notes, 9 May 2013), and Duncan Drasdo, speaking on behalf of the Manchester United Supporters' Trust. Both these clubs were considered Liverpool's traditional and 'hot' rivals (see Giulianotti 2002). Kevin Miles, representing the FSF, was also present at this meeting, pointing out the existence of the 'Twenty's Plenty' campaign although it seemed as if there was a mixed reaction to his plea to join this instead of setting up an alternative.

The June protest took place amidst strong enthusiasm from the 400 supporters who joined the march. SoS, Blue Union, Manchester United

Supporters' Trust, the Tottenham Hotspur Supporters' Trust, Arsenal fans' 'Black Scarf Movement', and Crystal Palace's Holmesdale Ultras all had strong, visible presences. Castells argues that people and relationships forged across both urban space and online discussions create and make real networked collective action. The 'mass self-communication' of digital technologies, including social media, is used in urban space—and connections made and strengthened (Castells 2015 [2012]). Hashtags that were used in connection to the protest included '#enoughisenough', '#footballwithoutfansisnothing', and '#StandAMF' ('Stand Against Modern Football', see Hill et al. 2016). Additionally, those who were not at the event could follow the protest through photographs and texts.

Measuring a collective action's direct outcomes is notoriously difficult (Giugni 1998). Indeed, the very constitution of 'success' emerges from the collective values and aspirations of those judging such. These values and aspirations are also the product of relationships. 'Success' thus becomes a reflection of the communication of ideas of 'success' in networks of networks of networks of networks, to paraphrase Crossley's (2011) argument. In the light of this the success of this protest was, predictably, debatable—perhaps according to the position of the actor who is doing the judging in the network. For instance, Football Supporters Europe (FSE, see Chap. 7) declared the protests to have 'reclaimed the game' for English fans (FSE 2013). Materially, the Premier League offered £12 million over three years to improve away fans' experiences of attending games to be distributed through each club in the way it saw fit (BBC 2013). However, on the other hand, at a northwest (England) FSF branch meeting in April 2014, attendees refrained from declaring this intervention a direct result from the protests. One audience member suggested that these moves should not be recognized as 'enough' given that the Premier League's broadcasting agreements had grown in value for three years and that—in reality—the budget amounted to small financial savings for each travelling fan over a full season (field notes, 3 April 2014).[1] Nevertheless, the money therefore offered from broadcast deals was a thin slice of contracts valued at £5.5 billion for the 2013/14–2015/16 seasons (David and Millward 2014).

On 14 August 2014, this physical protest was followed with another which had 250 people in attendance. This time the protest had not been organized through a fluid coalition of supporter groups (led by SoS) but by the FSF. The same hashtags were used, but FSF outlined another official hashtag in line with its campaign title: '#Twentysplenty'. Afterwards FSF member and Tottenham Hotspur Supporters' Trust member Martin Cloake (2014: 16) wrote that expecting ticket prices to immediately change is 'as futile as waiting for "the football bubble to burst"—a prediction popular a few years ago but also not likely to pass any time soon. What matters is that the discussion is happening, and that fans are organizing around it [...]. The fact that a cross-club campaign is actively supported by a wide selection of fan groups and that the football authorities felt the need to be seen to at least pretend to take it seriously, indicates progress'. Thus, Martin Cloake, possibly guided through his networks of association, saw the protest as indicating 'progress'; however, Hill et al. (2016) capture the voices of other fan activists, potentially in other networks, who saw it as lacking the energy of the previous year, possibly because it was organized in a hierarchical way.

Alongside these accounts, we also capture the structures of the loosely overlapping networks that connect the 'Twenty's Plenty' campaign and SoS' 'Walk Out on 77' protests, on the social media platform Twitter. This is important because Twitter has an underlying structure that is fundamentally a social network (Murthy 2012, 2013) and as such can be measured using the tools of SNA (Hansen 2011). As Himelboim et al. (2013) note, Twitter represents a network of users who are connected to one another via relationships displayed when one user 'follows' another user, exposing themselves primarily to the messages authored by the people they select. Such a network allows the examination of 'tweets' as the mode of open communication on the platform. The architecture of Twitter communication has several functions that allow for such conversations and information to flow through these connections, namely, @replies, @mentions, and #hashtags. It is the later concept that this chapter focuses on. The hashtags ('#') function was created as descriptive keywords to form conversational communities on a given topic that may otherwise be disperse (Himelboim et al. 2013). Alperstein (2013) views those who tweet with the same hashtag as within an issue-bound amorphous group, not in a 'relationship' (also Crossley (2011) points out that there are different strengths and forms of 'relationship'). 'Twenty's Plenty' campaign and SoS' 'Walk Out on 77' protest both used a hashtag to coordinate action and generate flow of information, in doing so created a network.

#Twentysplenty and #Walkouton77

FSF (2013) claim that their 'Twenty's Plenty' campaign aim is to ensure football clubs recognize and reward the contribution of away fans by getting together to agree an across-the-board price cap on away match tickets of £20. After the first and second ticket price marches we earlier detailed, on 3–4 October 2015, FSF planned and coordinated 'a weekend of action' protesting on ticket prices at football stadia across the UK under the banner of 'Twenty's Plenty'. Fans were asked to tweet pictures and evidence using #Twentysplenty. The offline protest involved fan groups at all Premier League and many Football League matches unfurling banners demanding that ticket prices for away games be capped at £20. Coverage was widespread and appeared in several of the weekend editions of the many leading British media sources, including *BBC*, *The Guardian*, and *The Telegraph*. Across the weekend Twitter was a medium for communicating ideas, tactics, and images of the protest as FSF's Director of Communications Michael Brunskill noted: 'the significance of social media in growing and sustaining the campaign' (quoted *BBC* 2015).

Early in 2016, 'Walk Out on 77' took place during Liverpool's home match against Sunderland (6 February). This protest was orchestrated by the Spion Kop 1906 group—a group of 1906 supporters who watch homes match together on Liverpool famously vociferous 'Spion Kop' end of their Anfield ground—but was backed by the SoS, with whom it shares many overlapping memberships and can be considered to be related to their earlier outlined campaign. The fans' collective consternation was that with 'no explanation' (SoS 2016) the football club announced that there would be an increase from £59 to £77 for each single top-priced match ticket in its newly redeveloped Main Stand from 2016/17. In a series of tweets in the week preceding the match, Spion Kop 1906 communicated to fans:

'Saturday is your chance to make your feelings known. Unhappy with the prices for next season? Then #WalkOutOn77'

'77—a number associated with @LFC. From Rome '77 [when Liverpool won the European Cup] to £77 a ticket. Let's give the number 77 a meaning on Saturday. #walkouton77'

'If the club want to charge up to £77 a ticket, make your feelings known and walk out on 77 minutes'

'Up to a £13 increase in the Anfield Road [an end of the Anfield stadium] next season. If you're not happy then show your anger.'

'Up to a £116 increase in The Main Stand next season. If you're not happy then show your anger.'
'Centenary Stand [a stand on the side of the Anfield stadium] increasing to £66 when we told @LFC £59 was too expensive.'

The tactic was that in front of a global television, audience supporters from across the ground would leave their seats and head for exit 13 minutes before the end of the match, on the 77th minute. As thousands of supporters left the stadium, Liverpool led Sunderland by two goals to nil. However, with the loss of their fans' support, Liverpool's playing team collapsed and ended up drawing the game as Sunderland, occupying a lowly place in the Premier League table, scored two late goals. Rob Guttman (2016), a prominent Liverpool supporter who owns several bars and social spaces wrote in *The Guardian*:

I've never seen a crowd finish a football team like that. The match was won, Liverpool 2 Sunderland 0. Then the 77th-minute protest began. About half the Kop walked, and a significant portion of the rest voted with their feet too. The dissenting mass totally sucked the life out of their team, Sunderland seized the moment, and the win was stolen. The point, emphatically made.

No witnesses could have failed to draw the inference. Crowds matter. People matter. Without fans it's just 22 fools in a field. Even [Liverpool playing team manager] Jürgen Klopp has referenced this in the past.

Before the game there was plenty of talk but no real sense of what might actually unfold in the ground. The week was tense: plans were hatched, black flags prepared.

The point we were making was this: we're worth more. An £8.5 billion TV windfall [which was the next television rights contract, to be shared between all Premier League clubs] deserved to be shared and the launch of a new 8,500-capacity main stand at Anfield represented a major opportunity to do that. The planets were aligning: this was the moment when our club could have made us proud. We could have been first to the punch.

I've been giving Liverpool my money as a season-ticket holder for 30 years. They've got me. Like all of us, a slave to football's rhythm. We'd just like to feel they weren't laughing at us.

Today felt like a flag had been planted, and maybe things will never be the same again. I expected sadness but there was mainly stoic pride. The Kop, defiantly mute for an hour, roused itself with trademark angry majesty on 75 minutes and cheered the faithful home. Never so literally.

77 and out. So many of us gone—hopefully not forever. But enough is enough.

The fans vowed to continue the protests with future games that season. SoS' Jay McKenna reported that:

> We have got Manchester City and Chelsea at Anfield so those two league matches—where prices are still going to be on the forefront of people's minds—will be opportunities where we will discuss what action we take next. For us, it is unequivocal: this is the start. A walkout of Anfield is unprecedented—it has never happened before—and I can't think of an occasion where it has happened in such numbers in another league ground in the UK. We don't have a firm idea of what we will do yet as this has all happened very quickly, so we will take the next two days to take stock and talk to the supporters about what we do next. But we will be taking action because we need to. Yesterday wasn't about letting off steam, and saying we are a bit angry but we will carry on. We really need Liverpool Football Club, the owners, and the executives to think to themselves: 'Is this the right approach?' (Quoted in *The Guardian*, 7 February 2016)

The club seemingly did ask themselves 'is this the right approach?'. In the wake of the media coverage of the protest, Labour Party MP Clive Efford asked then-Prime Minister David Cameron (from the Conservative Party) to meet with the FSF to discuss possible solutions and legislative changes to ensure lower ticket prices for supporters. Cameron did not commit to this but recognized the high price of match admission to be 'a problem' (Riach 2016). On 10 February, Liverpool's financial owners, Fenway Sports Group (FSG) (principally made up of a consortium of John W. Henry, Tom Werner, and Mike Gordon), published an open letter to the club's supporters in which they 'would like to apologize for the distress caused by our ticket pricing plan for the 2016–17 season [… which they] got wrong' and froze ticket prices. Many fans, in their networks of association, saw this as a sign of 'success'. What is more, one month later, and with *BBC* (2016) breaking the news with a photograph of the 'Walk Out on 77' protest, the Premier League announced that it was inserting a £30 price cap on away match tickets at all games in its competition. While FSF had initially declared 'Thirty's Dirty' and Labour's shadow Minister for Sport Clive Efford said the £30 cap is 'still £10 above the level that fans have called for', Kevin Miles said the organization was 'very pleased the voice of fans has been listened to'. SoS followed this up by calling it 'a very good step in the right direction' (*BBC* 2016), and such meetings continue with the Premier League Chief Executive Richard Scudamore (Turner 2017: 129). The networks within the networks of this association reasonably saw their actions as playing a role in the yielding of this 'success', affording them the opportunity to tell the story of their relationships which has a point to 'pause' the narrative on a point that generates emotions of happiness and pride. In the next section we move towards a network theory approach utilizing formal SNA to show the Twenty's Plenty campaign pulled affiliated fan groups into the social media campaign that crossed historical rivalries and diverse geographic places across Britain, drawing in supporters from clubs.

STRUCTURING THE PROTEST NETWORK

Our interest in protest movement networks online architecture's structures took us to use the main hashtags of #Twentysplenty and #Walkouton77 as a proxy for patterns of communication in the network. This is not, as Rainie and Wellman (2012) caution against, technologically reducing the network to online communication but simply to find an online proxy for its measures of connections between those involved. A graphical representation of the two Twitter network structures is shown in Figs. 6.2 and 6.3, and Table 6.1 shows an overview of the graph metrics on these socio-graphs.

As the two networks in each of the columns demonstrate, there are complex patterned relationships that structure these communities. Of the two, #Twentysplenty has a greater level of actors engaged in the online communication than #Walkouton77, perhaps reflecting a proportion of the wider population of 'football fans' as opposed to a proportion of 'Liverpool fans' it engaged. Indeed, as the metrics in Table 6.1 show, there were 4689 individuals within the #Twentysplenty community in comparison to 941 within the latter, as such the information flow (measured by communication 'ties' of tweeting/responding to tweets with the hashtag) is certainly much greater. However, while these structures are differentiated by volume, the patterns of structure are similar with a cluster of centrally engaged actors surrounded by an outer layer of more peripheral actors (see both Figs. 6.2 and 6.3). This claim is supported by the graph metrics where the two graphs share a very low density level (being the proportion of potential ties that are realized). Table 6.1 illustrates that the average geodesic distance—as the average path length information has to travel to connect any two individuals—for #Twentysplenty (3.78) and #Walkouton77 (3.32). This reinforces the similarities of structure and network flow within these two communities but also suggests that although

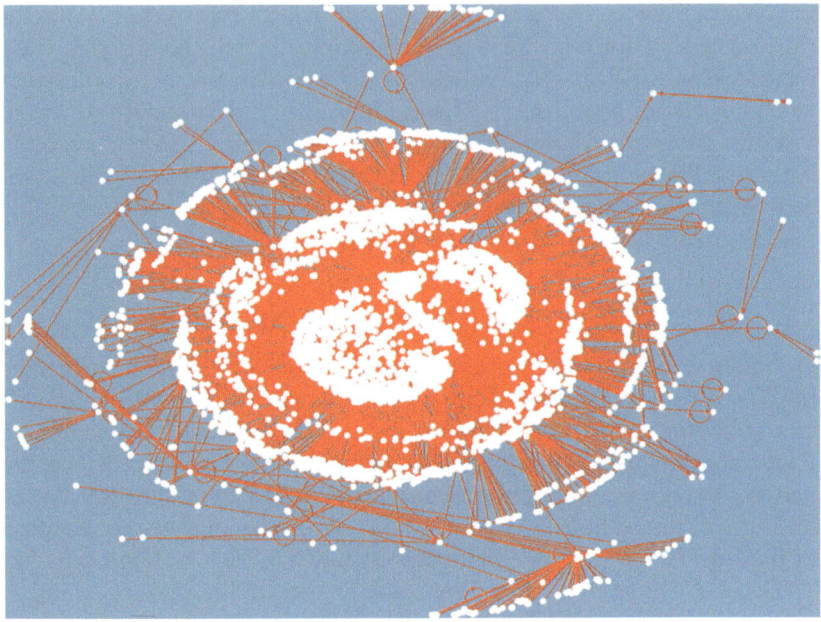

Fig. 6.2 Twitter network of #Twentysplenty campaign

being low in density, these communities have quite short paths for information to pass between all members. This means that information can pass relatively quickly through these networks as it does not have a great deal of distance to travel. On a related note, the average weighted degree, which records the number of connections of each actor in the network, their degree, and derives its average, also demonstrates both the similarities of the networks. Indeed, across both communities the average degree is very low, which indicates that actors within the network in general (on average) are loosely connected. The final measure on Table 6.1 is the 'clustering coefficient', which is a measure of the degree to which actors/nodes in a network tend to cluster together. Furthermore, this measure describes the strength of the connections between the nodes, that is, it measures the proportion of weak/strong ties in the network (on a scale 0–1, 0 being low and 1 high), and a low clustering coefficient is indicative of a network comprised of numerous weak ties. Both these networks show low average clustering, which suggests that these structures are built on

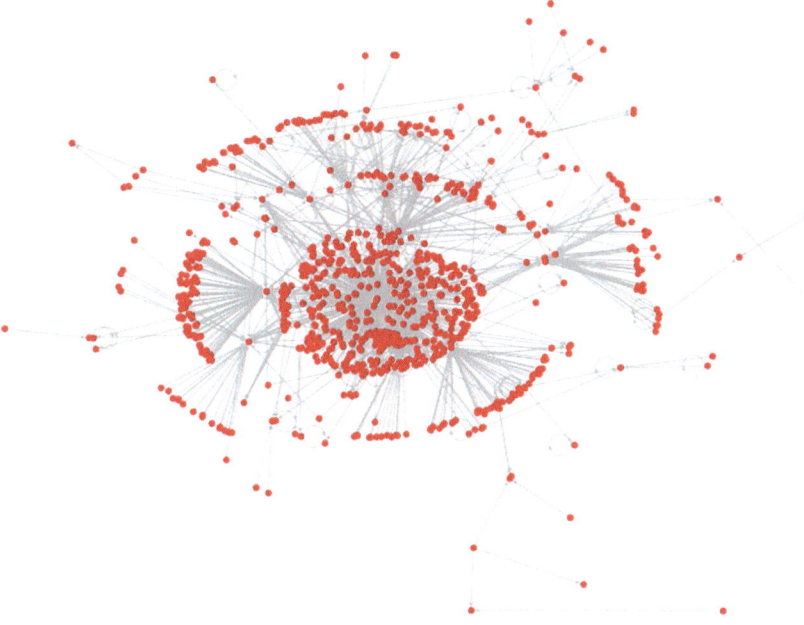

Fig. 6.3 Twitter network of #Walkouton77 campaign

Table 6.1 Graph metrics

	#Twentysplenty	#Walkouton77
Actors	4689	941
Edges (ties)	7953	1170
Density	0.00035	0.0012
Average geodesic distance	3.78	3.32
Average degree	1.7	1.4
Clustering coefficient	0.15	0.06

connections of weak relationships. Cumulatively this evidence supports the notion that contrary to much of the literature on social movements (see González-Bailón and Wang 2016), these networks are built on weak ties (measured by low density and clustering coefficients), yet information can still traverse the network quickly (measured by the relatively small average geodesic distances).

The metrics presented in Figs. 6.2 and 6.3 give an overview of the whole network but are unable to determine or identify clusters or sub-networks within them, in which nodes are substantially more connected to one another than to nodes outside that sub-group (see Carrington et al. 2005; Newman 2004). As noted by Himelboim et al. (2013), clusters on Twitter are the context in which users are exposed to messages, therefore offering the potential to generate capital and mobilize resources. Equally, these different networks may be exposing different communications to other members that might be at odds with the centralized message of the protest movements. By applying the Clauset-Newman-Moore cluster algorithm to these two protest networks, we can draw out the partitions of sub-networks, exposing the divisions within the protest movements (for more information, see Clauset et al. 2004; Hansen et al. 2010; Millward et al. 2017). These two socio-graphs (networks) are presented in Figs. 6.4 and 6.5, with the nodes/actors have been sized by a centrality measure (*betweenness*—discussed in next section) to illustrate the important actors in the clusters.

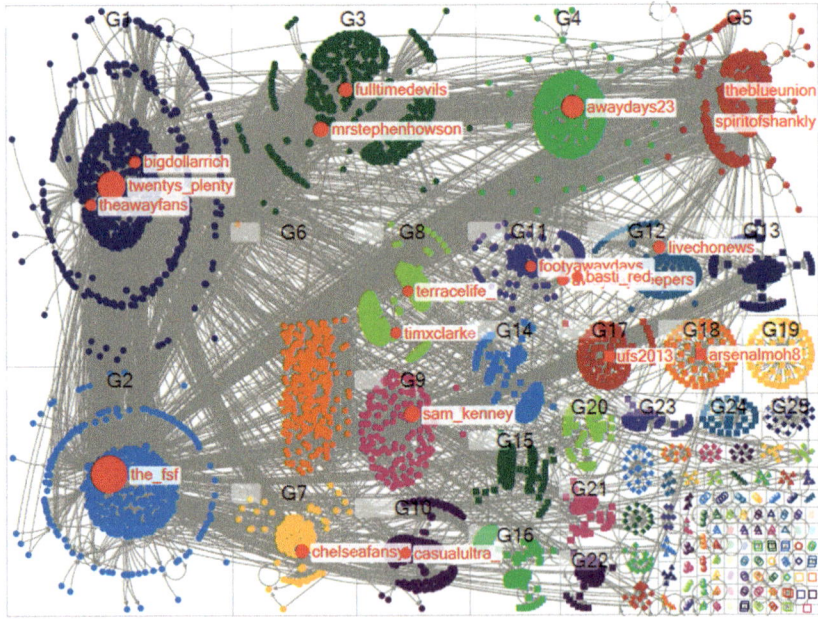

Fig. 6.4   Cluster network of #Twentysplenty

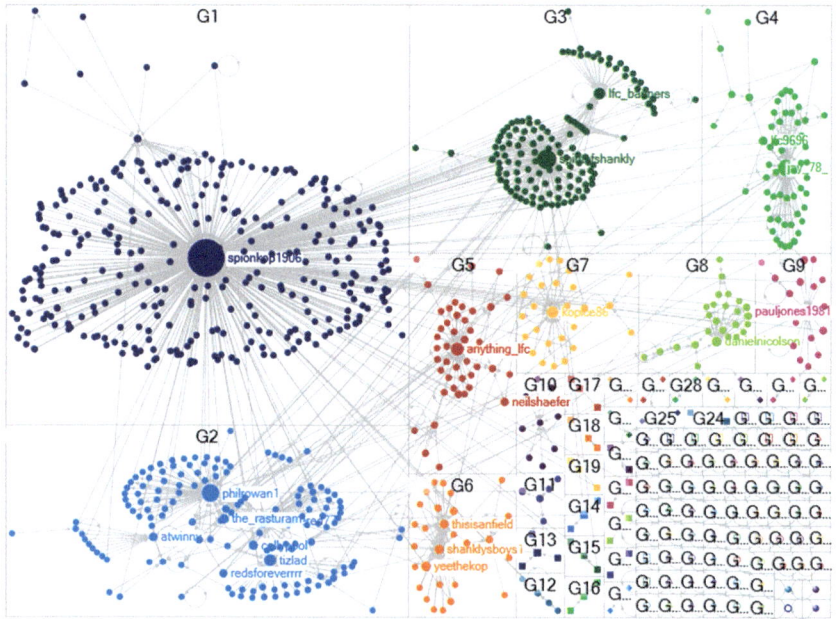

Fig. 6.5 Cluster network of #Walkouton77

CONNECTED SUB-NETWORKS OF ACTION

The #Twentysplenty network, presented in Fig. 6.4, has in total 118 community clusters, although the actual network is dominated by 19 sub-networks, with G1–G5 being the most significant. The remaining clusters are on the fringes of the whole network. It is important to note that while we focus on the most dominant clusters here, these groups on the fringes form a very important contingent for social movements. Indeed, for Himelboim et al. (2013) these individuals are potential recruits to the movement and can be drawn into the centre of the network and increase the size and level of activism in future campaigns. The following breaks out core characteristics of G1–G5.

Making up the cluster in G1 are 771 individual actors, 16 per cent of the network. The community is focused around three highly central actors: the 'Twenty's Plenty' Twitter handle, along with 'The Away Fans' account which describes itself as 'a community celebrating football supporters that travel across the country following their team' in its Twitter description, and 'BigDollarRich' who is a Swedish-based Norwich City supporter that regularly tweets about enterprises that could be reasonably be described as from the political left. The wider-tweeted content from this group shows that they mainly directed individuals towards news media sources on the protest rather than voicing their own opinion/reports on the event. Furthermore, analysis of key words circulating around this community was based around the ticket pricing issues, with the most mentioned and replied to being supporter groups affiliated with football issues rather than football clubs (i.e., it was supporter welfare groups rather than the traditional fan groups affiliated to a specific club). G2 made up 11 per cent of the network and centred around the FSF who are information 'brokers' (Diani 2015) and important in linking other clusters in the network together. G2 was much more engaged with those organizations and individuals with political capital such as the *BBC*, football TV pundits, key journalists, and politicians than G1. Indeed, Granovetter (1973) argued that weak ties help to build trust and coordination among a large group of loosely affiliated members (Lehrer 2010), and this might have occurred in this large sub-network as it reached out to organize the campaign to other actors.

G3 was made up of 490 actors, accounting for 10 per cent of the total network and was mainly made up of fan groups and individuals that followed Manchester United. While they still engaged in the key message of the protest, messages were often framed in relation to Manchester United and its supporters although not usually negatively against their 'rivals' on this day. Two fan journalist accounts were central in this group, and they created and generated news content for their followers, mostly made up of other Manchester United supporters. G4 was a sub-network defined by their dissemination pictures of the football supporters at the protest, and they make up 8 per cent of the whole network. They tweeted and retweeted photographs of supporters engaged in the protest in urban spaces (Castells 2015 [2012]) of the stadiums across the UK.

G5 was made up of 315 actors (7 per cent of the whole network) and was made up of the fans closely connected to 'SoS' and 'Blue Union' at Liverpool and Everton. These groups were discussed in the storied dimensions of the movement earlier in this chapter and were highly prominent in the first protest march and the earlier meeting at Static Gallery in Liverpool. Although linking into the main themes of the protest, this group regularly added their own hashtagged slogans to communications such as #ScouseSolidarity and #ScousersStrongerTogether[2] to their tweets with #Twentysplenty. Like G2, G5 also included journalists who either then or had previously worked for the *Liverpool Echo* (some of these journalists now worked for national newspapers). The group was connected to the urbane locale of the city of Liverpool but was well connected to other groups in the whole network; indeed, both 'SoS' and 'Blue Union' had connections to the key actors in G1 and G2 which were not defined by any strong support for other teams. The other clusters were much smaller and tended to congregate along football club allegiances. For example, G7 was comprised of Chelsea supporters and its 'official' news channel broadcast through the club's media platforms; G9 was made up of Manchester City fans and supporter groups; G17 was centred on supporters of Leicester City, and G18 was similarly associated to Arsenal. Connections between these groups existed but only on a loose way perhaps hinting at coalitions of convenience but still facilitating the transfer of information and ideas. These connections were not as strong as might have been suggested at the cross-group meetings that were held in 2013.

A temporal dimension of cultural relational sociology outlined in Chap. 1 is that relationships formed in previous interactions in the past may be able to reactivate in the future. Networks established in earlier bouts of collective action can be used to mobilize new campaigns. Accordingly, 65 of the actors who formed the #Twentysplenty network were part of the Twitter presence for #Walkouton77 action. Therefore, the campaigns drew upon some of the same actors. However, as visually through Figs. 6.2 and 6.3, these networks had both 'cores' and 'peripheries', structurally defined as through connections to other actors in the protest. When this is taken into account only four actors were in the 'core' of both: these are 'SoS', the '*Liverpool Echo*' newspaper, 'Twenty's Plenty', and 'FSF'. These actors are organizations rather than individuals. The 65 actors who tweeted with both hashtags included journalists (such as Tony Barrett, then working at *The Times* but who had previously worked at the *Liverpool Echo* and who Millward, 2011, discussed as being well connected to SoS), television and digital media agencies (*BBC Sport, The Daily Mail*), football pundits and presenters (such as Colin Murray and Robbie Savage), and current players (including Joey Barton). Each of these may have had different reasons for tweeting under the hashtag and may not have necessarily been 'involved' (recognizing 'involvement' to mean a range of different actions) with the protest campaign away from social media. Each also had a different set of social connections and 'communication power' (Castells 2013 [2009]), in that they have access to different media, political channels, and the number of 'Twitter' followers the reach to whom would be otherwise unobtainable.

#Walkouton77 had a total 109 sub-networks ('G's), although nine sub-networks made up the bulk of the majority of the whole network (presented visually in Fig. 6.5). Smith et al. (2014) describe a 'broadcast network structure' to exist when the best connected actor is in a powerful position in agenda setting and dictating the flow of information. G1 is the largest sub-network in the whole network and represents a broadcast network structure, and the lead organizing fan group '@SpionKop1906' was its best connected actor. In G1 the top paired words centred on distributing of leaflets and meeting points (i.e., 'handing pub', 'leaflets ground') with @SpionKop1906 a 'go-to' reference point for other members of G1 and the whole network. Fifteen per cent of the whole network were in G2. This is the sub-network where 15 per cent of the network had no clearly defined 'leader'. Key words that actors within it used included 'Scouse-Spring' (a reference to the Arab Spring) and discussed the protest as it unfolded rather than its organization and coordination, as found in G1 and G3. The latter of these sub-networks, G3, made up 14 per cent of the whole network and involves those strongly connected to 'SoS'. This is of little surprise given that the storied dimension of the 'football without fans' ticket price movement saw it and its members heavily involved in its organization, with Hill et al. (2016) describing some of the individuals involved in its network being 'soft leaders' in the UK Stand Against Modern Football movement. Key paired words in G3's tweets included 'print and leaflets', 'leaflets and give', 'give and out', 'out and pubs', 'pubs and coaches', and 'ground and Walkouton77': these were all indicative of spreading out information for dissemination of campaign materials at certain physical meeting space 'foci'. Given the connections SoS had worked hard to achieve with mainstream media organizations across its lifespan (highlighted earlier in this chapter and Millward 2011, 2012, 2016b), it is unsurprising such actors (*BBC*, *BT Sport*, and *The Daily Mail*) are connected to this group even if they might not be part of the tactics SoS openly communicates. As such, they might be considered to be part of 'submerged networks' (Melucci 1989) where experienced campaign groups recognize that they have to forge connections with established media channels through multiple means, including in social media space.

G4 is a much smaller sub-network, accounting for less than 5 per cent of the whole network, and is built around two actors with much smaller followings than the organizations involved in G1, G2, and G3 (and the individuals who comprise them). A key word within the information from this group was based around issues associated with 'solidarity'—showing support for the protest but not organization of its action. The other main sub-networks G5–G9 centred on one key individual often members of more traditional supporter groups spreading out information, much like the broadcast structure network of G1 but on a much smaller scale.

STRUCTURED NETWORKS: CENTRAL ACTORS INVOLVED COLLECTIVE ACTION

This section explores the actors according to the metrics of centrality measures to deeply evidence who were the most connected individuals involved in these bouts of collective action. Three measures of centrality are discussed. First, *betweenness* centrality which is a measure of prestige or brokerage is derived from how often an actor/node falls along the shortest path connecting two other actors, such that they may broker between these individuals (Crossley et al. 2014). Second, *in-degree* centrality which is simply the number of connections going into an actor, as such a high in-degree is indicative of a receiver of information. Third, out-degree centrality is the flipped version of in-degree in that it is messages going out from an actor to other actors. Within social media these three nodes are important, in that they can influence behaviour and ultimately restrict or facilitate information flowing through it.

Tables 6.2 and 6.3 present the central actors in the network in each of these measures on the #Twentysplenty and #Walkouton77 network. There is a *betweenness* tendency that in #Twentysplenty's whole networks and sub-networks the best connected actors are organizations rather than individuals. This pattern is only partially repeated in #Walkouton77 where the best connected actors are @spionkop1906 and @spiritofshankly, but then after them, many of the individuals involved in these fan groups are the best connected. This might reflect that #Twentysplenty was a nationally set campaign which, to paraphrase Anderson's (1991 [1983]) idea, was an 'imagined community' where actors had never met or even previously exchanged messages. On the other hand, #Walkouton77 spread from a group of people who watched football matches together and therefore

Table 6.2 Centrality measures for #Twentysplenty—underlined names have a high betweenness and high out-degree centrality

Actor	Betweenness	Actor	In-degree	Actor	Out-degree
The_FSF	8,604,879	The_FSF	949	Twentys_plenty	161
Twentys_plenty	4,993,728	Twentys_plenty	478	The_FSF	131
awaydays23	3,114,115	awaydays23	428	markmarriott7	55
sam_kenney	1,315,824	FullTimeDEVILS	279	roybentham1	51
Mrstephenhowson	1,218,098	spiritofshankly	234	BigDollarRich	49
FullTimeDEVILS	1,076,716	theawayfans	183	sebderay_1894	34
chelseafansyt	908,364	Theblueunion	173	Telfordblues	34
livechonews	732,369	Mrstephenhowson	170	Nwprogrammes	30
theblueunion	679,535	Chelseafansyt	146	Awaydaysyt	28
BigDollarRich	676,081	sam_kenney	145	Theblueunion	25
Awaydaysleepers	649,764	Livechonews	115	Susanwtid	23
spiritofshankly	648,595	david_conn	100	blefuscu74	22
theawayfans	621,443	Thefootballrep	84	Drasdo	20
Footyawaydays	545,340	ufs2013	76	tfeditor1892	19
Timxclarke	524,485	Timxclarke	75	Davefckelly	17
casualultra_	471,933	terracelife_	74	brianmiller216	16
arsenalmoh8	471,309	casualultra_	71	barbs_paul	12
terracelife_	469,218	footyawaydays_	68	sammcbride98	12
basti_red	463,232	Mancitymen	67	villa_trust	11
ufs2013	462,041	arsenalmoh8	65	1894group_mcfc	11

Table 6.3 Centrality measures for #Walkouton77—underlined names have a high betweenness and high out-degree centrality

Actor	Betweenness	Actor	In-degree	Actor	Out-degree
spionkop1906	518,152.060	spionkop1906	393	philrowan1	15
spiritofshankly	128,449.332	spiritofshankly	109	tedthered77	12
philrowan1	107,255.116	jay_78_	56	Collypool	7
jay_78_	87,496.143	philrowan1	55	Iphobin	7
tedthered77	59,356.533	tedthered77	43	danigennard91	7
anything_lfc	46,127.932	lfc_banners	40	Tenovatenchido	7
Tizlad	41,481.496	anything_lfc	35	Tizlad	6
lfc_banners	35,922.433	Tizlad	35	Yeethekop	6
kopice86	34,178.372	kopice86	25	the_rasturam	6
pauljones1981	22,764.257	shanklysboys1	24	Atwinny	5
danielnicolson	21,651.877	Thisisanfield	24	Redsforeverrrr	5
Yeethekop	18,538.285	Lfc	22	Jacquessantucci	5
the_rasturam	17,497.846	danielnicolson	19	Indiankopite	5
Collypool	17,148.406	pauljones1981	16	2014winners	5
shanklysboys1	15,969.216	liver16bird	15	Doolez	5
Thisisanfield	15,969.216	Atwinny	11	Huytonbad	5
Atwinny	14,019.938	Indykaila	8	Kolotoure	5
Redsforeverrrr	12,596.920	lost_sophist	7	kopgirl1991	5
lfc9696	11,408.000	Livechonews	7	Lfcwool	5
Neilshaefer	9795.965	19red	7	Spezialuruguaya	5

knew each other—even if only slightly—than was the case in the national campaign. *In-degree* relates to messages directed at an actor, that is, tweets heading to a Twitter user from another. Unsurprisingly, the central players on this measure are a mirror image of the betweenness scores with some adjustment in ranking. Clearly, on both networks these individuals hold key brokerage positions, information flow is like a magnate to these individuals within their clusters, and there are soft leaders in both communities' use of online communication. However, *out-degree* differs from the other measures on both the #Twentysplenty and #Walkouton77 network. First, those names underlined in both Tables 6.2 and 6.3 have a high *betweenness* and high out-degree centrality. Second, the out-degree values are relatively lower in comparison to in-degree. This means many more messages are coming into these actors from different parts of the network, but only a fraction is going out. In other words, these key actors with high *betweenness* centrality are absorbing tweets, as in information gatherers, but they are not necessarily passing this information directly onto other tweeter users. This type of structure may minimize the overall effectiveness as information can become locked into certain clusters.

Conclusions: The Relational Contours of Ticket Price Campaigns

This chapter has drawn together qualitative field material and quantitative analysis of intertwining campaigns to that fought against the high price of live football match attendance costs. The national and Liverpool-specific ticket price campaigns (including #Twentysplenty and #Walkouton77 but also the storied dimensions of the protest) drew upon the resources offered by members which were mobilized in the networks of collective action. In empirically capturing these campaigns the chapter drew upon storied, structured, and temporal dimensions of cultural relational sociology, as outlined in Chap. 1. In all cases of mobilization in this chapter, the campaigns reasonably claimed successes, although the qualification of what made the 'success' is understood within the relations of those actors involved and reporting on such campaigns. 'Success' is not an objective term but culturally constructed through the values created in networks of association (Mische 2003).

As discussed in Chap. 1, Borgatti and Halgin (2011) claim that much of the theory associated with social relations can ultimately be traced to the mechanisms and processes that interact with network structures to yield certain outcomes for individuals and groups. Three key mechanisms are advanced from the analysis presented in this chapter. First, ties come in different strengths. At meeting places such as the Static Gallery and The Horseshoe Inn, ties of varying strengths were formed in lived urban space that cut across traditional rivalries, a defining cultural feature of football fandom. Messages from these meetings were tweeted out and a protest in the lived urban space of Gloucester Place emerged. This was anticipated, reported upon, and commemorated in the way Urry (2005 [1990]) suggests tourists do as they 'gaze' upon places: in other words, they spread emotions of affect. Through social media, networks and sub-networks can be built upon 'weak ties' (Granovetter 1983) that facilitate the rapid sharing of such forms of information and generate feelings of unity and 'hope' (Castells 2015 [2012]). While there has been much criticism of these types of ties for activism (Gladwell 2010; Giraldi 2016), we would suggest that this type of tie was important in sending out the messages and images of the protests outlined in this chapter across the world, including the 212 countries in which the Premier League is broadcast. In making this point we argue that weak ties can be formed as 'submerged networks' in collective action (Melucci 1989) to media agencies as a means of gaining coverage of protests. These connections could be strategic, as a tactic of raising awareness and recruiting members, but may not be declared by protesting actors. The weak tie ensures that selective information can be passed to the media very quickly across the network and its sub-networks.

Second, related to this, protest movements can be considered to be strategic coalitions in pursuit of a broadly shared (and relationally conceived) aim. While some organizations documented in this chapter are comprised of individuals who are tightly bound together, others are not. The protest networks are usefully broken down qualitatively through fieldwork or quantitatively through algorithms such as the Clauset-Newman-Moore into their sub-networks. 'Unity' and 'solidarity' between sub-networks may be entirely situational but can be used as mechanisms to excite individuals. As Crossley (2005) stated, emotions—that for Burkitt (1997, 2014) are relationally generated—make movements 'move'. The clustering of the whole network into smaller sub-networks is also an interesting complexity in the second half of the chapter adds to this point. When networks can be partitioned into clusters, information flow can be impaired if there is an absence of ties across communities, this will result in information becoming trapped in the areas of high internal density (González-Bailón and Wang 2016). However, the networks here are characterized by low density and short paths. Interestingly, and perhaps at odds with the current literature, rather than the often portrayed flat decentralized structures of online worlds, there does appear to be more of a loosely adhered-to hierarchical structure, with communities being built up around key actors, or 'soft leaders', with a loose connection between them. A further feature of these clusters is that the key actors are what Burt describes as brokers and play a major role in the flow of information throughout the network.

Third, networks and sub-networks have well-connected actors within them. Our storied account in this chapter showed SoS, FSF, and some of their key members to hold these roles. SoS may be structured more informally and non-hierarchically than FSF, but in both instances key individuals—who are well connected—have key roles. One such role is as a 'broker', forging new connections with other (sub-)networks and offering out information to the networks of networks of networks of actors involved in collective action. The formulation of a protest movement requires coordination and an effective efficient flow of communication and information between those involved. Therefore, it requires connection between actors and a structure that allows information to travel quickly across the network. It is evident that the protest movements in this chapter, in terms of overall structure, are characterized by weak ties and short paths of information flow. Well-connected actors played an important role in this action. As Crossley (2011) notes, individuals in brokerage positions can mediate between otherwise unconnected parts of the network, which leads them to many advantages but can be constraining when trying to mediate between two communities. It is evident that both #Twentysplenty and #Walkouton77 networks are built around brokers. For González-Bailón and Wang (2016), the success of communities utilizing online spaces depends on the willingness of brokers to spread information. They argue networks afford but do not determine dynamics of information diffusion. If information brokers do not engage, information is lost or restricted. The diffusion of information is relevant because it helps organize protests. Therefore, connectivity often taken for granted in online networks depends on the existence of these central actors who connect communities and link to other well-connected actors (structural holes). The fact that these networks can be clustered into communities the absence of these brokers would result in a collapse of the wider group. They are essential actors in holding the online protests together. In effect these soft leaders with brokerage positions are to some degree what Castells (2013 [2009]) terms switchers, whose power lies in their ability, 'to connect and ensure the cooperation of different networks by sharing common goals and combining resources'. Yet González-Bailón and Wang (2016) argue that actors occupying brokerage positions need to be engaging in actual network exchanges to become information brokers, rather than network brokers. Switchers only become powerful in connecting and coordinating information. This subtle difference is of vital importance, we noted earlier that many of the central actors often have limited information emanating outwards (out-degree), to that end they are brokers but not information brokers. Therefore, protest information diffusion was not maximized. Interestingly, in the #Twentysplenty community, the big players in G1 and G2 ('The_FSF', 'twentys_plenty', and 'BigDollarRich') have very large centrality out-degree scores; they are clearly information brokers and driving the information within the network. Conversely, in #Walkouton77 the key actors ('jay_78_', 'spiritofshankly', and 'spionkop1906') do not appear to be information brokers. The failure of these groups to diffuse information may have limited the overall effectiveness of the network. Perhaps this was a reason why the #Twentysplenty campaign had a greater level of engagement.

Themes of space and place emerged across this chapter, too. National and club networks interacted with geography in alternative ways. While #Twentysplenty campaign involved a geographically diverse set of actors, the #Walkouton77 used social media to coordinate action in physical space (i.e., handing out leaflets at certain locations). In understanding these networks, it is worth reiterating again that these communities formed out of—and through—a hybrid of offline and online spaces, using a hashtag that linked to protests happening in a physical space. Therefore, these structures are being built in real time, which may reflect the tactics used in their construction and dissemination of information. Furthermore, given the nature of the national protest of #Twentysplenty, with over 20 urban protest sites, social media was essential in shrinking geography, creating spatial compressions (Harvey 1989). In this space support groups belong to different movements, with different approaches, policies, and tactics, but were able to come together in a space and exchange views, share information, and share tactics (Crossley 1999). The hybrid nature of modern movements in urban and virtual worlds was identified by Castells, and their interconnection is a crucial element. We demonstrate that just as the online connection of football supporters were essential in the Egyptian revolution (Costanza-Chock 2014), the online manifestation of these physical supporter protests was a key tactic in bringing geographically diverse groups into one space. Here the nature of the structure of weak ties, brokers, and small path distances supported the communication flow, without the obstacle of geography. Therefore, although different support groups were involved the key messages were universal and centrally organized. Technology and social media have actually made it possible to shrink geography in a way that was impossible before social media, pulling together very geographically separate groups into a network which is supported by the communicative architecture of Twitter. As such, Castells (2013 [2009], 2015 [2012]) is right to note informational capital as important in forging relations that establish counter-power.

Supporters are connected in many ways. From offline urban spaces where they meet, to online worlds where they share and coordinate information and tactics. These online spaces remove geographical boundaries and are structured and influenced by various network mechanisms that facilitate information flow. The Introduction to this chapter set out the neo-liberal economic position for setting prices for football matches. In that tradition supporters are too many and too small for individual action to affect price, which is set at the intersection of supply and demand. Football supporters are not isolated individuals using rational judgement in pursuit of consumption. We have shown that supporters or more precisely fan movements are embedded structurally in networks and these structures can facilitate communication between supporters and their interconnectedness is central in their resistance of accesses of capitalism. It is evident that, rather than being an isolated group of consumers, these supporters did come together in offline and online spaces to create action and claim 'success' in influencing ticket prices in the ways traditional economists would not have anticipated.

NOTES

1. The cumulative value of Premier League broadcasting rights was £3.182 billion across the previous three seasons, compared to £5.5 billion across the three seasons from 2013 to 2014 (see David and Millward 2014; Millward 2017).
2. 'Scouse' is a term associated with those who hail from the elastic boundaries of cultural understandings of Liverpool as a city (see Belchem 2006; Boland 2008; Millward 2009b; Rookwood and Millward 2011).

CHAPTER 7

Football Supporters Across Europe: Cooperation and Solidarities in Networks of Fan Movements

INTRODUCTION

Shortly after the tragic photographs showed three-year-old Alan Kurdi's lifeless body on the shoreline of Lesbos, hundreds of fan groups across Europe displayed banners that stated 'Refugees Welcome'. In the following weeks, other fan groups displayed the opposite sentiment by declaring 'Refugees Not Welcome'. We could look at this brief outpouring of humanity or protectionism as mere coincidence collectively reacting to the emotional events of a child's death that symbolized the 'refugee crisis' during 2015. Yet deeper relational sociological analysis demonstrates how football fans across Europe are engaged in complex and variable networks of interaction where they share information or seek to assert their difference. Traditional and social media helped disseminate the images of Alan Kurdi and also the images of fans displaying their banners. Many are members of fan organizations locally, nationally, and internationally and regularly interact with fans of many different clubs. These acts of cooperation and solidarity are not restricted to helping refugees but also relate to activities to challenge discrimination and resist police repression and general 'Against Modern Football' campaigns. Social media facilitates these interactions, but face-to-face meetings at fan congresses and football matches help foster collaborative networks within the social world of football fandom. Ideas get shared and collaborative campaigns emerge from what is often considered to be rival fan groups.

© The Author(s) 2018
J. Cleland et al., *Collective Action and Football Fandom*,
Palgrave Studies in Relational Sociology,
https://doi.org/10.1007/978-3-319-73141-4_7

As discussed in Chaps. 1, 3, and 6, the cultures of football fandom have usually been made and remade based upon rivalries. As De Biasi and Lanfranchi (1997) observed, fan identity in Italy is based upon 'the importance of difference'. In Argentina, Archetti (2001: 154) highlighted that 'no identity can ever exist by itself and without an array of opposites, negatives and contradictions'. Despite Armstrong and Giulianotti (2002: 1) stating that 'The history of football is the story of rivalry and opposition', football, like many social relations, is a complex web of conflicting and collaborating interactions. Just as Becker (2008 [1982]) observed in the art world, 'collective action' comprises of networks of competing and cooperating individuals and groups. Clubs have to compete against each other in competition but cooperate in order to hold those leagues and cups. Likewise, fans are placed in the same situation. Football fan culture predominantly focuses on the competition with other fans, in particular, the symbolic domination over rivals. Despite this, there is a long history of fans cooperating with rivals, particularly when faced with a different common enemy. In some cases, this was due to hooliganism as rival firms from a particular city would unite against a common rival from a different city. In Italy, the practice of *gemellaggio* would see networks of friendships form around common rivals (Doidge 2015). Both conform to what Murphy et al. (1990) call 'Bedouin syndrome' where the 'friend of a friend is a friend and the friend of an enemy is an enemy'.

Semi-formal and formal fan relationships have developed across Europe since the late 1990s (as also discussed in Chap. 6). Increasingly, fans are cooperating with rival groups over significant changes affecting their clubs. There is a growing awareness that financial problems, changes to policing, or growing commercialism are not issues that are restricted to one particular club but affect fans of many football clubs. In this way, fans cooperate to contest the changes. There are increasing examples of rival fans cooperating to challenge larger issues, such as Borussia Dortmund and Schalke 09 fans campaigning together on behalf of their local club Duisburg who faced financial problems. In 1997, in the UK, a Plymouth Argyle fan invited fans of many clubs to support Brighton and Hove Albion when they faced problems with management (North and Hodson 2011 [1997]); this favour was reciprocated when Argyle faced financial problems 14 years later. Rival Italian ultras have consistently united against a common enemy, especially the police (Doidge 2015, 2017). On a grander scale, fans of the three Istanbul teams joined forces in the Gezi Park protests (Nuhrat 2017; Turan and Özçetin 2017), and Egyptian ultras collaborated during the Arab Spring (Castells 2015 [2012]; El-Zatmah 2012). More formal collaborative networks are also forming across Europe, especially including Football Supporters Europe (FSE).

It is also important to note the internal power dynamics of these organizations as well as the broader social, political, and economic changes. There are complex interactions both within and between organizations (Nash 2000). Externally, economic and political power still overwhelmingly resides with the clubs and governing bodies despite agitation from Supporters' Trusts and fan groups. Within organizations, there are power struggles and egos that do not always keep the key activities focused. This can be manifested in different ways. In many ultras groups, power is hierarchical and resides in the capo (head) and his (and very rarely, her) supporters. For other fan groups there are more formal procedures which mean that power is dissipated across the group in a different manner. For democratic organizations like FSE, the guiding principle is to empower fan groups across Europe and to do this through cooperation. Yet power is still relative to that of the clubs and federations.

As we have seen elsewhere in this book, fans have been organizing political movements and associations in order to challenge and influence various aspects of football. Principally, this book has shown how fans of specific clubs have mobilized around issues affecting their clubs. King (2003: 184) argued:

> While it is possible that fans can be mobilized on a national level for certain critical developments such as the introduction of all-seater stadiums, it is almost impossible to sustain national fan groups beyond a period of crisis.

While there is some truth to King's assertions that it is difficult to maintain a national focus, formal organizations can help create a sustained network that can be mobilized according to varying issues affecting football. Fans mobilize around local issues pertinent to their club such as stadium redevelopment, ownership issues, or name changes. Yet linking to a broader network helps provide information and solidarity, as well as mobilizing fans from other clubs who are sympathetic. Fans are not hermetically sealed units that eschew any interaction with other fans. This chapter acknowledges that having shared crises does help engender an emotional focus for fans of different clubs together. It also suggests that regular interaction and a growing awareness of similar issues, as well as a shared solidarity in being a football fan, do sustain some relationships beyond local, national, or European-wide issues. While this is not true for all fans, there is a sizeable group of fans who engage in various political activities that go above and beyond their own club, including supporting refugees, anti-discrimination activities, and Supporters' Trusts or running fan embassies that welcome fans to their city.

ACTIVIST FAN GROUPS IN EUROPE

There is also a growing formalization of activist fan groups. It is possible to see a shift towards national organizations that are providing a formal network for local groups. This is also occurring on a European level. Throughout the 1990s in Britain we can see how national organizations formed to challenge a range of issues in football. Of those related to racism, Let's Kick Racism Out of Football was formed in 1993 and changed to Kick It Out in 1997. Football Unites Racism Divides was formed in Sheffield in 1995 and a year later Show Racism the Red Card was established. The Gay Football Supporters Network was formed in 1989 and the Justin Campaign started in 1998. The National Association of Disabled Supporters was formed in 1998 before changing to Level Playing Field in 2011. A similar pattern emerged in Germany. KOS Fanprojekte became the unifying organization for the network of fan projects in Germany (Giulianotti and Millward 2013; Doidge 2014). These fan projects do not have an equivalent in the UK and combine social work and fan engagement with education to challenge anti-social behaviour in football, like violence and racism. BAFF, the *Bündnis antifaschistischer Fanclubs und Faninitiativen* (Association of Anti-fascist Fan Clubs and Fan Initiatives), was also formed in the early 1990s. Five years later in 1998 it changed its name to the less political *Bündnis aktiver Fußballfans* (Association of Active Football Fans) but retained the acronym of BAFF.

These national organizations help overcome some of the issues of wider fan cooperation. As King (2003) stated, fans predominantly mobilize over local issues. As Nicolai Mäurer (FSE 2015) observes in Germany:

> cooperation between fans of different clubs is quite uncommon, too, especially within a city or a local area. There are some cases of friendly relations between different communities, i.e. Hertha and Karlsruhe, or Schalke and Nuernberg, which are rather to consider as exceptions, or between single groups which are parts of different communities. Aside from that, it's possible to work together within a countrywide operating organization like

ProFans or 'Unsere Kurve' or BAFF, or in the framework of an action or event given by the football association or maybe by an NGO. ... However, the main activities are done within the own community.

In Germany, as elsewhere, cooperation is the exception rather than the rule. The culture of football is predicated on the formation of in-groups and out-groups and 'the importance of difference' (De Biasi and Lanfranchi 1997: 174). What this quote shows, however, is that fans from different clubs can mobilize collectively when there is a common focus provided by a particular campaign, such as #RefugeesWelcome, or linking to a national fan organization, like BAFF. The critical aspect of these national campaigns, however, is to ensure that they do not stifle the creativity or dynamism of the grassroots movements (Hill et al. 2016).

The process of national formation of fan organizations varies according to specific national factors. While fans in Germany and England have been actively engaged with changes to their club since the 1990s, political economic transformations have affected other clubs at different times. The approach has spread across Northern Europe. As King (2003) observes, fans mobilize when their team becomes affected. Jasper (1997, 1998) calls this a 'moral shock'. National fan federations occur when a change to regulations or ownership potentially affects fans of all clubs, regardless of the teams they support. And they are influenced by similar movements elsewhere in Europe. The Federation of Danish Football Fan Clubs (DFF) was formed in 2003, while the Swedish Football Supporters Union (Svenska Fotbollssupporterunionen) formed in 2008 with support from the DFF. The SFSU was crystallized when there was a threat the Swedish '50+1' ownership model. Fans of the Jupiler Pro League in Belgium organized themselves as the Supporters Federatie Profclubs (SfP) in 2005. They demonstrate the power of fans working together as successive campaigns have united SfP and they have successfully resisted the introduction of a supporters' identity card and negotiated an agreement about maximum ticket prices.

Austria is a good example of the lack of national coordination. While there are a number of diverse fan scenes in Austria, many of which are incredibly active, there is not a national, well-organized network that links them together. As in other nations, many fan groups face similar situations and similar issues. Pro supporters was established in 2012 and linked to a broader organization called FairPlay, but fans do not run this. Pro supporters provides a link and enables a dialogue between clubs, police, and football authorities and attempts to speak on behalf of the fans, yet fans do not drive this (Giulianotti and Millward 2013, 2014). Active campaigns tend to organize on a local basis with fan scenes within clubs organizing events and campaigns independently. As Alexander Fontó from Vienna Supporters (of First Vienna FC) states, 'Fans tend to stick to what they know, not considering the advantages of cooperation' (FSE 2015). Germany and England can provide examples of good practice at establishing national links between fan groups, not just organizations like Pro supporters where fans are just one voice among the clubs and football authorities.

France and Turkey demonstrate how new national federations are emerging, but in parallel. As we have seen in England with Supporters Direct and FSF, and in Europe with SD Europe and FSE, France and Turkey have two fan federations representing slightly different constituents. National fan cooperation is relatively new in both countries. In 2015 the Association Nationale des Supporters (ANS) was formed to represent ultras and other active fan groups. The same year the Conseil National des Supporters de Football (CNSF) was formed to help Supporters' Trusts. French fans have faced further complications through the refusal of the French Football Federation to engage in dialogue with fans, even through the ANS and CNSF. Aggressive policing and the authorities' focus on violence have ensured that security has become the focus of fans in France.

A similar situation has occurred in Turkey as the authorities attempt to eliminate violence particularly after the Gezi Park protests in 2013 (Nuhrat 2017; Turan and Özçetin 2017). Fans of Fenerbahçe and Galatasaray joined with Istanbul rivals Beşiktaş to protest the development of Gezi Park, but broadly symbolizing the growing authoritarian approach of President Erdoğan. Some fans were even charged with 'attempting to overthrow the Turkish Government', although this was overturned in court. As has occurred elsewhere in Europe, the authorities proposed fan identity cards. This Passolig system is a combined e-ticket and credit card but linked to a progovernment bank, thus raising concerns about access to personal data. The Passolig system provided the catalyst to bring fans from different clubs together. Fans joined forces to boycott games. Attendances fell by 50 per cent across the Super Lig and by two-thirds among the big three Istanbul clubs. Strong attachment to local teams in Turkey has traditionally hindered any collaboration. Yet, these national issues have helped fans cooperate. The fans' rights network, Taraftar Haklari Derneği (THD), was formed in 2012, while TarafDer (Taraftar Hakları Dayanışma Derneği—Fan Rights Solidarity Association) formed a year later.

Reinforcing how a local issue can act as a 'moral shock' for mobilization, THD was established by fans from Izmir-based clubs to challenge the proposed demolition of their football stadium. They have broadened to encompass other issues affecting football fans. TarafDer was set up in Ankara and has predominantly concentrated on legal issues and has a strong membership of lawyers who provide legal aid to fans. Both organizations have cooperated since they were established and successfully pushed for the Constitutional Court to hear the case against the Passolig system. What these cooperative networks demonstrate is that there is greater power for fans when they work together. It is notable that these networks formed outside of Istanbul, the power centre of Turkish football. Despite this, both networks are in discussion to merge their resources into one organization. The first cooperative action undertaken was to host a FSE networking meeting in Izmir in July 2016 (more of which is outlined below). As Castells (2013 [2009]) argues, power is relational and resides within the network of interactions. When fans combine their effort and focus on specific goal, then they can wield substantial power over clubs, government, or authorities.

There are also specific historical and national factors that inhibit the formation of national associations. For example, in Italy, a strong local attachment to clubs, combined with a weak national identity, can impede national cooperation (Doidge 2015). Although a formal agreement was made between ultras in 1992 (see below), this did not sustain beyond an agreement around violence. Early attempts to bring fans together focused on the ultras in Italy. Progetto Ultra was formed in the 1990s to break down some of the barriers between ultras groups and prevent violence. Although funding has ceased, one lasting legacy is the Mondiali Antirazzisti anti-racist World Cup that takes place near Bologna every July. As has occurred elsewhere in Europe, government or police repression helps coalesce fan activism. In Italy, the introduction of the *tessera del tifoso* (fan identity card) in 2009 in the wake of the death of a policeman led to widespread resistance from fans (Doidge 2015). The *tessera* helped unite fans, but this has not led to a more formal national network emerging. Wider political economic changes did not lead to any wider cooperation in Italy until 2013, when Supporters' Trusts of smaller clubs formed Supporters in Campo to share information. This is similar to Spain. Even though the law affecting club ownership in Spain was introduced in 1992, it was not until 2008 that FASFE (Federación de Accionistas y Socios del Fútbol Español), the federation of Supporters' Trusts in Spain was formed.

Unlike Italy, members are not restricted to smaller clubs but come from throughout the league.

European supporter federations formed in parallel to the formation of national fan associations. Throughout the 1990s and early 2000s there was a growing awareness of European partners (King 2000, 2003). This is reflected in the growth of European fan organization. The earliest group was the European Gay and Lesbian Supporters Federation (EGLSF) that was formed in Germany in 1989. Ten years later, anti-racist groups from across Europe, including Kick It Out, BAFF, and Never Again in Poland agreed to have a pan-European network called Football Against Racism in Europe (FARE). This has been followed by Supporters Direct Europe in 2007 and Football Supporters Europe a year later. The Centre for Access to Football in Europe (CAFE) was formed in 2009 to champion the rights of disabled football fans across Europe. The location of the headquarters of these organizations helps to reiterate the Anglo-German lead in fan activism. CAFE, FARE, and Supporters Direct Europe are all based in London, while FSE and the EGLSF are both based in Germany.

While the location of these pan-European organizations denotes a North European focus to fan activism, they also provide a repository of activists and information that can help and support fan groups across Europe, including those who want to set up national networks. FASFE and Supporters in Campo were both established as national networks of Supporters' Trusts in Spain and Italy respectively and were done so with the support of SD Europe. The formation of Turkish organization THD was facilitated by FSE and reinforced through the annual networking event in Izmir in 2016. Certain anti-racism groups will look to FSE or FARE in order to help challenge racism in their respective nations. It is important that these groups recognize their North European cultural and political context and support fans across Europe. FARE's anti-racism conference in Barcelona in 2015 and FSE's networking event in Izmir in 2016 both made important contributions to expanding the dialogue.

Referring to wider European fan organizations can provide protection for fans' freedom of expression in their home nation. In 2015, in a match against, fans of Balçovaspor in Izmir unveiled a banner declaring ACAB. The police charged the fans for unfurling an offensive banner as ACAB stands for 'All Cops Are Bastards'. The fans successfully defended the charge by arguing that ACAB actually stood for 'All Colours Are Beautiful', the campaign for FSE's Anti-Discrimination Division. These broader interactions across local and national borders can provide more than solidarity but strategic information that supports and empowers fans.

FOOTBALL SUPPORTERS EUROPE: WORKING UTOPIAS AND EXPANDING THE NETWORK ACROSS EUROPE

FSE is central to these networks. Founded in July 2008 when FSF hosted the first European Football Fans' Congress at Arsenal's Emirates Stadium, it drew upon membership from Football Supporters International, who provided information, assistance, and advice at fan embassies/parks at international tournaments (see Curi 2008; Frew and McGillivray 2008; McGillivray and Frew 2015; Millward 2009a; Selmer and Sulze 2010). FSE is an independent, representative, and democratically organized grassroots network of football fans in Europe with members in 48 countries across the continent that is recognized as an association of supporters by the confederation of European football, UEFA, and, away from sport, the Council of Europe. It has members that are networked within national and club-specific bouts of collective action across the continent. FSE is an organized network that links fans and fan groups across Europe. Membership is open to local and nation fan groups, as well as individuals on the premise that individuals pledge to 'proactively support' principles of (1) opposition to any form of discrimination that is based on grounds such as ethnic origin, ability, religion and belief, gender, sexual orientation, and age; (2) a rejection of physical and verbal violence (both physical and verbal); (3) the empowerment of grassroots actions of football supporters; and (4) the promotion of a positive football and supporters' culture, including values such as 'fair play' and 'good governance'. Notions of what is 'positive' and 'fair' are not held by the group in a rigid way but created through the networks of networks to mean anti-discriminatory. This is intended to allow for communication across a wide number of supporters.

Both of the threads of fan embassies and fan representation remain. FSE is a democratic organization with a committee that is elected from members from across Europe. It also has two divisions: Fan Embassies and the Anti-Discrimination Division (ADD). Each year FSE leads in the organization of European Football Fans' Congress (held in a different city each year) in which workshops that focus on issues related to combating discrimination, ticketing, 'fair' policing, and the promotion of vibrant but inclusive 'fan culture' are held.

As outlined in Chap. 2, Crossley (1999) talks about movements of collective actors drawing upon 'working utopias' that they can visit to 'top up' their beliefs in the movements' aims and give the 'illusio' that is needed for continued action. In other words they are spaces where the movement's culture is reformed/reproduced and where 'people visit them in order to learn how to practice differently; how to perceive, think and act' (Crossley 1999: 817). FSE works hard to provide a variety of spaces for fans to physically interact and these serve a purpose in refreshing its activists' views in the earlier outlined beliefs that FSE is based upon. Every year there is an annual fans' congress or networking event. From 2008, FSE has held an annual congress. Most of these have been in Northern Europe (London 2008, Hamburg 2009, Copenhagen 2011, Amsterdam 2013, Belfast 2015, Gent and Lokeren 2017), which reflects where the active fan groups are based. Yet these have also tried to reach out to different nations by going to Barcelona in 2010, Istanbul in 2012, and the Mondiali Antirazzisti in Italy in 2014. At Belfast the following year, it was proposed that due to the time constraints of organizing an annual congress, FSE should move to a biennial congress. It was acknowledged that regular interaction was still required, so an annual networking event was instigated for the alternate years to the congress. This would be organized by the local fans and would be smaller in scale.

For Crossley, those who visit working utopias use the material and sets of 'knowledge' generated through interactions in such spaces as a means to attempt to persuade others away from the space as to their specific views. Effectively, they establish the conventions of a movement. At the congress, fans' views and stories are dialogically shared. Many of these (sometimes from previous congresses) are made into material form in the bases of information leaflets, 'fanzines' (see Chap. 1 and Jary et al. 1991; Millward 2008), and stickers that symbolize members' collective thoughts and endeavours. FSE highlights the importance of conventions of fandom when communicating with fans. As Becker (2008 [1982]) highlighted, conventions are important at helping people within a shared activity work efficiently together. FSE uses forms of communication that are conventionally understood by fans across Europe. Not only is social media used, particularly Facebook and Twitter, but FSE uses traditional forms of fan communication such as newsletters and fanzines. With their *Revive the Roar* fanzine, FSE draws together different contributors from across

Europe to showcase their work and highlight the successes and difficulties.

Crossley (1999: 815) argues that the communion experienced in working utopias gives rise to commonly shared feelings of affect such as 'excitement', 'stimulation', 'enthusiasm', 'evangelism', feeling 'right', and having 'heads blown'. Crossley argues (1999: 822) that working utopias are 'places of pilgrimage, they become meeting grounds for key movement activists and intellectuals, and thus sites of debate and discussion'. The workshops and, just as importantly, the social events where members can meet and solidify their bonds generate an excitement or hope at what other fan projects can achieve, providing the space where positive emotions—along with negative emotions such as anger at injustice (Jasper 1998)—can be generated. Crossley (1999: 822) also claims working utopias offer 'different national movements, with different approaches, policies and tactics were able to exchange views, learning from each other even when they could not agree and borrowing from each other, thus enhancing their discursive and tactical repertoires'. This is precisely what the activists from across 48 different national contexts offer at the congress as new tactics are formed and others exported in, for instance, fighting high ticket prices—particularly in the context of English fans seeking to incorporate selective elements of football in Germany into their national cultures (see Chap. 6). As FSE is officially recognized by UEFA as the official dialogue partner for European fans, it has access to its political structures, but that does not necessarily mean that they will be listened to. Hill et al. (2016) observed the paradox of formal fan networks. In relation to the FSF and the campaign against high ticket prices in England and Wales, formal networks can be perceived as taking over or stifling grassroots initiatives. Yet they also have official access to the governing structures of the game. Organizations like FSE have to walk a difficult fine line between access to political structures and representing the voices of a heterogeneous group of fans. Providing adequate opportunities for communication is important to limit accusations of empire building or quashing dissent.

Networks are an important link between micro and macro aspects of social life (Granovetter 1973; Putnam 2000). The strength of these ties within a network is based on time, emotional intensity, intimacy, and reciprocal exchange (Granovetter 1973). Obviously, these will vary depending on individual feelings and expectations within the relationships in the network. Homans (1950: 133) suggests that 'the more frequently persons interact with one another, the stronger their sentiments of friendship for one another are apt to be'. While regular repetitive contact is important, the quality and emotional content of the interactions is important. Just regularly interacting with people does not automatically mean that we become friends; otherwise, our work colleagues would constitute most of our friends.

The strength of FSE is providing an extensive, pan-European network of 'weak ties'. The organization is effectively a formal network that links various affiliated individuals and groups. This allows fans or fan groups from anywhere in Europe to link with others across many different networks. Granovetter (1973) highlights the importance of wider networks in communicating information. 'The strength of weak ties' lies in the 'bridges' that link across to other groups and networks. 'Weak ties', as Granovetter (1973: 1378) argues, 'are here seen as indispensable to individual's opportunities and to their integration into communities; strong ties, breeding social cohesion, lead to overall fragmentation'. In his analysis of social capital, Putnam (2000) also emphasized the difference between dense relations within a group, or 'bonding social capital', and wider links to other groups, or 'bridging social capital'. Groups that remain too closed, no matter how strong and tight the relationships within the group, often do not successfully challenge wider power structures. This has been one of the problems that have historically afflicted football fans when they refuse to work with rivals (Doidge 2015; Hill et al. 2016). Bridging links to other groups helps information get diffused and strengthens the overall network.

Castells (1996, 1997, 1998) argues that digital technologies produce a 'space of flows'. These spaces operate across time and space and allow people to share information from anywhere in the world at any time. These networks are more horizontal as users can communicate directly with others without going through a formal hierarchy. Castells (2015 [2012]) suggests that these 'spaces of flows' help drive social movements. Grassroots movements, like the various fan movements described in this book, are 'rhizomatic', growing like roots and connecting to a variety of other groups and networks. Like other social movements, these rhizomatic movements bypass conventional political parties and are non-hierarchical. Hill et al. (2016) observe that 'soft leaders' emerge that help bridge various nodes in the networks. They have the social and cultural capital to link individuals and groups outside of their core group.

This strengthens the network by expanding it, which, as we shall see, enables members to utilize a wide range of weak ties throughout the network.

While the internet and social media have facilitated communication and sustained relationships across Europe, face-to-face interaction is still important. One of the important aspects of football fandom is the collective emotional energy of attending a match. As Durkheim (1915) demonstrated, the collective effervescence of the group contrasts with the mundanity of everyday life. Regular, ritualistic interaction produces this emotional sense of belonging. Having a focal point for the ritual produces solidarity from the group. In football, this focus is the team or rival groups of fans. Football matches help fan groups differentiate themselves from their rivals, both through the performance of the fans and the performance of the team. As Marx (1932 [1846]: 189) noted, we become more aware of ourselves as a 'solitary individual ... [in] precisely the epoch of the (as yet) most highly developed social ... relations'. The greater range of interactions fans have with other fan groups helps differentiate them from each other and gives them a higher sense of self-identity. Until the 1990s, this was predominantly achieved within local and national leagues and within the physical space of the stadium.

Regular European football has helped form pan-European relationships between fans and fan groups. King (2000, 2003) has shown how the formation of the UEFA Champions League has helped restructure fan rivalries across the continent. Not only does the league format provide regular opportunities to play across Europe, the financial transformation, to which the Champions League has contributed, ensures there is a hegemonic group of clubs who regularly compete. This resulted in fans developing new rivalries across Europe, as well as becoming familiar with European cities. Cheap air travel has also facilitated the increased travel to away games across Europe. The result is a shifting cultural awareness of different cultures and a sharpening of particularistic identities. King (2000) observes how Manchester United fans became more focused on their local Mancunian identity, rather than an English national identity. At the same time, there was a growing awareness of being part of a broader imagined community of Europe. This is also occurring on a political level. Regular interaction through traditional media, social media, and matches helps expand this imagined community into a broader political movement. Fans are becoming increasingly aware that they are having similar shared experiences with fans across Europe. Increasing commercialization and changes to ownership, combined with changes to regulations and legislation, is affecting fans. As Tsoukala (2009) has argued, police are cooperating across Europe and similar repressive measures are being introduced by police and governments. The Council of Europe has introduced new 'Convention on an Integrated Safety, Security and Service Approach at Football Matches and Other Sports Events' in 2017 that lays out best practice guidelines for policing across Europe. FSE's recognition by the Council of Europe ensured that it was part of the discussions that developed the Convention.

REFUGEES WELCOME: SMALLER NETWORKS

Smaller networking meetings also provide additional focus and maintain the network throughout the year emerging from the two divisions of the Fan Embassies and the ADD. The former focuses on organizing the fan embassies at World Cups and European Championships. These bring together fans of national teams who want to support fellow fans of national teams at international events. The ADD organizes regular meetings to bring together fans that are campaigning against discrimination across Europe. There are four subdivisions within the ADD: Anti-racism and the Far Right, Refugees Welcome, Anti-homophobia, and Women in Football. The ADD works with other groups to organize these events. For example, ADD coorganized their network meeting in Munich in October 2015 with Football Fans Against Homophobia. Similarly, they worked with Queer Football Fanclubs to host a Football Pride event in Berlin in 2016. Giulianotti and Millward (2013) suggested that FSE needed to prioritize expanding its network to increase its influence to avoid dialogue including only the same engaged voices. This opportunity emerged at the Berlin event when the German-born Russian international men's football player Roman Neustädter attended as a 'regular' delegate. His presence, along with messages from the conference, was tweeted and retweeted using the event hashtag ('#footballprideweek') by fans at the event and then across Europe, especially in Russia—a country in which state-sponsored homophobia exists although it is clear that it needs more than these communications to change these deep-seated prejudices (Lenskyj 2014; Müller 2014).

Collaborations and regular meetings create sustained focused interactions that maintain solidarity and help share information across Europe. Collaboration with the University of Brighton in June 2016 brought fans together in Paris for an event to understand how to make Refugees

Welcome. The Paris event linked groups who had set up grassroots initiatives where refugees could be supported through playing football with fan groups who had led campaigns, volunteered, or set up other initiatives. As one participant stated:

> It was very inspiring to hear the struggles other organizations deal with and the different solutions that come up with as well as to hear about the great job the fan club societies do for the integration of refugees in their countries. (Danish fan, female, personal interview, June 2016)

Participants learned from each other and, more importantly, drew confidence from the work of others. Again, paralleling Crossley's (1999) working utopias physical face-to-face meetings help share best practice and ideas. The Refugees Welcome event clearly showed that fans forming relationships with refugees was where the real value of football rested. The personal contact and interaction with new migrants were the only way that fans could bridge divides and help people feel comfortable in their new home city. A German fan demonstrated that a few fans from their group actively tried to build relationships with new migrants to their city: 'They helped them with learning German or going to the authorities and filling out some bureaucracy stuff ... there are also a lot of refugees playing now on their [the fans] teams. And, yes, sometimes they also invite them to our stands' (German fan, male, focus group, June 2016). Building those relationships is more important in the stadium. As another German fan stated:

> The club does quite a few things for refugees, invites them, gives out free tickets and from the beginning we thought that it's not enough, just to invite them, but there should be people there explaining stuff, include them and meet them; form some relationships. (German fan, female, focus group, June 2016)

While it is important that clubs and football federations have a variety of initiatives to widen the fan base of clubs, the real way that these initiatives can be sustained is through fans being friendly with refugees. These fans collect refugees, sit with them, talk to them, and explain the culture and history of the club and its fans.

> At Elfsborg in North Sweden, when the refugees get tickets, fans go to their camps, meet them, have a talk with them and fix people that can speak their languages. And then coming to the terraces where the supporters are and

going and standing with them and making them included. (Swedish fan, male, focus group, June 2016)

In this way, the refugees are provided with a more rounded and friendly experience. One German fan reinforces this point by stating that 'it's always important to make the people not only welcome, but to belong' (German fan, female, focus group, June 2016). This emotional sense of belonging is what sustains football fandom and extending it to new fans is the best way to integrate (Stone 2013).

Forming personal relationships with refugee also demonstrates the 'strength of weak ties' (Granovetter 1973). When clubs provide free tickets, they are often for individual matches, and often the refugees are left alone, sometimes marginalized in a separate section of the stadium. Building relationships is the way to make this sustainable.

It takes a longer time, but then those people talk to other refugees and it becomes a kind of chain reaction and they start inviting people to games ... this empowers the people to help themselves and they become more self-confident and they start helping each other's languages. (German fan, female, focus group, June 2016)

Chain reactions are important network developments. It is not necessarily the immediate friends and family or 'strong ties' that recruit new fans; it is the extended network of 'weak ties'. This was also observed in Denmark with recruiting female players.

Often you can find a few women who are very into it. So you have to find some role models amongst them. ... And they are so committed that they want to go to the [refugee] centre to get the other women. (Danish fan, female, focus group, June 2016)

Trust is important in networks (Crossley 2011). Most importantly, the 'role models' become the important trusted bridge between the football project and potential recruits. Allied to this, the wider network of refugees is better connected into the social network which works better for social integration (Granovetter 1973; Putnam 2000). It is also important for fan groups to be connected to broader networks and partnerships. McCarthy and Zald (1977) identified that mobilizing political allies was a key activity within social movements. Many groups working with refugees across

Europe identified the lack of engagement from national football federations. For many fans engage in social activism, engagement with the authorities has always been arduous (Taylor 1992; Millward 2012; Doidge 2015). This is also true when fans work with refugees. When working together, fans share best practice and identify strategies of how fans created a dialogue with national federations. When fans identified best practice from football associations, other fans felt able to use this information to challenge their own federations. Ultimately, relationships are fundamental within the group, to share ideas and recruit new members and to engage in a dialogue with those in power.

The Importance of Collective Emotions

As with all social engagement, outside factors can provide the ingredients to enhance emotional relations. FSE's 2016 annual networking meeting was held in the Turkish port city of Izmir from 14 to 17 July. The event was organized by a local committee of fan groups from rival teams in Izmir. It was intended to have two days of workshops, meetings, and evening social events to create a space where fans could share experiences and ideas. Like other FSE events, the focus of the events was on issues faced by fans across Europe, including police repression, stadium moves, and anti-discrimination. Yet many of these activities did not take place as late in the evening of Friday 15 July, an attempted military coup took place in Istanbul and Ankara. The local organizing committee had to adjust their plans accordingly. Despite this, the event still provided the space for fans to relate and share experiences.

The incident provided an excellent example of intergroup dynamics, stratification, and solidarity among a wide range of football fans, many of whom had never met each other before. When news of the attempted coup broke, it was still unclear about the details. Fans were attending the launch party, socializing, and eating and drinking. Members of the FSE committee informed all the attendees that a potential situation was taking place in Istanbul, possibly a terrorist attack, and that they recommended letting friends and family back home know so that they would not worry. Information throughout the night was sketchy as the story was unfolding in real time. Social media proved to be both a boon and a hindrance as it was becoming increasingly clear that there were many different stories emerging. The FSE committee and members of the local organizing team agreed to organize the coaches to take the attendees back into Izmir city centre and to their hotels. All fans agreed to return and the coach journey was uneventful. Certainly, it was not clear that a coup was taking place in Izmir, and in the circumstances most fans agreed to stick together.

Group solidarity was vital in this situation. Daniela Wurbs, the Chief Executive of FSE, suggested that all fans 'stick together', rather than isolate themselves in their hotel rooms. Some fans did return to their hotels and many of them took early flights home. Not sticking with the group isolated them, and they did not benefit from the collective emotion, effervescence, and solidarity of the wider group. For the remaining 30–40 fans, it was suggested that we go to the pub we had been in the night before. It had Wi-Fi and this would allow people to communicate. One group of about 20 fans went off to the pub, while Daniela Wurbs and the local organizing team stayed behind to round up any other fans. The first group ended up outside a kebab shop as many people wanted to eat. Food and alcohol helped unite the group. Some individuals were concerned about what was occurring in Istanbul and Ankara. Others were checking social media and trying to pass on information. Potentially, this could have fuelled anxiety, as some of the stories were sensationalist (and turned out to be not true). Others sought to keep the group united.

The key thing in these group situations is not simply the collective emotional energy that unites people but the work that is done by members of the group to keep the group focused. Durkheim (1915) argued that a ritual focus helped generate the collective effervescence that helped unite the group. In football, the game provides a ready ritual focus. In social movements, especially around football, work needs to be done by members to keep the group focused. During the failed coup in Turkey, members of the group worked hard to keep moral high and provide a different focus to the political events that were unfolding. In this way, group solidarity was produced in a positive manner. If the coup had become the focus, and in a negative way, then different emotions, like anxiety and fear, would have been allowed to flourish. This would have fragmented the group.

When it became clear that the coup had failed, it was agreed that fans could return to their hotels. Some fans chose to sleep in the rooms of their friends, rather than return alone to their own hotels. Times were agreed for congregating to decide what should happen on the following day. Rather than run the workshops, it was agreed that attendees could do something social. Of the fans that stayed behind, it was suggested that fans could go to the beach. Some Turkish fans were staying at a communal campsite near a beach, about two hours south of Izmir. FSE hired a coach and many of the fans who decided to stay in Turkey opted to travel to the beach. The solidarity that had been created the previous night was enhanced through the shared activity of coach travel and relaxing on the beach. It provided a space where fans from different clubs and nations could come together as fans and share their experiences as people and as fans.

The group unity was enriched because the form of travel matched football fandom. Thousands of fans across Europe will hire coaches to travel to away games. The trip to the beach echoed many away matches. Even for the seasoned and well-travelled supporter, not every traveller to an away match will be known to each other. There is always a slow process of getting to know the others in the coach. Songs and jokes help fuel the atmosphere, and as the fans approach the stadium, the atmosphere heightens and intensifies. When fans from across Europe ended up sharing the coach to a beach, then the focus changed. Despite this, the shared rituals of football help unite and join the group together. Fans from the local Izmir clubs took the lead in singing various chants. This helped to create a 'typical' fan experience, even if many of the fans did not know the words. One non-Turkish fan suggested that the local fans should teach the others a Turkish song. After some discussion, a chant entitled *Sik Bakalim* was chosen that was relatively easy for the non-Turkish speakers to sing. Taking part in this shared activity united all the fans, regardless of team, nation, or gender in a shared aspect of football culture. As one FSE member said, 'this is what it's all about!'. The return trip was fuelled with more alcohol and songs, as fans from different clubs tried to get their chants taken up by others on the coach. The jovial and supportive approach helped create a special atmosphere that united fans independently of the political situation unfolding around the fans.

Jokes were made in Izmir about how a unifying experience for the 2017 fan congress in Belgium could be created. It was suggested that specially branded FSE T-shirts bearing the slogan 'we survived the coup' would create a sense of unity. Many conversations were had that acknowledged how the situation had helped unite fans despite the lack of workshops and meetings that the networking event was supposed to engender. At the following congress in Gent and Lokeren, the topic of Izmir came up among those who had experienced the previous year's attempted coup. Once again, many remarked on what would happen in Gent or Lokeren to better the dramatic experiences of Izmir. On the coach trip to the opening party, the chant *Sik Bakalim* was started again. Ultimately, Izmir was supposed to be a networking event and the attempted coup provided many alternative opportunities to network with fans from across Europe.

CONCLUSIONS: RELATIONSHIP AND COLLECTIVE EMOTIONS IN A EUROPEAN NETWORK

Just as the photographs of the drowned Syrian child provoked an emotional outpouring for refugees, external political events can provide the emotional ingredients to bring a group together. Jasper (1997, 1998) refers to these events as 'moral shocks' and they can provide the necessary components for a network to coalesce and solidify. Football provides an important emotional vehicle for fans. It has long been acknowledged that football provides a sense of emotional belonging to a wider social collective. As has been demonstrated elsewhere in this book, fans are now mobilizing politically around activities associated with their club. This emotional attachment works with the 'moral shock' to motivate people to engage. This chapter has argued that emotion is a fundamental ingredient to fandom and political mobilization and is necessary for a network to form and endure.

Significantly, fan networks are spreading across Europe. The growing interconnectedness of European football is resulting in a greater awareness by fans of developments across the continent (King 2003). The formation of Football Supporters Europe provides a hub and formal structure that creates important channels of communication for disparate fan groups. This means that fans can mobilize relatively easily around momentous political activity, such as the 'refugee crisis'. Significantly, FSE ensures the continuation of the network through face-to-face activity. Fan congresses, networking activities, and meetings around significant activity mean that fans have a chance to build friendships and contacts across Europe and beyond constituting experiences of 'working utopias' (Crossley 1999), conjured through the stories told by the presence of networks of protestors, for its congress delegates. This provides a hub for network activity (Castells 2000 [1996], 2004 [1997], 1998) and this provides access to an extensive web of 'weak ties' (Granovetter 1973). This gives fans the potential to access information and strategies from a wider group of people and potentially gives more power to individual fan groups.

CHAPTER 8

Conclusion: Connections More Than Matter!—Relational Understandings of Football Fans' Collective Actions

Our conclusion begins at the same temporal and spatial location as the opening vignette in this book—the FSF and Supporters' Direct Supporter Summit in July 2017. While the short story that opened Chap. 1 took us to the opening address of the conference, we have now fast forwarded to the closing keynote, and journalist David Conn, whose work on the political economy of football has been mentioned across this book, is giving his address. This speech unites themes ranging from 'Clubs in Crisis', the Supporters' Trust movement, to the fans' fight against the injustices associated to 1989s Hillsborough disaster. He is 'weakly tied' (Granovetter 1973, 1995) into fan activist networks and is speaking to an audience that includes those from non-league football (Chap. 3), Coventry City (Chap. 4), Swansea City (Chap. 5), and many of those who devised the 'Twenty's Plenty' campaign (Chap. 6). In total, there are supporters from around 90 different football clubs in the audience. The conversations, debates, and talks that have taken place in the space undergird a renewed 'illusio' in the fan activists' belief in the supporters' movement. The audience of social actors loudly applaud him, their energy for social change topped up one day after the same people collectively launched plans to challenge Rupert Murdoch's news outlet, *The Sun*, on account of its reportage of football supporters across four decades. For Castells (2013 [2009]), Murdoch is emblematic of hegemonic power in a transnationally networked society, but the supporters in the room have generated a mood where they believe

© The Author(s) 2018

J. Cleland et al., *Collective Action and Football Fandom*,
Palgrave Studies in Relational Sociology,
https://doi.org/10.1007/978-3-319-73141-4_8

a 'better future' can be fashioned through their collective action. The terms of reference for that 'future' are imprecise, allowing many to buy into it.

FSE's congress was held a week later across venues in Lokeren and Gent, Belgium, where similar processes of glueing together weakly connected networks and actors in the movement took place. Once more, talks and workshops were important, but—equally crucially—so were the social spaces of nearby coffee bars and public houses. This was the third football supporter activist conference held in less than three weeks—the week before the Supporter Summit, Pride in Football's 'Call It Out' conference was held, which also provided similar functions to sociality. Indeed, some people attended all three events—many attended more than one.

Chapter 7 includes reference to FSE's coordinator, Daniela Wurbs who, from its launch in 2008 until winter 2016, led the organization. Prior to this, she had worked for FSF and provided an initial link between the two groups. Kevin Miles, FSF's chief executive, is another tie, as he sits on FSE's organizing committee. The links stretch further, as numerous other members of Supporters Direct and FSF attended FSE's 2017 congress, as they have done so in the past. Social actor's memberships crosscut the groups. The strength of ties inside the organizations varies with those who attend all of the congresses and is at least known to the organizers: some are firm friends, others just know each other through following on Twitter and a nod and smile when they meet in the 'lived urban spaces' of conferences or protests (Castells 2015 [2012]).

As Crossley (2011) notes, networks know no boundaries in place or politics. FSF's (2017: 36–37) 'Annual Review 2016–17', given to each delegate at the Supporters Summit, names 32 British MPs, from five different political parties, that they liaise with to 'give fans a voice in Westminster'. Some of those in the audience at the Supporters Summit are actively involved with frontline politics and heard Conn's keynote address ends with the following statement:

> It is important we recognize that a football club is still a *club* [Conn's emphasis] even though it may be a PLC [public liability company], floated on the New York stock exchange and registered in the Cayman Islands. [...] Clubs have membership, in this case drawn from fans, and has a collective identity that reflects its communities. (Field notes, 1 July 2017)

Conn rallied the audience by showing that despite commercial and business interests, they, as football fans, were part of a 'club' that underpins the football team. In other words, he drove forward the enthusiasm of supporters by reminding them that *they* were of crucial importance to *their* club. In doing so, his commentary resembled that offered by former England manager Sir Bobby Robson, whom—ironically—the room Conn was speaking in was named after, who wrote:

> What is a club in any case? Not the buildings or the directors or the people who are paid to represent it. It's not the television contracts, get-out clauses, marketing departments or executive boxes. It's the noise, the passion, the feeling of belonging, the pride in your city. It's a small boy clambering up stadium steps for the very first time, gripping his father's hand, gawping at that hallowed stretch of turf beneath him and, without being able to do a thing about it, falling in love. (Robson 2009: 2)

Akin to Conn, Robson was correct to state supporters are part of the football club—although as Dunning (1999: 126) argued that 'fans are, individually, the least powerful person in the football figuration'—but was wrong to assume that those who are paid employees are not part of it. All are part of its networks of relations, although they perform very different roles in its operations. A football club, and the social worlds it gives rise to, is a clear expression of the multiplicity of actors collectively engaged in the cultural relational actions outlined in Chap. 1 and all subsequent chapters across this book. As we noted in Chap. 4, a football club's board of directors is made up networks of actors each engaged in their own relationships with others who are internal and external to it. We do not want to dispute their engagements in being part of the social world of a football club, but the empirical focus of this book has been on football fans. The proposition that a football club is a business has been discussed elsewhere (King 1997c; Morrow 1999; Millward 2013; Doidge 2015). Although money is generated by its business operations, revenue does not always (or even normally) transfer into profits. Even considering this, the relationships in a football show it to be different from other business entities.

Fans are important stakeholders in football. In the terms we proposition in cultural relational sociology, they are deeply part of the effective and storied dimensions of a football club's social world. Although they hand over money in the form of ticket prices, television subscriptions, and the purchase of consumer goods, their investment is their support (including its wide range of practices). Fans' return on this investment comes in the form of the emotional gratification remembered both individually (such as attending an important match with a much valued relative) and collectively (including winning a trophy). To guarantee this return, all a football club needs to do is to continue to exist as individual and collective memories will be made through the relationships in its social spaces. Football clubs might reasonably be described in legal, business, or administrative terms or as a collection of players and managers (i.e., the 'team'). However, it might also be understood in cultural terms—in terms of the symbolic dimensions made and remade by fans, players, and their relationships with remembrance of previous fans and players that is concretized in the form of a football club crest, team colours, its name, or—as discussed in Chap. 4—the urbanity in which it plays 'home matches'. As one of the political slogans discussed in Chap. 6 stated: 'Football with fans is nothing'. Without them it would be a semi-vacuous entity.

Cultural Relational Sociology: Collective Action and Football Fandom

The theoretical approach of cultural relational sociology takes inspiration from the ideas Crossley put down in *Towards Relational Sociology* (2011). As suggested in Crossley's book title, the approach he offers is still in development, but he further concretized it when he used it to explore punk and post-punk movements of musicians and artists in Manchester, London, Liverpool, and Sheffield (Crossley 2015b). Jenkins (2014) suggested that a theoretical approach is likely to refine when it is applied to empirical situations and subsequently reflected upon. Effectively, an approach means little without the social worlds it operates. Therefore we have picked up on many of Crossley's (2011) threads to understand the relational social worlds associated to the collective actions involved in some expressions of football fandom. Through applying of many of Crossley's ideas to our case studies, we devised three levels in which a cultural relational sociology could be developed. These are, first, the central concepts in the turn; second, its key dimensions; and third, seven touchstones that can be used for a cultural relational sociology in understanding the specifics of football fans' collective actions. The path cutting through these levels is of wide significance to the discipline of sociology as it provides ideas for both a cultural relational analysis of sociality and, as an example of this, the collective actions of football fans. Doing this moves the key contribution of this book beyond the specifics of the case studies in Chaps. 3, 4, 5, 6, and 7. This chapter now discusses these three levels of analysis in specific relation to the five case studies we have outlined.

The five central concepts in cultural relational sociology we outlined were (i) relations/relationships, (ii) interaction, (iii) networks, (iv) social actors, and (v) power/counter-power. Relations and relationships cut across our analysis and across the production and consumption of football. Relationships are made and remade between football fans in all case studies and are evidently made between football fans and journalists in Chaps. 4 and 6. Alternatively, the breakdown of a relationship between supporters and the business owners of a football club prompted fan action in Chap. 4. Without relations and relationships, the interaction needed to organize and carry out the collective actions in all chapters would not take place. Repeated interactions and the structuring of relationships become manifest as networks. This chapter opened up by noting that all case studies in this book—and many others across unquantifiable numbers of fans of football clubs spread across multiple countries—form networks of supporters engaged in sets of politics broadly framed to be 'progressive'. These networks can be periodically 'switched' together at temporal periods in which weakly connected social actors—which could be groups, agencies, or individuals—need to draw on each other's expertise or resources. Power represents the social, economic, and cultural interests embedded in the relationships that control supporters such as the government, the FA, and football clubs. Counter-power is found in the acts of 'doing things differently'. This takes the form of forging visions of alternative social futures (Chaps. 3 and 6), opposition to networks of owners who govern clubs in ways that jars with the values of many supporters (Chap. 4), Supporters' Trusts (Chap. 5), and organized resistance to hegemonic practices operating in the sport, such as expensive match admission prices (Chap. 6). This counter-power might also include not paying for live streamed broadcasts of football matches (David and Millward 2012; David et al. 2017).

Cutting across these concepts we outline six dimensions of cultural relational sociology, which are (i) temporal, (ii) spatial, (iii) symbolic, (iv) emotional, (v) narrative, and (vi) structured aspects. First, networks, relationships, and interactions all have histories. Unsurprisingly, each of the socialities discussed in the chapters shows the forms of collective actions to have enduring and sedimented histories. If FSE's founding chief executive had not spent time working for FSF, she would not be so connected into that movement (Chap. 7). If the social actors in SoS had not mobilized through a range of movements, they would not have been in a position to forge with Spion Kop (with whom they have many cross-cutting memberships) to challenge ticket prices through the 'Walk Out on 77' protest (Chap. 6). If Swansea City supporters had not engaged in the discursive spaces afforded by internet forums, it is contestable whether a Supporters' Trust would have emerged (Chap. 5). Similarly, the sedimented history of supporters' groups' rivalries may present some difficulties in making cross-football club action 'happen' (Chaps. 3, 6, and 7). As Crossley (2011: 29) notes, 'what happens early on in the interaction may both facilitate and constrain what happens later'. Second, spatial dimensions of cultural relational sociology are important. Effectively, this is to say that the collective actions discussed through the book are often related to specific spaces. Online architectures are important in forging and representing relationships (see Chap. 6), but these ties become 'real' in lived urban space (see Chaps. 3, 6, and 7). It is in the spaces of public houses, protest sites, or congresses that social ideas of 'success' are made, tactics are forged, and emotions are topped up. It is also in such spaces where friends of friends become 'friends' and weakly connected individuals become more tightly connected.

Third, cultural relational sociology has symbolic dimensions as actors interact, classify, and typify each other. They also interpret the range of symbols in the social worlds of football fandom, submerging into their internal thoughts about themselves and others in that environment. An actor's reflective thoughts about himself/herself are as social and relational as those thoughts about others. Across the book, examples have been discussed about how football fans and those in positions of 'power' in football have reflected upon the things that they have done in the light of the counter-power actions of others. Examples of such reflection include Chap. 6's account of Liverpool's financial owners changing their ticketing plans in the light of protest and, in Chap. 5, Huw Cooze standing down as the Supporters' Trust representative on the board of directors at Swansea City. Fourth, cultural relational sociology involves a recognition that the social worlds, including those that football is located within, have affective dimensions. The 'moral shocks' prompted by the treatment of some people—such as refugees—outside of football (Chaps. 3 and 6) provide examples of dimension. Similarly, the relocation of a football club away from its 'home' locale (Chap. 4), fears about the long-term future of a football club (Chap. 5), and anger at high match admission prices (Chap. 6) provide the emotions needed to make a collective action 'move'. These emanating emotions, along with those coming from the excitement of communal protest activities, are arguably more social than physiological. They are created, recreated, and modified to form collective 'hope' for a 'better' future. Both the hope for and the design of that future are collectively generated and shaped by social processes that are inherently relational.

Fifth, cultural relational sociology involves the recognition of narratives. In each chapter, these narratives have begun with a socially conceived idea of 'injustice', including potential 'victims' and 'perpetrators', and have mobilized with the idea that this can be successfully overcome. In these narratives, a socially conceived idea of 'victory' (or 'success') must always be possible to ignite socially rooted ideas of collective 'hope'. Sixth, there is a recognition that structures of sociality matter and shape connections. The movements outlined in Chaps. 3, 6, and 7 are made up of coalitions of smaller networks of football supporters in which connections are 'switched on' and, through which, information flows. These structured networks make the collective actions of seemingly disparate actors possible through overt and 'submerged' networks (Melucci 1989, 1996a, b).

Chapter 2 outlines seven analytical touchstones to understand the collective actions of football fans. These are (i) the structures of and roles in collective action; (ii) affect, emotion, and collective effervescence; (iii) communication, cooperation, and conventions; (iv) mobilizing resources; (v) tactics; (vi) recruitment to collective action and 'outcomes' of mobilization; and (vii) the spaces and places of organization and action. Each is relationally defined. For instance, Chap. 4 shows how the role of the 'villain' is socially defined through networks and interactions of fans. Across the movements, some, such as those in Chaps. 4, 5, 6, and 7, have formally recognized roles, while many across the chapters and in Chap. 3 take on roles in networks of action informally. Communications with each other, the press, other fan groups, and politicians might forge, reinforce, and weaken connections between actors in the networks of that comprise 'football clubs'. Meanwhile conventions for protest are socially made and shared through, for instance, hashtags, and resources such as money and connections are mobilized but only become meaningful through interaction. Even ideas of 'success' are socially generated, such as in Chap. 6 when fans, despite complaining that 'thirty's dirty' accepted the cap of £30 for Premier League ticket prices as a marker of success in their

'Twenty's Plenty' campaign. Such ideas of what constitutes 'success' along with the generation of emotion, affect, and collective effervescence take place in the spaces of collective action, where ties are made and reinforced.

Last Words: Even Further Towards a Cultural Relational Sociology

This book puts down a significant marker in shaping cultural relational sociology, but the theoretical project is not complete and needs further engagements with other empirical case studies. By showing how networks of football fans adjoin in range of different strengths of connection, we have profiled the networks of networks of networks of interactions of interactions of football fans in what could be broadly fit under the banner of (relationally conceived) 'progressive politics'. This drift towards 'progressive politics' mirrors wider trends in the study of social movements (Edwards 2014). In other words, research such as that offered by McVeigh (2009) on the Ku Klux Klan is more unusual than those books and articles that explore environmental movements (such as Melucci 1996b). However, we recognize that collective actions of football fans are not always from the (broadly defined) socio-political 'left' (see, for instance, Armstrong 1998; Robson 2004; Garland and Treadwell 2010; Treadwell and Garland 2011). The cultural relational sociological approach—taking into account the three levels of theoretical analysis: concepts, dimensions, and touchstones—would potentially gain a great deal if it was used to explore more 'right-wing' football fan collective actions. Beyond this example, other ways to engage with the theoretical propositions through the concepts, dimensions, and touchstones might include non-political forms of collective fandom (in football, sport, popular culture or less popular culture), social movements in contexts that may be removed from football fandom, or forms of sociality that operate in entirely different social worlds to football or mobilizations. We set no limit on the number in the 'critical mass' needed to partake in collective action. Neither do we prescribe specific forms of theory or method that could be used, other than following Crossley (2011) in that they must have patterned connections between people at their core.

The cultural relational sociological approach we utilize can be important in governmental and political terms as well as those that 'only' talk about culture (if such a divide is even possible). For instance, several UK cross-party parliamentary inquiries (including their 'follow-ups') into governance in football have been held in the twenty-first century. Some of the actors detailed in their relationships, networks, and interactions in this book have given evidence to such inquiries, and several of the MPs that are weakly tied to the networks of collective action have heard their evidence. But weak ties can have strength (Granovetter 1973), forming the basis of 'being in touch', exchanging tactics, sharing success stories, and developing 'conventions' for action (Becker 2008 [1982]). Discussions do not merely take place on official platforms—weak and strong ties are formed 'back stage' at rallies, congresses, and social occasions and are strengthened through technologically enabled communications—and those who give evidence usually have the mobilized capital of connections to such figures. The call for 'improved governance' in the sport is made through the connections between fan activists and politicians. The umbrella term of 'improved governance' is framed and reframed in several socially rooted ways and, in many cases, involves pleas for a regulator in the sport and the mandatory presence of a supporters' representative (usually drawn from the network of fan/activists) on the networks of networks of football club's boards of directors. Effectively, calls through the political machinery of cross-party parliamentary inquiries ask for the free-market networks of actions to be disrupted by the potential blockages of social actors who are 'regulators', shifting the contours of 'power' in football. Asking for fans to be given a 'voice' in the running of the club is to alter the networks that, to varying degrees, are accused of shunning them in their present and historically sedimented iterations. The tools of cultural relational sociology are useful for the analysis of, and may hold some of the answers for, these political processes emerging through inherently social encounters. We do not anticipate that these processes of connection are particular to the social worlds that involve football but might be found in many forms of collective action.

Connections are clearly more important just 'mattering' in the social worlds that involve the consumption and production of football. To say connections are important to the ways in which power and counter-power operate in football and other social worlds is to underplay their significance. Indeed, to do this to any form of sociality would be an ontological error. As Rancière (2004) argued, the performance is itself political—and they are the performance. Therefore, following Tilly's (2002) lead, they *are* those power and counter-power arrangements. The collective actions of power and counter-power are those relationships including the networks of networks of networks that are made up of the interactions of interactions of interactions of unquantifiable social actors that are connected through differing strengths of ties.

References

Abiade, Y. (2015, February 17). Dulwich Hamlet Hope Anti-homophobia in Football Campaign Is Blueprint to Others in the Game. *The Guardian*. Available https://www.theguardian.com/football/2015/feb/17/dulwich-hamlet-anti-homophobia-campaign-stonewall-fc. Accessed 25 Apr 2016.

Adamic, L., Buyukkokten, O., & Adar, E. (2003). A Social Network Caught in the Web. *First Monday, 8*(6), 1–20.

Alinsky, S. (1971). *Rules for Radicals*. London: Vintage Books.

Allan, G. (1989). *Friendship. Developing a Sociological Perspective*. Hemel Hempstead: Harvester Wheatsheaf.

Alperstein, N. (2013, October 8). The New Twitter Conversation: Weak Ties That Bind. *Social Media Today*. Available http://www.socialmediatoday.com/content/new-Twitter-conversation-weak-ties-bind. Accessed 20 June 2017.

Anderson, B. (1991 [1983]). *Imagined Communities*. London: Verso.

Archetti, E. P. (2001). *Masculinities: Football, Polo and the Tango in Argentina*. Oxford: Berg.

Armstrong, G. (1998). *Football Hooligans: Knowing the Score*. Oxford: Berg.

Armstrong, G., & Harris, R. (1991). Football Hooligans: Theory and Evidence. *The Sociological Review, 39*(3), 427–458.

Aronowitz, S. (2003). *How Class Works: Power and Social Movement*. New Haven: Yale University Press.

Back, L., Crabbe, T., & Solomos, J. (1999). Beyond the Racist/Hooligan Couplet: Race, Social Theory and Football Culture. *The British Journal of Sociology, 50*(3), 419–442.

Bale, J. (1991). *The Brawn Drain*. Urbana: University of Illinois Press.

© The Author(s) 2018   191
J. Cleland et al., *Collective Action and Football Fandom*,
Palgrave Studies in Relational Sociology,
https://doi.org/10.1007/978-3-319-73141-4

Bale, J. (1993). *Sport, Space and the City*. London: Routledge.

Bale, J. (2000). The Changing Face of Football: Stadiums and Communities. *Soccer and Society, 1*(1), 91–101.

Barbalet, J. (2001). *Emotion, Social Theory and Social Structure: A Macrosociological Approach*. Cambridge: Cambridge University Press.

Barnes, J. (2006). Charlton FC – Back to the Valley. In D. Brimson (Ed.), *Rebellion: The Growth of Football's Protest Movement*. London: John Blake Publishing.

Bauman, Z. (2000). *Liquid Modernity*. Cambridge: Polity.

BBC. (2011, August 1). Clubs Reveal All in BBC Sport Price of Football Survey. Available http://www.bbc.co.uk/sport/football/14366574. Accessed 5 Apr 2017.

BBC. (2013, January 24). Football Supporters' Federation Calls for £20 Away Ticket Price Cap. Available http://www.bbc.co.uk/sport/football/21181709. Accessed 5 Apr 2017.

BBC. (2015, January 24). Supporters Stage Ticket Price Protests Across English Football. Available http://www.bbc.co.uk/sport/football/34435999. Accessed 10 Apr 2017.

BBC. (2016, March 9). Premier League to Cap Cost of Tickets for Away Fans at £30. Available http://www.bbc.co.uk/sport/football/35764007. Accessed 5 Apr 2017.

Becker, H. S. (1974). Art as Collective Action. *American Sociological Review, 39*(6), 767–776.

Becker, H. S. (1976). Art Worlds and Social Types. *American Behavioral Scientist, 19*, 703–718.

Becker, H. S. (2008 [1982]). *Art Worlds*. Berkeley: University of California Press.

Belchem, J. (2006). *Merseypride: Essays in Liverpool Exceptionalism*. Liverpool: Liverpool University Press.

Bhaskar, R. (1997 [1975]). *A Realist Theory of Science*. Abingdon: Routledge.

Blackshaw, T. (2008). Contemporary Community Theory and Football. *Soccer and Society, 9*(3), 325–345.

Blanton, R. E., & Fargher, L. F. (2016). *How Humans Cooperate: Confronting the Challenges of Collective Action*. Colorado: University of Colorado Press.

Blumer, H. (1951). Collective Behavior. In A. M. Lee (Ed.), *Principles of Sociology*. New York: Barnes & Noble.

Blumer, H. (1969). *Symbolic Interactionism: Perspective and Method*. Berkeley: University of California Press.

Boland, P. (2008). The Construction of Images of People and Place: Labelling Liverpool and Stereotyping Scousers. *Cities, 25*(6), 355–369.

Borgatti, S. P., & Halgin, D. S. (2011). On Network Theory. *Organizational Science, 22*, 1168–1181.

Borgatti, S. P., & Lopez-Kidwell, V. (2011). Network Theory. In J. Scott & P. J. Carrington (Eds.), *The SAGE Handbook of Social Network Analysis*. London: SAGE.

Borgatti, S. P., Everett, M. G., & Johnson, J. C. (2012). *Analyzing Social Networks*. London: Sage.

Bosi, L., & Uba, K. (2009). The Outcomes of Social Movement Action: An Introduction. *Mobilization, 14*(4), 405–411.

Bourdieu, P. (1977). *Outline a Theory of Practice*. Cambridge: Cambridge University Press.

Bourdieu, P. (1986). The Forms of Capital. In J. E. Richardson (Ed.), *Handbook of Theory of Research for the Sociology of Education*. London: Greenwood.

Bourdieu, P. (1998). Programme for a Sociology of Sport. In P. Bourdieu (Ed.), *In Other Words*. Cambridge: Polity Press.

Bourdieu, P. (2004 [1990]). *Distinction: A Social Critique of the Judgement of Taste*. Cambridge: Harvard University Press.

Bourdieu, P., & Passeron, J. C. (1990). *Reproduction in Education, Society and Culture*. London: Sage.

Bradbury, S. (2013). Racisms and the Experiences of Minorities in Amateur Football in the UK and Europe. In T. Blackshaw (Ed.), *Handbook of Sport and Leisure Studies*. London: Routledge.

Brimson, D. (2006). *Rebellion: The Growth of Football's Protest Movement*. London: John Blake Publishing.

Bromberger, C. (1995). Football as World-View and as Ritual. *French Cultural Studies, 6*(18), 293–311.

Brown, A. (2007). 'Not for Sale'? The Destruction and Reformation of Football Communities in the Glazer Takeover of Manchester United. *Soccer and Society, 8*(4), 614–635.

Brown, A. (2008). 'Our Club, Our Rules': Fan Communities at FC United of Manchester. *Soccer and Society, 9*(3), 346–358.

Brown, A., & Walsh, A. (1999). *Not for Sale: Manchester United, Murdoch and the Defeat of BSkyB*. London: Mainstream.

Buechler, S. M. (1995). New Social Movement Theories. *The Sociological Quarterly, 36*(3), 441–464.

Bunnage, L. A. (2014). Social Movement Engagement Over the Long Haul: Understanding Activist Retention. *Sociology Compass, 8*(4), 433–445.

Burdsey, D. (2006). 'If I Ever Play Football, Dad, Can I Play for England or India?' British Asians, Sport and Diasporic National Identities. *Sociology, 40*(1), 11–28.

Burdsey, D. (2009). Forgotten Fields: Centralizing the Experiences of Minority Ethnic Men's Football Clubs in England. *Soccer and Society, 10*(6), 704–721.

Burkitt, I. (1997). Social Relationships and Emotions. *Sociology, 31*(1), 37–55.

Burkitt, I. (2014). *Emotions and Social Relations*. London: Sage.

Burnham, A. (2000). Time for Change: Supporters Direct. *Soccer & Society, 1*(3), 45–48.

Burt, R. S. (1992). *Structural Holes: The Social Structure of Competition*. Cambridge, MA: Harvard University Press.

Burt, R. S. (2004). Structural Holes and Good Ideas. *American Journal of Sociology, 110*(2), 349–399.

Burt, R. S. (2005). *Brokerage and Closure: An Introduction to Social Capital.* Oxford: Oxford University Press.

Byrne, P. (1997). *Social Movements in Britain.* London/New York: Routledge.

Cable, J. (2016). *Protest Campaigns, Media and Political Opportunities.* London: Rowman and Littlefield International.

Callon, M. (1991). Techno-economic Networks and Irreversibility. In J. Law (Ed.), *A Sociology of Monsters? Essays on Power, Technology and Domination, Sociological Review Monograph.* London: Routledge.

Campbell, J. L. (2005). Where Do We Stand? In G. F. Davis & D. McAdam (Eds.), *Social Movements and Organization Theory* (pp. 41–48). Cambridge: Cambridge University Press.

Carder, T. (2006). Brighton AHA FC – The Brighton Stadium Mystery. In D. Brimson (Ed.), *Rebellion: The Growth of Football's Protest Movement.* London: John Blake Publishing.

Carrington, P. J., Scott, J., & Wasserman, S. (2005). *Models and Methods in Social Network Analysis.* Cambridge: Cambridge University Press.

Carroll, W. K., & Ratner, R. S. (2001). Sustaining Oppositional Cultures in 'Post-socialist' Times: A Comparative Study of Three Social Movement Organisations. *Sociology, 35*(3), 605–629.

Carthy, V. (2015). *Wired and Mobilizing: Social Movements, New Technology, and Electoral Politics.* Abingdon: Routledge.

Cashmore, E., & Cleland, J. (2011). Glasswing Butterflies: Gay Professional Football Players and Their Culture. *Journal of Sport and Social Issues, 35*(4), 420–436.

Cashmore, E., & Cleland, J. (2012). Fans, Homophobia and Masculinities in Association Football: Evidence of a More Inclusive Environment. *British Journal of Sociology, 63*(2), 370–387.

Casquette, J. (2006). The Power of Demonstrations. *Social Movement Studies, 5*(1), 45–60.

Castells, M. (1976). *The Urban Question. A Marxist Approach.* London: Edward Arnold.

Castells, M. (1983). *The City and the Grassroots: A Cross-Cultural Theory of Urban Social Movements.* Berkeley: University of California Press.

Castells, M. (1997). *The Power of Identity: The Information Age: Economy, Society, and Culture.* Oxford: Blackwell Publishers.

Castells, M. (1998). *End of the Millennium.* Oxford: Blackwell.

Castells, M. (2000 [1996]). *The Rise of the Network Society.* Oxford: Blackwell.

Castells, M. (2000). Materials for an Exploratory Theory of the Network Society. *British Journal of Sociology, 51*(1), 5–24.

Castells, M. (2004 [1997]). *The Power of Identity.* Oxford: Blackwell.

Castells, M. (2011). A Network Theory of Power. *International Journal of Communication, 5*, 773–787.

Castells, M. (2013 [2009]). *Communication Power.* Oxford: Blackwell.

Castells, M. (2015 [2012]). *Networks of Outrage and Hope: Social Movements in the Internet Age.* Cambridge: Polity Press.

Caudwell, J. (1999). Women's Football in the United Kingdom: Theorizing Gender and Unpacking the Butch Lesbian Image. *Journal of Sport and Social Issues, 23*(4), 390–402.

Caudwell, J. (2011). Gender, Feminism and Football Studies. *Soccer and Society, 12*(3), 330–344.

Chesters, G., & Welsh, I. (2010). *Complexity and Social Movements.* London/New York: Routledge.

Chesters, G., & Welsh, I. (2011). *Social Movements: The Key Concepts.* London/New York: Routledge.

Chomsky, N. (2003). Leaders and Movements. In P. R. Mitchell & J. Schoeffel (Eds.), *Understanding Power: The Indispensable Chomsky.* New York: The New Press.

Chong, D. (1991). *Collective Action and the Civil Rights Movement.* Chicago: University Of Chicago Press.

Clark, T. (2006). 'I'm Scunthorpe'til I die': Constructing and (Re) negotiating Identity Through the Terrace. *Chant'Soccer & Society, 7*(4), 494–507.

Clauset, A., Newman, M. E. J., & Moore, C. (2004). Finding Community Structure in Very Large Networks. *Physical Review E, 70*, 66–111.

Cleland, J. (2010). From Passive to Active: The Changing Relationship Between Football Clubs and Football Supporters. *Soccer and Society, 11*(5), 537–552.

Cleland, J. (2014a). Racism, Football Fans and Online Message Boards: How Social Media Has Added a New Dimension to Racist Discourse in British Football. *Journal of Sport and Social Issues, 38*(5), 415–431.

Cleland, J. (2014b). Association Football and the Representation of Homosexuality by the Print Media: A Case Study of Anton Hysén. *Journal of Homosexuality, 61*(9), 1269–1287.

Cleland, J. (2015a). *A Sociology of Football in a Global Context.* London: Routledge.

Cleland, J. (2015b). Discussing Homosexuality on Association Football Fan Message Boards: A Changing Cultural Context. *International Review for the Sociology of Sport Journal, 50*(2), 125–121.

Cleland, J., & Cashmore, E. (2014). Fans, Racism and British Football in the 21st Century: The Existence of a Colour-Blind Ideology. *Journal of Ethnic and Migration Studies, 40*(4), 638–654.

Cleland, J., & Cashmore, E. (2016). 'Football Fans' Views of Racism in British Football. *International Review for the Sociology of Sport, 51*(1), 27–43.

Cleland, J., & Dixon, K. (2015). 'Black and Whiters': The Relative Powerlessness of 'Active' Supporter Organization Mobility at English Premier League Football Clubs. *Soccer and Society, 16*(4), 540–554.

Cleland, J., Magrath, R., & Kian, E. (2016). Masculinity and Sexuality in Association Football: An Online Response by Fans to the Coming Out of Thomas Hitzlsperger. *Men & Masculinities*. First published online October 30, 2017. https://doi.org/10.1080/09589236.2017.1394278

Cloake, M. (2014, October). Cost Cutting. *When Saturday Comes, 332,* 16–17.

Coleman, J. S. (1973). *Resources for Social Change.* New York: Wiley.

Coleman, J. S. (1990). Rational Organization. *Rationality and Society, 2*(1), 94–105.

Coleman, J. S. (1993). *The Mathematics of Collective Action.* London: Aldine Transaction.

Collins, R. (1970). A Conflict Theory of Sexual Stratification. *Social Problems, 19*(1), 3–21.

Collins, R. (1990). Stratification, Emotional Energy, and the Transient Emotions. In T. D. Kemper (Ed.), *Research Agendas in the Sociology of Emotions.* New York: State University of New York Press.

Collins, R. (2004). *Interaction Ritual Chains.* Princeton: Princeton University Press.

Conn, D. (2002 [1997]). *The Football Business: The Modern Football Classic.* London: Mainstream.

Costanza-Chock, S. (2014). *Out of the Shadows, into the Streets! Transmedia Organizing and the Immigrant Rights Movement.* Cambridge, MA: MIT Press.

Couper, N. (2012). *This Is Our Time: The AFC Wimbledon Story.* London: Cherry Books.

Crabbe, T. (2008). Fishing for Community: England Fans at the 2006 FIFA World Cup. *Soccer and Society, 9*(3), 428–438.

Crawford, G. (2004). *Consuming Sport.* London: Routledge.

Crossley, N. (1999). Working Utopias and Social Movements: An Investigation Using Case Study Material from the Radical Mental Health Movement in Britain. *Sociology, 33*(4), 809–830.

Crossley, N. (2002). *Making Sense of Social Movements.* Buckingham: Open University Press.

Crossley, N. (2003). Even Newer Social Movements? Anti-corporate Protests, Capitalist Crises and the Remoralization of Society. *Organization, 10*(2), 287–305.

Crossley, N. (2004). On Systematically Distorted Communication: Bourdieu and the Socio-Analysis of Publics. *The Sociological Review, 52*(1), 88–112.

Crossley, N. (2005). How Social Movements Move: From First to Second Wave Developments in the UK Field of Psychiatric Contention. *Social Movement Studies, 4*(1), 21–48.

Crossley, N. (2008a). Pretty Connected: The Social Network of the Early Punk Movement. *Theory, Culture and Society, 25*(6), 89–116.

Crossley, N. (2008b). (Net) Working Out: Social Capital in a Private Health Club. *The British Journal of Sociology, 59*(3), 475–500.

Crossley, N. (2009). The Man Whose Web Expanded: Network Dynamics in Manchester's Post Punk Music Scene 1976–80. *Poetics, 37*(1), 24–49.

Crossley, N. (2011). *Towards Relational Sociology.* Abingdon: Routledge.

Crossley, N. (2013). Interactions, Juxtapositions and Tastes. In F. Dépelteau & C. Powell (Eds.), *Conceptualizing Relational Sociology.* London: Palgrave.

Crossley, N. (2014). Totally Wired: The Network Structure of the Post-Punk Worlds of Liverpool, Manchester and Sheffield, 1976–80. In N. Crossley, S. McAndrew, & P. Widdop (Eds.), *Social Networks and Music Worlds.* Abingdon: Routledge.

Crossley, N. (2015a). Relational Sociology and Culture. *International Review of Sociology, 25*(1), 65–85.

Crossley, N. (2015b). *Networks of Sound, Style and Subversion: The Punk and Post-punk Worlds of Manchester, London, Liverpool and Sheffield, 1975–80.* Manchester: Manchester University Press.

Crossley, N., & Bottero, W. (2015). Music Worlds and Internal Goods: The Role of Convention. *Cultural Sociology, 9*(1), 38–55.

Crossley, N., & Edwards, G. (2016). Cases, Mechanisms and the Real: The Theory and Methodology of Mixed-Method Social Network Analysis. *Sociological Research Online, 21*(2), 13.

Crossley, N., & Emms, R. (2016). Mapping the Musical Universe: A Blockmodel of UK Music Festivals, 2011–13. *Methodological Innovations, 9*(1), 1–14.

Crossley, N., & Ibrahim, J. (2012). Critical Mass, Social Networks and Collective Action: Exploring Student Political Worlds. *Sociology, 46*(4), 596–612.

Crossley, M. L., Crossley, N., & Crossley, M. (2001). 'Patient' Voices, Social Movements and the Habitus; How Psychiatric Survivors 'Speak Out'. *Social Science and Medicine, 52*(10), 1477–1489.

Crossley, N., McAndrew, S., & Widdop, P. (2014). *Social Networks and Music Worlds.* Abingdon: Routledge.

Curi, M. (2008). Samba, Girls and Party: Who Were the Brazilian Soccer Fans at a World Cup? An Ethnography of the 2006 World Cup in Germany. *Soccer & Society, 9*(1), 111–134.

Cutts, D., & Widdop, P. (2016). Reimagining Omnivorousness Consumption in the Context of Place. *Journal of Consumer Culture, 17*(3), 480–503.

David, M., & Millward, P. (2012). Football's Coming Home?: Digital Reterritorialization, Contradictions in the Transnational Coverage of Sport and the Sociology of Alternative Football Broadcasts. *British Journal of Sociology, 63*(2), 349–369.

David, M., & Millward, P. (2014). Digital Revolutions in Sport and the New Media. In R. Giulianotti (Ed.), *Routledge Handbook of the Sociology of Sport.* New York/Abingdon: Routledge.

David, M., Kirton, A., & Millward, P. (2015). Sports Television Broadcasting and the Challenge of Live-Streaming. In M. David & D. Halbert (Eds.), *Sage Handbook of Intellectual Property.* London: Sage.

David, M., Kirton, A., & Millward, P. (2017). Castells, 'Murdochization', economic counterpower and livestreaming. *Convergence: The International Journal of Research into New Media Technologies, 23*(5), 497–511.

Davies, W. (2016). *The Limits of Neo-liberalism*. London: Sage.

De Biasi, P., & Lanfranchi, P. (1997). The Importance of Difference: Football Identities in Italy. In G. Armstrong & R. Giulianotti (Eds.), *Entering the Field: New Perspectives on World Football*. London: Berg.

Della Porta, D. (1995). *Social Movements, Political Violence, and the State: A Comparative Analysis of Italy and Germany*. Cambridge: Cambridge University Press.

Della Porta, D., & Diani, M. (2006 [1999]). *Social Movements: An Introduction*. Oxford: Wiley.

Della Porta, D., & Reiter, H. (1998). *Policing Protest: The Control of Mass Demonstrations in Western Democracies*. Minneapolis: University of Minnesota Press.

Deloitte and Touche. (2003). *Annual Review of Football Finance*. London: Deloitte and Touche.

Denzin, N. K. (1984). *On Understanding Emotion*. London: Transaction Publishers.

Dépelteau, F. (2008). Relational Thinking: A Critique of Co-deterministic Theories of Structure and Agency. *Sociological Theory, 26*(1), 51–73.

Dépelteau, F. (2011). Nick Crossley, Towards Relational Sociology. *Canadian Journal of Sociology, 36*(4), 395–397.

Dépelteau, F. (2013). What Is the Direction of the Relational Turn? In F. Dépelteau & C. Powell (Eds.), *Conceptualizing Relational Sociology: Ontological and Theoretical Issues*. London: Palgrave.

Dépelteau, F. (2015). Relational Sociology, Pragmatism, Transactions and Social Fields. *International Review of Sociology, 25*(1), 45–64.

Dépelteau, F., & Landini, T. S. (2014). Introduction. In T. S. Landini & F. Dépelteau (Eds.), *Norbert Elias and Empirical Research*. Basingstoke: Palgrave.

Dépelteau, F., & Powell, C. (2013a). *Applying Relational Sociology: Relations, Networks, & Society*. New York: Palgrave Macmillan.

Dépelteau, F., & Powell, C. (2013b). *Conceptualizing Relational Sociology: Ontological and Theoretical Issues*. New York: Palgrave Macmillan.

Diani, M. (2003). "Leaders" or Brokers? Positions and Influence in Social Movement Networks. In M. Diani & D. McAdam (Eds.), *Social Movements and Networks. Relational Approaches to Collective Action*. Oxford: Oxford University Press.

Diani, M. (2015). *The Cement of Civil Society*. Cambridge: Cambridge University Press.

Diekmann, A., & Lindenberg, S. (2001). Sociological Aspects of Cooperation. In *International Encyclopedia of the Social & Behavioral Sciences*. New York: Elsevier Science.

Dixon, K. (2013). *Consuming Football in Late Modern Life*. Aldershot: Ashgate.

Dixon, K. (2014). The Football Fan and the Pub: An Enduring Relationship. *International Review for the Sociology of Sport, 49*(3–4), 382–399.

Doidge, M. (2013). "The Birthplace of Italian Communism": Political Identity and Action Amongst Livorno Fans'. *Soccer & Society, 14*(2), 246–261.

Doidge, M. (2014). *Anti-racism in European Football: Report to UEFA.* Brighton: University of Brighton.

Doidge, M. (2015). *Football Italia: Italian Football in an Age of Globalization.* London: Bloomsbury.

Doidge, M., & Lieser, M. (2017). The Importance of Research on the Ultras: Introduction. *Sport in Society.* First published online April 20, 2017. https://doi.org/10.1080/17430437.2017.1300377

Dominick, J. R. (1987). *Mass Media Research: An Introduction.* London: Wadsworth Publishing.

Donati, P. (1983). *Introduzione alla sociologia relazionale.* Milan: FrancoAngeli.

Donati, P. (2010). *Relational Sociology: A New Paradigm for the Social Sciences.* Abingdon: Routledge.

Donati, P. (2013). Relational Sociology and the Globalized Society. In F. Dépelteau & C. Powell (Eds.), *Applying Relational Sociology: Relations, Networks, & Society.* Basingstoke: Palgrave.

Donati, P. (2015). Manifesto for a Critical Realist Relational Sociology. *International Review of Sociology, 25*(1), 86–109.

Donati, P., & Archer, M. S. (2015). *The Relational Subject.* Cambridge: Cambridge University Press.

Downey, G. L. (1986). Ideology and the Clamshell Identity: Organizational Dilemmas in the Anti-nuclear Power Movement. *Social Problems, 33*(5), 357–373.

Dulwich Hamlet Supporters' Trust. (2017). *Celebrating International Women's Day.* Dulwich Hamlet Supporters Trust. Retrieved from: http://dhst.org.uk/international-womens-day-dhst-interviews/. Accessed 11 Jan 2018.

Dunn, C. (2014). *Female Football Fans: Identity, Community and Sexism.* Basingstoke: Palgrave Macmillan.

Dunn, C. (2017). The Impact of the Supporters' Trust Movement on Women's Feelings and Practices of Their Football Fandom. *Soccer and Society, 18*(4), 462–475.

Dunning, E. (1999). *Sport Matters: Sociological Studies of Sport, Violence and Civilization.* London: Routledge.

Dunning, E., Murphy, P., & Williams, J. (1986). Spectator Violence at Football Matches: Towards a Sociological Explanation. *British Journal of Sociology, 37*(2), 221–244.

Dunning, E., Murphy, P., & Williams, J. (1988). *The Roots of Football Hooliganism.* London: Routledge.

Dunning, E., Murphy, P., & Williams, J. (1991). Anthropological Versus Sociological Approaches to the Study of Soccer Hooliganism: Some Critical Notes. *The Sociological Review, 39*(3), 459–479.

Durkheim, E. (1915). *The Elementary Forms of the Religious Life*. London: George Allen & Unwin.

Earl, J., & Kimport, K. (2011). *Digitally Enabled Social Change: Activism in the Internet Age*. Cambridge, MA: MIT Press.

Edwards, G. (2014). *Social Movements and Protest*. Cambridge: Cambridge University Press.

Elias, N. (1978). *The Civilizing Process: The History of Manners* (Vol. 1). London: Wiley-Blackwell.

Elias, N. (2008 [1986]). Introduction. In N. Elias & E. Dunning (Eds.), *Quest for Excitement: Sport and Leisure in the Civilising Process*. Oxford: Blackwell.

El-Zatmah, S. (2012). From Terso into Ultras: The 2011 Egyptian Revolution and the Radicalization of the Soccer's Ultra-Fans. Soccer & Society, *13*, 5–6, 801–813.

Emirbayer, M. (1997). Manifesto for a Relational Sociology. *The American Journal of Sociology, 103*, 281–317.

Everitt, R. (2014). *Battle for the Valley*. London: Voice of the Valley.

Evrigenis, I. D. (2007). *Fear of Enemies and Collective Action*. Cambridge: Cambridge University Press.

Field, J. (2008). *Social Capital*. Abingdon: Routledge.

Fieldhouse, E., Cutts, D., John, P., & Widdop, P. (2014). When Context Matters: Assessing Geographical Heterogeneity of Get-Out-the-Vote Treatment Effects Using a Population Based Field Experiment. *Political Behavior, 36*(1), 77–97.

Fischer, C. (1982). *To Dwell Among Friends: Personal Networks in Town and City*. Chicago: University of Chicago Press.

Fisher, D., & McInerney, P. B. (2012). The Limits of Networks in Social Movement Retention: On Canvassers and Their Careers. *Mobilization: An International Quarterly, 17*(2), 109–128.

Flam, H., & King, D. (2007). *Emotions and Social Movements*. Abingdon: Routledge.

Fletcher, R., & Drillsma-Milgrom, D. (2005, November 13). Queen of Debt Won't Take No for an Answer. *The Times*. Available https://www.thetimes.co.uk/article/queen-of-debt-wont-take-no-for-an-answer-hlsfzncspk8. Accessed 10 July 2017.

Florida, R. (2002). *The Rise of the Creative Class*. New York: Basic Books.

Fominaya, F. (2010). Collective Identity in Social Movements: Central Concepts and Debates. *Sociology Compass, 4*(6), 393–404.

Forster, K. (2015). Dulwich Hamlet: London's Most Hipster Football Club. *The Observer*, 23 August. Available at: https://www.theguardian.com/global/2015/aug/23/dulwich-hamlet-londons-most-hipster-football-club. Accessed Jan 2018.

Freeman, J. (1973). The Origins of the Women's Liberation Movement. *American Journal of Sociology, 78*(4), 792–811.

Freeman, J. (1979). Resource Mobilization and Strategy: A Model for Analyzing Social Movement Organization Actions. In M. N. Zald & J. M. McCarthy (Eds.), *The Dynamics of Social Movements*. Cambridge, MA: Winthrop Publishers.

Frew, M., & McGillivray, D. (2008). Exploring Hyper-Experiences: Performing the Fan at Germany 2006. *Journal of Sport and Tourism, 13*(3), 181–198.

Friedman, M. (1999). *Consumer Boycotts: Effecting Change Through the Marketplace and the Media*. Abingdon: Routledge.

Frink, B., & Prinz, J. (2006). Crisis? What Crisis? Football in Germany. *Journal of Sports Economics, 7*(1), 60–75.

Frosdick, S., & Marsh, P. (2015 [2005]). *Football Hooliganism*. Abingdon: Routledge.

FSE. (2013, December 24). Against Modern Football. *New Statesman*. Available http://www.newstatesman.com/cultural-capital/2012/12/against-modern-football. Accessed 10 May 2016.

FSE. (2015, April). The State of the Game: Fan and Football Culture in Europe: The Fans' View. *Revive the Roar*, Issue 4.

FSF. (2012, October 18). Ticket Prices Rise at Four Times Rate of Inflation. *FSF*. Available http://www.fsf.org.uk/latest-news/view/ticket-prices-rise-at-four-times-rate-of-inflation. Accessed 10 Apr 2017.

FSF. (2013). *Twenty's Plenty*. http://www.fsf.org.uk/campaigns/away-fans/twentys-plenty/. Accessed Jan 2018.

FSF. (2014). The FSF Annual Report 2014. *FSF*. Available http://www.fsf.org.uk/assets/Downloads/Annual-reports/2014/FSF-Annual-Report-2014-web.pdf. Accessed 10 Apr 2017.

FSF. (2017). Annual Review 2016–17. London.

Gamson, W. A. (1990 [1975]). *The Strategy of Social Protest*. Belmont: Wadsworth.

Garcia, B., & Welford, J. (2015). Supporters and Football Governance, from Customers to Stakeholders: A Literature Review and Agenda for Research. *Sport Management Review, 18*(4), 517–528.

Garland, J., & Treadwell, J. (2010). 'No Surrender to the Taliban!' Football Hooliganism, Islamophobia and the Rise of the English Defence League. *Papers from the British Criminology Conference, 10*, 19–35.

Geertz, C. (1973). *The Interpretation of Cultures*. New York: Basic Books.

Gerbaudo, P. (2012). *Tweets and the Streets: Social Media and Contemporary Activism*. London: Pluto Books.

Gibson, O. (2015, October 2). Twenty's Plenty Campaign Sets Fan Sense Against Premier League Greed. *The Guardian*. Available https://www.theguardian.com/football/2015/oct/02/twentys-plenty-premier-league-football-supporters-federation-ticket-prices. Accessed 10 Apr 2017.

Giddens, A. (1991). *Modernity and Self-Identity: Self and Society in the Late Modern Age*. Cambridge: Polity Press.

Gilbert, S. (2016). *A Club Without a Home: The Fight Behind the Sky Blues' Return From Exile.* Worthing: Pitch Publishing.

Giraldi, N. A. (2016). *The Strength of Weak Social Ties: Social Activism and Facebook.* Doctoral Thesis, Old Dominion University.

Giugni, M. G. (1998). The Outcomes of Social Movements: A Review of the Literature. *Annual Review of Sociology, 24,* 371–393.

Giulianotti, R. (1991). Scotland's Tartan Army in Italy: The Case for the Carnivalesque. *Sociological Review, 39*(3), 503–527.

Giulianotti, R. (1995). Participant Observation and Research into Football Hooliganism: Reflections on the Problems of Entreé and Everyday Risks. *Sociology of Sport Journal, 12*(1), 1–20.

Giulianotti, R. (1999). *Football: A Sociology of the Global Game.* Oxford: Blackwell.

Giulianotti, R. (2002). Supporters, Followers, Fans and Flaneurs: A Taxonomy of Spectator Identities in Football. *Journal of Sport and Social Issues, 26*(1), 25–46.

Giulianotti, R., & Armstrong, G. (2002). Avenues of Contestation. Football Hooligans Running and Ruling Urban Spaces. *Social Anthropology, 10*(2), 211–238.

Giulianotti, R., & Millward, P. (2013). *End of Project Report: Pro-supporters – Prevention Through Empowerment.* Brussels: European Commission.

Giulianotti, R., & Millward, P. (2014). The Role of Fan Projects in Avoiding Conflict at Football Matches. *International Centre for Sport Security Journal, 1*(4), 56–61.

Giulianotti, R., & Robertson, R. (2004). The Globalization of Football: A Study in the Glocalization of the 'Serious Life'. *British Journal of Sociology, 55*(4), 545–568.

Giulianotti, R., & Robertson, R. (2007). Recovering the Social: Globalization, Football and Transnationalism. *Global Network, 7*(2), 166–186.

Giulianotti, R., & Robertson, R. (2009). *Globalization and Football.* London: Sage.

Gladwell, M. (2010, October 4). Small Change: Why the Revolution Will Not Be Tweeted. *The New Yorker.* Available http://www.newyorker.com/magazine/2010/10/04/small-change-malcolm-gladwell. Accessed 29 Mar 2017.

Goffman, E. (1967). *Interaction Ritual: Essays in Face-to-Face Behavior.* London: AldineTransaction.

Goffman, E. (1974). *Frame Analysis: An Essay on the Organization of Experience.* Plymouth: Penguin.

Goldblatt, D. (2007). *The Ball Is Round: A Global History of Football.* London: Viking.

Gonda, M. (2013). Supporters' Movement "Against Modern Football" and Sport Mega Events: European and Polish Contexts. *Przeglad Socjologiczny, 62*(3), 85–106.

González-Bailón, S., & Wang, N. (2013). The Bridges and Brokers of Global Campaigns in the Context of Social Media. SSRN Working Paper. Available http://ssrn.com/abstract=2268165. Accessed 8 July 2017.

González-Bailón, S., & Wang, N. (2016). Networked Discontent: The Anatomy of Protest Campaigns in Social Media. *Social Networks, 44*, 95–104.

Goodwin, J. (1997). The Libidinal Constitution of a High-Risk Social Movement: Affectual Ties and Solidarity in the Huk Rebellion, 1946 to 1954. *American Sociological Review, 62*(1), 53–69.

Goodwin, J., & Jasper, J. M. (2014). *The Social Movements Reader: Cases and Concepts*. Oxford: Blackwell.

Granovetter, M. (1983). The Strength of Weak Ties: A Network Theory Revisited. *Sociological Theory, 1*, 201–233.

Granovetter, M. S. (1973). Strength of Weak Ties. *American Journal of Sociology, 78*, 1360–1380.

Granovetter, M. S. (1985). Economic Action and Social Structure: The Problem of Embeddedness. *American Journal of Sociology, 91*, 481–510.

Granovetter, M. S. (1995). *Getting a Job*. Chicago: University of Chicago Press.

Granovetter, M. S. (2017). *Society and Economy: Framework and Principles*. Cambridge: Harvard University Press.

Guttman, R. (2016, February 6). Why I Walked: Liverpool Fan Explains Protest During Sunderland Draw. *The Guardian*. Available https://www.theguardian.com/football/2016/feb/06/why-i-walked-liverpool-fan-explains-protest-during-sunderland-draw. Accessed 27 May 2017.

Habermas, J. (1981). New Social Movements. *Telos, 49*, 33–37.

Habermas, J. (1986). *The Theory of Communicative Action (Vol. I): Reason and Rationalization of Society*. Cambridge: Polity.

Habermas, J. (1989). *The Theory of Communicative Action (Vol. II): Critique of Functionalist Reason*. Cambridge: Polity.

Ha-Ilan, N. (2017). The (Re)Constitution of Football Fandom: Hapoel Katamon Jerusalem and Its Supporters. *Sport in Society*. First published online April 6, 2017. https://doi.org/10.1080/17430437.2017.1300391

Hamil, S., Michie, J., Oughton, C., & Warby, S. (2001). *The Changing Face of the Football Business: Supporters Direct*. Abingdon: Routledge.

Hands, J. (2010). @ *Is for Activism: Dissent, Resistance and Rebellion in a Digital Culture*. London: Pluto Press.

Hansen, D. L. (2011). Exploring Social Media Relationships. *On the Horizon, 19*(1), 43–51.

Hansen, D. L., Shneiderman, B., & Smith, M. A. (2010). *Analyzing Social Media Networks with NodeXL: Insights from a Connected World*. Burlington: Morgan Kaufmann.

Hardin, R. (1982). *Collective Action*. Baltimore: Johns Hopkins University Press.

Harvey, D. (1989). *The Condition of Postmodernity*. Oxford: Blackwell.

Hayton, J., Millward, P., & Petersen-Wagner, R. (2015). Chasing a Tiger in a Network Society? Hull City's Proposed Name Change in the Pursuit of China and East Asia's New Middle Class Consumers. *International Review for the Sociology of Sport, 52*(3), 279–298.

Hebdige, D. (1979). *Subculture: The Meaning of Style*. London: Routledge.

Hendrix, C., Haggard, S., & Magaloni, B. (2009, August). Grievance and Opportunity: Food Prices, Political Regime and Protest. Paper Prepared for Presentation at the International Studies Association Convention, New York.

Hield, F., & Crossley, N. (2014). Tastes, Ties and Social Space: Exploring Sheffield's Folk Singing World. In C. Crossley, S. McAndrew, & P. Widdop (Eds.), *Social Networks and Music Worlds*. London: Routledge.

Hill, T., Canniford, R., & Millward, P. (2016). Against Modern Football: Mobilizing Protest Movements in Social Media. *Sociology*. First published online August 9, 2016. https://doi.org/10.1177/0038038516660040

Hills, M. (2002). *Fan Cultures*. Abingdon: Routledge.

Himelboim, I., McCreery, S., & Smith, M. (2013). Birds of a Feather Tweet Together: Integrating Network and Content Analyses to Examine Cross-Ideology Exposure on Twitter. *Journal of Computer-Mediated Communication, 18*(2), 40–60.

Hirsch, E. L. (1990). Sacrifice for the Cause: Group Processes, Recruitment, and Commitment in a Student Social Movement. *American Sociological Review, 55*(2), 243–254.

Holt, R. (1989). *Sport and the British: A Modern History*. Oxford: Oxford University Press.

Homans, G. C. (1950). *The Human Group*. New York: Harcourt, Brace & World.

Horne, J., & Malcolm, D. (2016). Sociology of Sport: United Kingdom. In K. Young (Ed.), *Sociology of Sport: A Global Subdiscipline in Review, Research in the Sociology of Sport* (Vol. 9). New York: Emerald.

Hughson, J., & Free, M. (2006). Paul Willis, Cultural Commodities and Collective Sport Fandom. *Sociology of Sport Journal, 23*, 72–85.

Ibrahim, J. (2015). *Bourdieu and Social Movements*. Basingstoke: Palgrave.

Jamieson, L. (1999). Intimacy Transformed? A Critical Look at the 'Pure Relationship'. *Sociology, 33*(3), 477–494.

Jary, D., Horne, J., & Bucke, T. (1991). Football 'Fanzines' and Football Culture: A Case of Successful 'Cultural Contestation'. *Sociological Review, 39*(3), 581–597.

Jasper, J. M. (1990). *Nuclear Politics: Energy and the State in the United States, Sweden, and France*. Princeton: Princeton University Press.

Jasper, J. M. (1997). *The Art of Moral Protest*. Chicago: University of Chicago Press.

Jasper, J. M. (1998). The Emotions of Protest. *Sociological Forum, 13*, 397–424.

Jasper, J. M. (2006). *Getting Your Way: Strategic Dilemmas in the Real World*. Chicago: University of Chicago Press.

Jasper, J. M. (2014). Introduction: Playing the Game. In J. W. Duyvendak & J. M. Jasper (Eds.), *Players and Arenas: The Interactive Dynamics of Protest.* Amsterdam: Amsterdam University Press.

Jasper, J. M., & Nelkin, D. (1992). *The Animal Rights Crusade: The Growth of a Moral Protest.* New York: The Free Press.

Jenkins, R. (2014). *Social Identity.* Abingdon: Routledge.

Jones, I. (2000). A Model of Serious Leisure Identification: The Case of Football Fandom. *Leisure Studies, 19*(4), 283–298.

Joyce, M. (2006). Wimbledon F.C. – No to Merton! And Off to Milton Keynes. In D. Brimson (Ed.), *Rebellion: The Inside Story of Football's Protest Movement.* London: John Blake.

Kádár, D. (2013). *Relational Rituals and Communication: Ritual Interaction in Groups.* Basingstoke: Palgrave.

Kahneman, D., & Tversky, A. (1984). Choices, Values, and Frames. *American Psychologist, 39*(4), 341–351.

Kanter, R. M. (1968). Commitment and Social Organization: A Study of Commitment Mechanisms in Utopian Communities. *American Sociological Review, 33*(4), 499–517.

Katz, J. (1999). *How Emotions Work.* Chicago: University of Chicago Press.

Kelly, C., & Breinlinger, S. (1996). *The Social Psychology of Collective Action: Identity, Injustice and Gender.* London: Routledge.

Kemper, T. D. (1978). Toward a Sociology of Emotions: Some Problems and Some Solutions. *The American Sociologist, 13*(1), 30–41.

Kennedy, D. (2012). Football Stadium Relocation and the Commodification of Football: The Case of Everton Supporters and Their Adoption of the Language of Commerce. *Soccer and Society, 13*(3), 341–358.

Kennedy, D., & Kennedy, P. (2007). Preserving and Extending the Commodification of Football Supporter Relations: A Cultural Economy of Supporters Direct. *Sociological Research Online, 12*(1). http://www.socresonline.org.uk/12/1/kennedy.html

Kennedy, P., & Kennedy, D. (2012). Football Supporters and the Commercialisation of Football: Comparative Responses Across Europe. *Soccer and Society, 13*(3), 327–340.

Kiernan, A., & Porter, C. (2014). Little United and the Big Society: Negotiating the Gaps Between Football, Community and the Politics of Inclusion. *Soccer & Society, 15*(6), 847–863.

King, A. (1997a). The Postmodernity of Football Hooliganism. *British Journal of Sociology, 48*(4), 576–593.

King, A. (1997b). The Lads: Masculinity and the New Consumption of Football. *Sociology, 31*(2), 329–346.

King, A. (1997c). New Directors, Customers and Fans: The Transformation of English Football in the 1990s. *Sociology of Sport Journal, 14*(3), 224–239.

King, A. (2000). Football Fandom and Postnational Identity in the New Europe. *British Journal of Sociology, 51*(3), 419–442.

King, A. (2001). Violent Pasts: Collective Memory and Football Hooliganism. *Sociological Review, 49*(4), 568–585.

King, A. (2002 [1998]). *The End of the Terraces: The Transformation of English Football in the 1990s.* London: Leicester University Press.

King, A. (2003). *The European Ritual: Football in the New Europe.* Aldershot: Ashgate.

King, A. (2010). The New European Stadium. In S. Frank & S. Streets (Eds.), *Stadium Worlds: Football, Space and Built Environment.* London: Routledge.

King, A. (2012 [2004]). *The Structure of Social Theory.* Abingdon: Routledge.

Klandermans, B. (1997). *The Social Psychology of Protest.* Oxford: Wiley-Blackwell.

Klandermans, B. (2002). How Group Identification Helps to Overcome the Dilemma of Collective Action. *American Behavioral Scientist, 45*(5), 887–900.

Kossakowski, R. (2017). From Communist Fan Clubs to Professional Hooligans: A History of Polish Fandom as a Social Process. *Sociology of Sport Journal, 34*(3), 281–292.

Knoke, A. (2012). *Economic Networks.* Cambridge: Polity Press.

Kossakowski, R. (2017). From Communist Fan Clubs to Professional Hooligans: A History of Polish Fandom as a Social Process. *Sociology of Sport Journal, 34*(3), 281–292.

Kriesi, H., Koopmans, R., Duyvendak, J. W., & Giugni, M. (1995). *New Social Movements in Western Europe.* Minneapolis: University of Minnesota Press.

Latour, B. (1987). *Science in Action: How to Follow Scientists and Engineers Through Society.* Harvard: Harvard University Press.

Latour, B. (2005). *Reassembling the Social: An Introduction to Actor-Network-Theory.* Oxford: Oxford University Press.

Lauman, E. O., & Pappi, F. U. (1976). *Networks of Collective Action.* New York: Academic Press.

Law, J. (1991). Introduction: Monsters, Machines and Sociotechnical Relations. In J. Law (Ed.), *A Sociology of Monsters.* London: Routledge.

Law, J. (2004). *After Method: Mess in Social Science Research.* Abingdon: Routledge.

Le Bon, G. (2008 [1895]). *The Crowd.* BiblioBazaar, LCC. Online at http://www.bilbliobazaar.com/opensource

Leach, D., & Haunss, S. (2009). Scenes and Social Movements. In H. Johnston (Ed.), *Culture, Social Movements, and Protest.* Burlington: Ashgate Publishers.

Leguina, A., Widdop, P., & Tampubolon, G. (2016). The Global Omnivore: Identifying Musical Taste Groups in Austria, England, Israel and Serbia. *Sociological Research Online, 21*(3), 15.

Leguina, A., Arancibia-Carvajal, S., & Widdop, P. A. (2017). Musical Preferences and Technologies: Contemporary Material and Symbolic Distinctions Criticised. *Journal of Consumer Culture, 17*(2), 242–264.

Lehrer, J. (2010, May 29). Weak Ties, Twitter and Revolution. *Wired*. Available https://www.wired.com/2010/09/weak-ties-twitter-and-revolutions/. Accessed 1 Mar 2017.

Lenskyj, H. (2014). *Sexual Diversity and the Sochi 2014 Olympics: No More Rainbows*. Basingstoke: Palgrave.

Lestrelin, L. (2012). Entering into, Staying, and Being Active in a Group of Football Supporters: A Procedural Analysis of Engagement. The Case of Supporters of a French Football Club. *International Review of Sociology, 22*(3), 492–513.

Lin, N. (2002). *Social Capital: A Theory of Social Structure and Action*. Cambridge: Cambridge University Press.

Lomax, B. (2000). Democracy and Fandom: Developing a Supporters' Trust at Northampton Town FC. *Soccer & Society, 1*(1), 79–87.

Löw, M., & Weidenhaus, G. (2017). Borders That Relate: Conceptualizing Boundaries in Relational Space. *Current Sociology, 65*(4), 553–570.

Luhmann, N. (2017 [1979]). *Trust and Power*. Cambridge: Polity.

Lull, J. (1995). *Media, Communication, Culture: A Global Approach*. Cambridge: Polity.

Malcolm, D. (2011). Sociology of Sport. In *Key Articles in British Sociology: BSA 60th Anniversary Special Collection*. London: Sage.

Malcolm, D. (2012). *Sport and Sociology*. Abingdon: Routledge.

Malcolm, D. (2014). The Social Construction of the Sociology of Sport: A Professional Project. *International Review for the Sociology of Sport, 49*(1), 3–21.

Marin, A., & Wellman, B. (2011). Social Network Analysis: An Introduction. In J. Scott & P. Carrington (Eds.), *The Sage Handbook of Social Network Analysis*. London: Sage.

Marren, B. (2016). *We Shall Not Be Moved: How Liverpool's Working Class Fought Redundancies, Closures and Cuts in the Age of Thatcher*. Manchester: Manchester University Press.

Marsh, P., Rosser, E., & Harré, R. (1978). *The Rules of Disorder*. London: Routledge.

Martin, P. (2007). Football, Community and Cooperation: A Critical Analysis of Supporter Trusts in England. *Soccer & Society, 8*(4), 636–653.

Martin, G. (2015). *Understanding Social Movements*. Abingdon: Routledge.

Marwell, G., & Oliver, P. (1993). *The Critical Mass in Collective Action*. Cambridge: Cambridge University Press.

Marx, K. (1932 [1846]). *The German Ideology*. Moscow: Marx-Engels Institute.

Mason, T. (1988). *Sport in Britain*. London: Faber and Faber.

Mathers, A. (2014). Book Review: Manuel Castells, Networks of Outrage and Hope: Social Movements in the Internet Age. *Sociology, 48*(5), 1063–1064.

Mauss, M. (1967). *The Gift: Forms and Functions of Exchange in Archaic Societies*. New York: Norton.

McAdam, D. (1982). *Political Process and the Origins of Black Insurgency.* Chicago: University of Chicago Press.

McAdam, D. (1983). Tactical Innovation and the Pace of Insurgency. *American Sociological Review, 48*(6), 735–754.

McAdam, D. (1986). Recruitment to High-Risk Activism: The Case of Freedom Summer. *American Journal of Sociology, 92*(1), 64–90.

McAdam, D. (1988). *Freedom Summer.* Oxford: Oxford University Press.

McCarthy, J. D., & Zald, M. D. (1977). Resource Mobilization and Social Movements: A Partial Theory. *American Journal of Sociology, 82*(6), 1212–1241.

McCarthy, J. D., & Zald, M. N. (2001). The Enduring Vitality of the Resource Mobilization Theory of Social Movements. In J. H. Turner (Ed.), *Handbook of Sociological Theory: Handbooks of Sociology and Social Research.* Boston: Springer.

McGillivray, D., & Frew, M. (2015). From Fan Parks to Live Sites: Mega Events and the Territorialisation of Urban Space. *Urban Studies, 52*(14), 2649–2663.

McQuail, D. (1985). Sociology of Mass Communication. *Annual Review of Sociology, 11*(1), 93–111.

McVeigh, R. (2009). *The Rise of the Ku Klux Klan: Right-Wing Movements and National Politics.* Minneapolis: University of Minnesota Press.

Medina, L. (2009). *A Unified Theory of Collective Action and Social Change.* Ann Arbor: University of Michigan Press.

Melucci, A. (1980). The New Social Movements: A Theoretical Approach. *Social Science Information, 19*(2), 199–226.

Melucci, A. (1984). An End to Social Movements? *Social Science Information, 23*(4/5), 819–835.

Melucci, A. (1988). New Perspectives on Social Movements. In A. Melucci (Ed.), *Nomads of the Present.* London: Hutchinson Radius. (1989).

Melucci, A. (1989). *Nomads of the Present.* London: Hutchinson Radius.

Melucci, A. (1995). The Process of Collective Identity. In H. Johnston & B. Klandermans (Eds.), *Social Movements and Culture.* London: UCL Press.

Melucci, A. (1996a). *Challenging Codes: Collective Action in the Information Age.* Cambridge: Cambridge University Press.

Melucci, A. (1996b). *The Playing Self: Person and Meaning in the Planetary Society.* Cambridge: Cambridge University Press.

Merkel, U. (2012). Football Fans and Clubs in Germany: Conflicts, Crises and Compromises. *Soccer and Society, 13*(3), 359–376.

Meyer, D. S., & Whittier, N. (1994). Social Movement Spillover. *Social Problems, 41*(2), 277–298.

Michie, J., & Oughton, C. (2005). The Corporate Governance of Professional Football Clubs in England. *Corporate Governance: An International Review, 13*(4), 517–531.

Miles, S., Cliff, D., & Burr, V. (1998). 'Fitting in and Sticking Out': Consumption, Consumer Meanings and the Construction of Young People's Identities. *Journal of Youth Studies, 1*(1), 81–96.

Millar, J. (2016, March 17). Dulwich Hamlet Fans Raise Thousands for Syrian Refugees. *Southward News.* Available https://www.southwarknews.co.uk/news/dulwich-hamlet-fans-raise-thousands-for-assyrian-refugees/. Accessed 25 Apr 2017.

Millward, P. (2008). The Rebirth of the Football Fanzine: Using E-zines as Data Source. *Journal of Sport and Social Issues, 32*(3), 299–310.

Millward, P. (2009a). Glasgow Rangers Supporters in the City of Manchester: The Degeneration of a 'Fan Party' into a 'Hooligan Riot'. *International Review for the Sociology of Sport, 44*(4), 381–398.

Millward, P. (2009b). *Getting 'into' Europe: Identification, Prejudice and Politics in English Football Culture.* Saarbrücken: VDM Verlag.

Millward, P. (2011). *The Global Football League: Transnational Networks, Social Movements and Sport in the New Media Age.* Basingstoke: Palgrave Macmillan.

Millward, P. (2012). 'Reclaiming the Kop: Analysing Liverpool Supporters' Twenty-First Century Mobilisations. *Sociology, 46*(4), 633–648.

Millward, P. (2013). 'New' Football Directors in the Twenty-First Century: Profit and Revenue in the English Premier League's Transnational Age. *Leisure Studies, 32*(4), 399–414.

Millward, P. (2016a). World Cup 2022 and Qatar's Construction Projects: Relational Power in Networks and Relational Responsibilities to Migrant Workers. *Current Sociology, 65*(5), 756–776.

Millward, P. (2016b). Football and Social Media: Fanzines, Fan-Scenes and Supporter Protest Movements in Elite English Football. In J. Hughson, J. Maguire, & R. Spaaij (Eds.), *Routledge Handbook of Football Studies.* New York/Abingdon: Routledge.

Millward, P. (2017). A Whole New Ball Game: The Premier League and Television Broadcast Rights. In R. Elliott (Ed.), *The English Premier League: A Socio-Cultural Analysis.* New York/Abingdon: Routledge.

Millward, P., & Poulton, G. (2014). Football Fandom, Mobilisation and Herbert Blumer: A Social Movement Analysis of F.C. United of Manchester. *Sociology of Sport Journal, 31*(1), 1–22.

Millward, P., Widdop, P., & Halpin, M. (2017). A 'Different Class'?: Homophily and Heterophily in the Social Class Networks of Britpop. *Cultural Sociology, 11*(3), 318–336.

Minkoff, D., & McCarthy, J. (2005). Reinvigorating the Study of Organizational Processes in Social Movements. *Mobilization: An International Quarterly, 10*(2), 289–308.

Mische, A. (2003). Cross-Talk in Movements. In M. Diani & D. McAdam (Eds.), *Social Movements and Networks.* Oxford: Oxford University Press.

Mische, A. (2008). *Partisan Publics: Communication and Contention Across Brazilian Youth Activist Networks.* Princeton: Princeton University Press.

Mische, A. (2011). Relational Sociology, Culture, and Agency. In J. Scott & P. Carrington (Eds.), *The Sage Handbook of Social Network Analysis*. London: Sage.

Mische, A., & White, H. (1998). Between Conversation and Situation: Public Switching Dynamics Across Network Domains. *Social Research, 65*(3), 695–724.

Monaghan, F. (2014). Seeing Red: Social Media and Football Fan Activism. In P. Seargeant & C. Tagg (Eds.), *The Language of Social Media: Identity and Community on the Internet*. Basingstoke: Palgrave.

Morrow, S. (1999). *The New Business of Football: Accountability and Finance in Football*. Basingstoke: Palgrave.

Müller, M. (2014). After Sochi 2014: Costs and Impacts of Russia's Olympic Games. *Eurasian Geography and Economics, 55*(6), 628–655.

Murphy, P., Williams, J., & Dunning, E. (1990). *Football on Trial: Spectator Violence and Development in the Football World*. London: Routledge.

Murthy, D. (2012). Towards a Sociological Understanding of Social Media: Theorizing Twitter. *Sociology, 46*, 1059–1073.

Murthy, D. (2013). *Twitter*. Cambridge: Polity.

Nash, R. (2000). Contestation in Modern English Professional Football: The Independent Supporters Association Movement. *International Review for the Sociology of Sport, 35*(4), 465–486.

Nash, R. (2001). English Football Fan Groups in the 1990s: Class, Representation and Fan Power. *Soccer and Society, 2*(1), 39–58.

Newman, M. (2004). Detecting Community Structure in Networks. *The European Physical Journal B, 38*, 321–330.

North and Hodson. (2011 [1997]). *Build a Bonfire: How Football Fans United to Save Brighton and Hove Albion*. London: Mainstream Publishing.

Nuhrat, Y. (2017). Ultras in Turkey: Othering, Agency, and Culture as a Political Domain. *Sport in Society*. First published online April 28, 2017. http://www.tandfonline.com/doi/abs/10.1080/17430437.2017.1300388

Numerato, D. (2015). Who Says "No to Modern Football?" Italian Supporters, Reflexivity, and Neo-liberalism. *Journal of Sport and Social Issues, 39*(2), 120–138.

Numerato, D. (2016). Behind the Digital Curtain: Ethnography, Football Fan Activism and Social Change. *Qualitative Research, 16*(5), 575–591.

Offe, C. (1985). New Social Movements: Challenging the Boundaries of Institutional Politics. *Social Research, 52*(4), 817–868.

Oliver, P., & Johnston, H. (2000). What a Good Idea! Ideologies and Frames in Social Movement Research. *Mobilization: An International Quarterly, 5*(1), 37–54.

Olson, M. (1968). *The Logic of Collective Action*. Cambridge: Harvard University Press.

Opp, K. D. (2009). *Theories of Political Protest and Social Movements: A Multidisciplinary Introduction, Critique, and Synthesis.* Abingdon: Routledge.

Pearson, G. (2012). *An Ethnography of English Football Fans: Cans, Cops and Carnivals.* Manchester: Manchester University Press.

Perasović, B., & Mustapić, M. (2017). Carnival Supporters, Hooligans, and the 'Against Modern Football' Movement: Life Within the Ultras Subculture in the Croatian Context. *Sport in Society.* First published online April 12, 2017. https://doi.org/10.1080/17430437.2017.1300395

Petersen-Wagner, R. (2016). Cultural Consumption Through the Epistemologies of the South: 'Humanization' in Transnational Football Fan Solidarities. *Current Sociology.* First published online August 4, 2016. https://doi.org/10.1177/0011392116658339

Petersen-Wagner, R. (2017). The Football Supporter in a Cosmopolitan Epoch. *Journal of Sport and Social Issues, 41*(2), 133–150.

Pilz, G. A., & Wölki-Schumacher, F. (2010). Overview of the Ultra Culture Phenomenon in the Council of Europe Member States in 2009. International Conference on Ultras, Hannover, Germany (Vol. 6), Council of Europe.

Polletta, F. (2006). *It Was Like a Fever: Storytelling in Protest and Politics.* Chicago: University of Chicago Press.

Porter, C. (2015). Loyal to What? FC United's 'Shaping Walk' Through Football's 'Muck of Ages'. *Sport in Society, 18*(4), 452–465.

Poulton, G. (2013). *F.C. United of Manchester: A Social Anthropological Study of Protest and Consumption in Everyday Life.* Unpublished PhD Thesis, The University of Manchester.

Prandini, R. (2015). Relational Sociology: A Well-Defined Sociological Paradigm or a Challenging 'Relational Turn' in Sociology? *International Review of Sociology, 25*(1), 1–14.

Prinz, J. (2004). Emotions Embodied. In R. Solomon (Ed.), *Thinking About Feeling.* Milton Keynes: Open University Press.

Putnam, R. (2000). *Bowling Alone: The Collapse and Revival of American Community.* New York: Simon and Schuster.

Rainie, L., & Wellman, B. (2012). *Networked: The New Social Operating System.* Cambridge, MA: MIT Press.

Rancière, J. (2004). *The Politics of Aesthetics.* London: Continuum.

Riach, J. (2016). David Cameron Asked to Meet Football Supporters' Group Over Ticket Pricing. *The Guardian,* February 10. Available at: https://www.theguardian.com/football/2016/feb/10/david-cameron-football-ticket-pricing-premier-league-problem-mp-clive-efford-fsf. Accessed Jan 2018.

Robson, G. (2004). *'No One Likes Us, We Don't Care': The Myth and Reality of Millwall Fandom.* Oxford: Berg.

Robson, B. (2009). *Farewell But Not Goodbye: My Autobiography.* London: Hodder & Stoughton.

Rookwood, J., & Millward, P. (2011). 'We All Dream of a Team of Carraghers': Comparing the Semiotics of 'Local' and Texan Liverpool Fans' Talk. *Sport in Society, 14*(1), 37–52.

Rosie, M., & Gorringe, H. (2009). 'The Anarchists' World Cup': Respectable Protest and Media Panics. *Social Movement Studies, 8*(1), 35–53.

Rt. Hon. Lord Justice Taylor. (1990). *The Hillsborough Stadium Disaster, 15 April 1989: Final Report.* London: HMSO.

Rucht, D. (2005). Appeal, Threat, and Press Resonance: Comparing Mayday Protests in London and Berlin. *Mobilization: An International Quarterly, 10*(1), 163–182.

Russell, D. (1997). *Football and the English: A Social History of Association Football in England, 1863–1995.* Preston: Carnegie.

Ryan, C. (1991). *Prime Time Activism.* Boston: South End Press.

Sanders, A., Heys, B., Ravenscroft, N., & Burdsey, D. (2014). Making a Difference: The Power of Football in the Community. *Soccer & Society, 15*(3), 411–429.

Sandfield, A., & Percy, C. (2003). Accounting for Single Status: Heterosexism and Ageism in Heterosexual Women's Talk About Marriage. *Feminism and Psychology, 13*(4), 475–488.

Scannell, P. (2007). *Media and Communication.* London: Sage.

Schrank, Z., & Running, K. (2018). Individualist and Collectivist Consumer Motivations in Local Organic Food Markets. *Journal of Consumer Culture, 18*(1), 184–201.

Schulke, H. J. (2010). Challenging the Stadium: Watching Sport Events in Public Stadium and Architecture. In S. Frank & S. Streets (Eds.), *Stadium Worlds: Football, Space and Built Environment.* London: Routledge.

Schumann, S. (2015). *How the Internet Shapes Collective Actions.* Basingstoke: Palgrave.

Schutz, A. (1972). *The Phenomenology of the Social World.* London: Heinemann Educational Books.

Schutz, A., & Sandy, M. (2011). *Collective Action for Social Change: An Introduction to Community Organizing.* Basingstoke: Palgrave.

Scott, A. (1990). *Ideology and the New Social Movements.* Sydney: Allen and Unwin.

Scraton, P. (2016). *Hillsborough: The Truth.* London: Mainstream.

Senaux, B. (2008). A Stakeholder Approach to Football Club Governance. *International Journal of Sport Management and Marketing, 4*(1), 4–17.

Shepard, B. (2011). *Play, Creativity and Social Movements.* Abingdon: Routledge.

Shepard, B. (2015). *Rebel Friendships: 'Outsider' Networks and Social Movements.* Basingstoke: Palgrave.

Shott, S. (1979). Emotion and Social Life: A Symbolic Interactionist Analysis. *American Journal of Sociology, 84*(6), 1317–1334.

Silverstone, R. (2006). *Media and Morality: On the Rise of the Mediapolis.* Cambridge: Polity.

Simmel, G. (1950). *The Sociology of George Simmel*. London: Free Press of Glencoe.

Smith, A. (1937). *An Inquiry into the Nature and Causes of the Wealth of Nations*. New York: Modern Library.

Smith, C. (2000). Strengthening the Voice of Supporters. *Soccer & Society, 1*(3), 13–16.

Smith, M. A., Rainie, L., Himelboim, I., & Shneiderman, B. (2014). *Mapping Twitter Topic Networks: From Polarized Crowds to Community Clusters*. Washington, DC: Pew Research Center.

Smithey, L. A. (2009). Social Movement Strategy, Tactics, and Collective Identity. *Sociology Compass, 3*(4), 658–671.

Snow, D. A., Zurcher, L. A., & Ekland-Olson, S. (1980). Further Thoughts on Social Networks and Movement Recruitment. *Sociology, 17*(1), 112–120.

Snow, D. A., Rochford, B., Worden, S. K., & Benford, R. D. (1986). Frame Alignment Processes, Micromobilization and Movement Participation. *American Sociological Review, 51*, 464–481.

SoS. (2016, February 2). *Response to LFC Ticket Prices*. http://www.spiritofshankly.com/news/response-to-lfc-ticket-prices. Accessed Jan 2018.

Spencer, D., Walby, K., & Hunt, A. (2012). *Emotions Matter: A Relational Approach to Emotions*. Toronto: University of Toronto Press.

Spirit of Shankly. (2010, October 15). Spirit of Shankly Statement on LFC Takeover. Available http://www.spiritofshankly.com/news/2010-10-15-spirit-of-shankly-statement-on-lfc-takeover. Accessed 9 July 2017.

Stevenson, R., & Crossley, N. (2014). Change in Covert Social Movement Networks. *Social Movement Studies, 13*(1), 70–91.

Stone, C. (2007). The Role of Football in Everyday Life. *Soccer and Society, 8*(2/3), 169–184.

Stone, C. (2013). *Football: A Shared Sense of Belonging*. Sheffield: FURD.

Stott, C., & Pearson, G. (2007). *Football "Hooliganism": Policing and the War on the "English Disease"*. London: Pennant Books.

Stott, C., Adang, O., Livingstone, A., & Schreiber, M. (2007). Variability in the Collective Behaviour of England Fans at Euro2004: 'Hooliganism', Public Order Policing and Social Change. *European Journal of Social Psychology, 37*(1), 75–100.

Stott, C., Hoggett, J., & Pearson, G. (2012). 'Keeping the Peace': Social Identity, Procedural Justice and the Policing of Football Crowds. *British Journal of Criminology, 52*(2), 381–399.

Sumbler, P. (2013). *From Graveyard to Ambition: The Official History of the Swansea City Supporters' Trust*. Stroud: Amberley Publishing.

Swank, E. (2000). In Newspapers We Trust? In P. G. Coy (Ed.), *Research in Social Movements, Conflicts and Change*. Bingley: Emerald Group Publishing Limited.

Sztompka, P. (2003 [1999]). *Trust: A Sociological Theory*. Cambridge: Cambridge University Press.

Tarrow, S., & Tilly, C. (2007). Contentious Politics and Social Movements. In C. Boix & S. C. Stokes (Eds.), *The Oxford Handbook of Comparative Politics*. Oxford: Oxford University Press.

Taylor, I. (1971a). Soccer Consciousness and Soccer Hooliganism. In S. Cohen (Ed.), *Images of Deviance* (pp. 134–164). Harmondsworth: Penguin.

Taylor, I. (1971b). Football Mad: A Speculative Sociology of Soccer Hooliganism. In E. Dunning (Ed.), *The Sociology of Sport: A Selection of Readings* (pp. 352–377). London: Frank Cass.

Taylor, I. (1987). Putting the Boot into a Working Class Sport: British Soccer After Bradford and Brussels. *Sociology of Sport Journal, 4*, 171–191.

Taylor, L. (2013, January 14). Manchester City Fan's Protest Over £62 Ticket Falls Foul of Arsenal. *The Guardian*. Available https://www.theguardian.com/football/2013/jan/14/manchester-city-protest-ticket-arsenal. Accessed 1 Mar 2017.

Taylor, R. (1992). *Football and Its Fans: Supporters and Their Relations With the Game, 1885–1939*. Liverpool: Liverpool University Press.

Taylor Report. (1990). The Hillsborough Stadium Disaster: 15 April 1989: Inquiry by the Rt Hon Lord Justice Taylor: Final Report: Presented to Parliament by the Secretary of State for the Home Department by command of Her Majesty, January 1990. London: HM Stationery Office.

Taylor, V., & Whittier, N. E. (1992). Collective Identity in Social Movement Communities: Lesbian Feminist Mobilization. In A. D. Morris & C. M. Mueller (Eds.), *Frontiers in Social Movement Theory*. New Haven: Yale University Press.

TenHouten, W. D. (1996). Outline of a Socioevolutionary Theory of the Emotions. *International Journal of Sociology and Social Policy, 16*(9/10), 190–208.

Testa, A., & Armstrong, G. (2010). *Football, Fascism and Fandom: The UltraS of Italian Football*. London: A and C Black Publishers Ltd.

Themen, K., & Van Hooff, J. (2017). Kicking Against Tradition: Women's Football, Negotiating Friendships and Social Spaces. *Leisure Studies, 36*(4), 542–552.

Thornton, S. (2008). *Seven Days in the Art World*. London: Granta Books.

Thurnell-Read, T. (2016). 'Real ale' Enthusiasts, Serious Leisure and the Costs of Getting 'Too Serious' About Beer. *Leisure Sciences, 38*(1), 68–84.

Tilly, C. (1978). *From Mobilization to Revolution*. Reading: Addison-Wesley.

Tilly, C. (1999). From Interactions to Outcomes in Social Movements. In M. Giugni, D. McAdam, & C. Tilly (Eds.), *How Social Movements Matter*. Minneapolis: University of Minnesota Press.

Tilly, C. (2002). *Stories, Identities, and Political Change*. New York: Rowman & Littlefield Publishers.

Tilly, C. (2008). *Credit & Blame*. Oxford: Princeton University Press.

Tilly, C. (2009). *Social Movements: 1768–2008* (2nd ed.). London: Paradigm Publishers.

Tonkonoff, S. (2017). *From Tarde to Deleuze and Foucault*. Basingstoke: Palgrave.

Touraine, A. (1977). *The Self-Production of Society*. London: Wildwood House.

Touraine, A. (1981). *The Voice and the Eye*. Cambridge: Cambridge University Press.

Touraine, A. (1988). *Return of the Actor: Social Theory in a Post Industrial Society*. Minneapolis: University of Minnesota Press.

Touraine, A. (1989). Is Sociology Still the Study of Society? *Thesis Eleven, 23*(1), 5–34.

Touraine, A. (1990). The Idea of Revolution. *Theory, Culture and Society, 7*(2), 121–141.

Touraine, A. (1992). Beyond Social Movements? *Theory, Culture and Society, 9*(1), 125–145.

Treadwell, J., & Garland, J. (2011). Masculinity, Marginalization and Violence: A Case Study of the English Defence League. *The British Journal of Criminology, 51*(4), 621–634.

Treharne, D. (2016). Ten Years of Supporters Trust Ownership at Exeter City AFC: An Overview. *Soccer & Society, 17*(5), 732–743.

Tsoukala, A. (2009). *Football Hooliganism in Europe: Security and Civil Liberties in the Balance*. Basingstoke: Palgrave.

Turan, Ö., & Özçetin, B. (2017). Football Fans and Contentious Politics: The Role of Çarşı in the Gezi Park Protests. *International Review for the Sociology of Sport*. First published online April 6, 2017. http://journals.sagepub.com/doi/abs/10.1177/1012690217702944

Turner, M. (2017). "Football Without Fans Is Nothing": Contemporary Fan Protests and Resistance Communities in the English Premier League. In R. Elliott (Ed.), *The English Premier League: A Socio-Cultural Analysis*. New York/Abingdon: Routledge.

Urry, J. (1995). *Consuming Places*. London/New York: Sage.

Urry, J. (2005 [1990]). *The Tourist Gaze*. London: Sage.

Van Laer, J., & Van Aelst, P. (2010). Internet and Social Movement Action Repertoires: Opportunities and Limitations. *Information, Communication & Society, 13*(8), 1146–1171.

Veg. (1992). New Year Portion. *Red Issue, 4*(6), 3.

Waddington, I., Roderick, M., & Naik, R. (2001). Methods of Appointment and Qualifications of Club Doctors and Physiotherapists in English Professional Football: Some Problems and Issues. *British Journal of Sports Medicine, 35*(1), 48–53.

Walters, G., & Tacon, R. (2010). Corporate Social Responsibility in Sport: Stakeholder Management in the UK Football Industry. *Journal of Management & Organization, 16*(4), 566–586.

Watkins, T. (2000). *Cherries in the Red: How One Football Fan Saved His Club and Became Its Chairman.* London: Headline Book Publishing.

Weber, M. (2001 [1930]). *The Protestant Ethic and the Spirit of Capitalism.* Abingdon: Routledge.

Webber, D. (2017). 'Playing on the Break': Karl Polanyi and the Double-Movement 'Against Modern Football'. *International Review for the Sociology of Sport, 52*(7), 875–893.

Weed, M. (2007). The Pub as a Virtual Football Fandom Venue: An Alternative to 'Being There'? *Soccer & Society, 8*(2–3), 399–414.

Wellman, B. (1988). Structural Analysis: From Method and Metaphor to Theory and Substance. In B. Wellman & S. D. Berkowitz (Eds.), *Social Structures: A Network Approach.* Cambridge: Cambridge University Press.

White, H. (1992). *Identity and Control: A Structural Theory of Social Action.* Princeton: Princeton University Press.

White, H. (1993). Cases Are for Identity, for Explanation, or for Control. In C. Ragin & H. S. Becker (Eds.), *What Is a Case: Issues in the Logic of Social Inquiry.* Cambridge: Cambridge University Press.

White, H. (1995). Network Switchings and Bayesian Forks: Reconstructing the Social and Behavioral Sciences. *Social Research, 62,* 1035–1063.

White, H. (2002). *Markets from Networks: Socioeconomic Models of Production.* Princeton: Princeton University Press.

White, H. (2008). *Identity and Control: How Social Formations Emerge.* Princeton: Princeton University Press.

Widdop, P., & Cutts, D. (2012). The Importance of Place: A Case Study of Museum Participation. *Cultural Trends, 21*(1), 47–66.

Widdop, P., Jarvie, G., & Cutts, D. (2016). Omnivorousness in Sport: The Importance of Social Capital and Networks. *International Review for Sociology of Sport, 51*(5), 596–616.

Williams, J. (2007). Rethinking Sports Fandom: The Case of European Soccer. *Leisure Studies, 26*(2), 127–146.

Williams, J. (2012). Walking Alone Together the Liverpool Way: Fan Culture and 'Clueless' Yanks. *Soccer and Society, 13*(3), 426–442.

Williams, R. (2016 [1962]). *Communications.* Harmondsworth: Penguin.

Williams, J., Dunning, E., & Murphy, P. (1992 [1984]). *Hooligans Abroad: The Control of English Fans in Continental Europe.* London: Routledge.

Yang, G. (2006). Emotions and Social Movements. In G. Ritzer (Ed.), *Blackwell Encyclopedia of Sociology.* Oxford: Blackwell.

Young, K. (2016). *Sociology of Sport: A Global Subdiscipline in Review.* Bingley: Emerald Group Publishing.

Zald, M. N., & Ash, R. (1966). Social Movement Organizations: Growth, Decay and Change. *Social Forces, 44*(3), 327–341.

INDEX

© The Author(s) 2018   217
J. Cleland et al., *Collective Action and Football Fandom*,
Palgrave Studies in Relational Sociology,
https://doi.org/10.1007/978-3-319-73141-4

Printed by Printforce, the Netherlands